The Singing Heart

The Autobiography of Thomas Allen Rector

Edited By
Laura Wayland-Smith Hatch

Salmon Creek Publishing
Williamson, New York
2010

The Singing Heart
The Autobiography of Thomas Allen Rector

Edited by Laura Wayland-Smith Hatch

First Edition

Copyright 2010 by Laura Wayland-Smith Hatch
All rights reserved. No part of this book may be reproduced by any means without the written consent of Laura Wayland-Smith Hatch.

Published by:
Salmon Creek Publishing
7580 Salmon Creek Road
Williamson, New York 145898-9501

ISBN: 978-0-9716794-3-6
Library of Congress Control Number: 2010931174

Thomas Allen Rector

"Take hands and part with laughter."
Algernon Charles Swinburne

Foreword

Thomas Allen Rector was born on the 22nd of July in 1881, in Vicksburg, Mississippi. His father, George Pickett Harrison Rector, was originally from Virginia and descended from German and English settlers of the early 1600s. His mother, Emma Shearer, was from Mississippi, her family having lived there for well over 100 years.

Historically, as the oldest son of rather patrician, Southern parents, the role of preserver of the family's traditions and continuation of the family line should have been his. He, however, chose another path in life and followed his singing heart to the world of music and dance. His father never seemed to truly understand Tom's need to dance and sing. In letters written to Tom over the years, he often referred to Tom's performing career as his "dancing thing" and seemed rather relieved when the dancing became a part of Tom's past.

What follows is the story of Thomas Allen Rector, from his birth to his enlistment, at the age of 36, in the Allied's cause upon the United States' involvement in World War One. The time was one of change and excitement. The Gay Nineties carried over into the turn of the century. New York was a whirlwind of social and artistic activity. Opera and theater stars were among the social elite. Vaudeville was at its peak. Hollywood was just beginning to get a grip on the country. Movie stars were just being born with the advent of silent films.

The manuscript for this book was given to me by my grandmother and Tom's niece, Leonora Crook Wayland-Smith. It had spent many years in an old manila envelope, buried in an old box at the back of a closet, forgotten until its rediscovery during a grand "clearing out." My grandmother, an artist, loved and admired her uncle very much, being a bit of a soulmate with him. She loved to tell me fascinating stories of her early years in New York City and of the adventures she had had with her mother, Leonora Rector Crook, her Aunt Natalie, and her Uncle Tom. It is for her that I have dusted off Tom's narrative.

The story is Tom Rector's, written when he was 58 years old and at a time when he was looking back upon the accomplishments of his life. I have been very selective in the rewriting and editing processes. No facts, thoughts or impressions have been changed. The spirit and soul of the book remain true to Tom. I can only hope that his heart sings knowing that others are being allowed to share in the adventures and awakenings of his youth.

Laura Wayland-Smith Hatch

Thomas Allen Rector
6 months old

Chapter One

My father, George Pickett Harrison Rector, always referred to himself as the last of the Cavaliers. Now, as a young boy I hadn't the vaguest of ideas as to just what a Cavalier might be, and it was not until I had reached the ripe old age of seven that I was able to muster the courage to admit my ignorance and query my father regarding this rather mysterious title of his. I can still see the amused look that appeared upon his face, his widening smile, and the twinkle in his eye as he replied.

"Sonnybuck," for that was his pet name for me, "a Cavalier is a man who loves good liquor, horse racing, fox hunting, and pretty women, but also one who always retains his sense of honor and humor—especially his humor." Pausing for a moment, he laughingly added, "The motto of our family has always been to get mellow before the fiddlers come."

Now, upon some reflection, I truly don't feel that the customs prevalent in today's society have changed that much since that family motto first came into use over one hundred years ago. People today still seem to enjoy getting a little bit tight and, in some instances, just plain, outright drunk.

Emanating from an extremely interesting, but rather eccentric family near Rectortown, Fauquier County, Virginia, the Cavalier was born and reared in the Blue Ridge Mountains. At the age of nineteen, he left his family behind and moved from his beautiful rolling hills to the deep South, entered the banking business, and settled down in the small city of Vicksburg, Mississippi, built upon the banks of the great river. The enduring love the Cavalier carried for his home state of Virginia was one of the most beautiful things I have ever known. He always referred to it as home, although his house, his family, and his business were all in Mississippi, and he constantly expressed his desire to return there to live, although he never did. In the family, the story is told of how he, upon his first return visit to Fauquier County, stepped down from the train, knelt, and kissed the ground of his birthplace.

It was in Vicksburg that The Cavalier met my mother and fell in love. Emma was her name, the daughter of Phares Waldo Shearer, a Captain in the Confederate Army. Her mother was Sallie Sivley, a descendant of one of the early pioneer families of Mississippi. My mother was a modern young girl for her times, very beautiful, with a magnificent suit of red-gold hair, perfectly chiseled Grecian features upon milk-white skin, and a personality that radiated a sparkling wit and charm. And so they were married and, in the 1880s, to this dashing Cavalier and his vivacious lady, their first child was born. A son. Me.

I must have been a spoiled little brat, because the first story I remember my parents telling me of my very early youth described an outbreak of temper.

I had almost reached the age of three and had just begun to realize that, by insisting loudly enough, I might even get the moon. Until that time, I had been an extremely healthy and moderately well-behaved youngster, but suddenly, for some reason unknown to my parents, I decided that I would refuse to eat. As time passed, my refusal became not only determined but most definitely stubborn in nature. My poor mother tried pleading with me, my father threatened dire consequences, and my black mammy coaxed and cooed. Their efforts to entice me to eat, however, were all in vain. In desperation, all seemingly convinced that I would soon starve to death, although my chubby little cheeks and body certainly indicated otherwise, they turned to the family doctor who finally prescribed a trip to some mineral wells a few hours distant from Vicksburg.

So, on one scorching July day, my father, my mother, and my mammy departed with me on a hot, stuffy train, determined to right whatever was seemingly wrong with their precious little boy. My father, knowing most of the countryside folk, quickly found several companions willing to join him for a mint julep or two. My mother became engaged in a small game of cards, and I snuggled in my mammy's arms, assuming the pose of a little blonde cherub. At some point during the trip, I must have suddenly realized the seriousness of this expedition and decided that I had best take matters into my own little hands before who knew what remedies were tested on me. Surveying the entire situation with my wide blue eyes, and then clutching my mammy's black arm, I proceeded to shriek at the top of my little lungs, "Meat. I want meat."

The intensity of my screams succeeded in immediately startling the whole coach into chaotic action. My mother rushed over to me, terrified that some terrible harm had befallen her child. My father became so alarmed that he almost lost his Southern dignity. Mammy, petrified at my sudden outburst and the surrounding crowd that had come to my rescue, clutched me tighter to her chest.

"Honey Chile," she crooned to me in a shaky voice, "that ain't no way fur a littl' gent'man to act. You can't hav' no meat. Meat pisens littl' babies."

Most probably enjoying the attention I had now attracted, I undauntedly continued to demand in a shrill little voice, "Meat. Give me meat."

It was at this point that my father swept me into his arms and—his six-feet three and one-half inches of height draped by his firstborn—proceeded to pace up and down the aisle, parting my would-be rescuers to one side or the other. All the time I kept repeating my demand in a most belluine manner.

One of my father's companions, most annoyed at being disturbed from the enjoyment of his sixth mint julep, more commanded than suggested, "For God's sake, George, give the boy some meat. Can't you see that he wants to be a man?"

My mother, who never seemed to lose her sense of humor, whatever the

Emma Shearer Rector

situation might be, answered him with, "Sir, that seems to be the cry of all men. The meat might kill him."

"Yes, and it just might cure him," my father replied most authoritatively. "By God! He's acting like a man so let's give the young man some meat."

Apparently not hearing, or just choosing to ignore my mother's pleas to the contrary, The Cavalier ordered a large porterhouse steak for, in his eyes, his rapidly growing young son. My father swore upon his honor as a Virginia Cavalier that I, despite my size, ate every morsel of that steak and then went blissfully to sleep in my mother's arms, instantly and completely cured.

So, as you can no doubt see, I started my life seeming to know most definitely what I wanted and yelping for it in such a loud and obtrusive manner that I always, or almost always got it. In my later years, however, I cannot honestly say that the satisfaction of my desires always brought with it such instant and complete contentment. In many cases, the wait was a long one, and the supposed satisfaction produced the exact opposite affect.

At the age of seven, I was entered into a private school with my little sister, Leonora, who was two and one-half years younger. Living as we did in the country, it was necessary that we be driven the several miles to and from school by Uncle Abe, who was our coachman. Formerly, he had been a slave of my grandmother Shearer's. His family made up the rest of the servants of our household; in fact they had all remained with us in a capacity not unlike that which they had enjoyed for many years with the Sivley and Shearer families. His wife was our laundress, his eldest daughter the cook, his second daughter acted as nurse, his eldest son worked in the garden, and the little pickaninnies toted and carried.

The road to school meandered along the banks of the Mississippi. With murky river waters flowing by on one side and green rolling farmlands stretching into the distance on the other, it was a tableau that I am sure we did not appreciate as we should have. Leonora and I were far too busy chattering away, discussing anything and everything, to take in our surrounding. It was Uncle Abe, and not the lush countryside, who truly fascinated us. Daily, he would entertain us with tales of his youthful adventures, spinning his yarns on the way to school and finishing them up on the all-too-short ride home. Every afternoon, we would beg him to drive a little slower, demanding that he make the horses walk instead of trot so that the time spent with him would not end so quickly. These daily treks soon became the high points of our days and were sorely missed when vacations or illness robbed us of them. School hours forced the two of us to submit to set schedules and disciplines, which we despised. We studied subjects in which we had little or no interest and conformed to the expectations of teachers for whom we had no respect. Uncle Abe placed no such restrictions on us, nor did he ever judge the thoughts and feelings we so

Thomas Allen Rector
7 years old

freely expressed to him. His was an attitude of live and let live, and we loved him for it.

Having no neighbors living near to us, Leonora and I grew up with no playmates of our own color. Our association with other children was limited to school hours, and our play there was regimented by the teachers of that loathsome institution. Living isolated from others of our own age, we rapidly became intense individualists, disliking the toys that so enamored other youngsters. Instead of idle hours being wasted with foolish things such as dolls and tin soldiers, we spent most of our free time dramatizing life, creating new games, and living in our own imagined worlds.

As often happens with young children, we entered a stage where we became entranced with the glitter and excitement of the circus. In fact, we became so obsessed with the idea of circus life that we actually assembled a miniature one of our own. We had Uncle Abe save us the empty oat sacks from the stables, and with the help of Uncle Abe's grandchildren we sewed them together to create a large tent. With great effort, we dug a ring, erected our tent, and gave performances unequaled anywhere but in our imaginations. Our animal menagerie consisted of my pony "Pinky," an old cow named "Welcome," Father's pedigreed pointer bitch he called "Beulah," and a billy goat I had gotten for Christmas that I named "Santa Claus." To create a performing troop, we dressed the little pickaninnies as wild men of Borneo and Zulu chiefs using brightly colored pieces of cloth and many feathers collected from unsuspecting roosters and hens. Leonora, though tomboyish at heart, yet still very feminine in appearance, persuaded our nurse to make for her a pink tarlatan dress that was profusely decorated with silver paper stars. She then, unequivocally insisted upon riding on Pinky's back and jumping through paper hoops, just as the beautiful ladies did in the big rings.

All of our shows went along in a masterly fashion until one afternoon, when we were giving a special performance for all the servants of the neighborhood. Glad for any excuse to get out of work on a hot summer day, they had filled our little tent to capacity. Leonora, wearing her pink, star-spangled dress, was proudly perched upon Pinky's back and was just about to make her breath-taking jump when, suddenly, a terrific baying of the hounds and yelping of the beagles filled the air, startling the performers and audience alike. As the baying approached, a scared little rabbit burst into the tent, rapidly followed by the entire pack of about seventy-five, or so it seemed to our wide little eyes, excited canines. The rabbit managed to jump to safety upon Santa Claus' back, who then gave two swift kicks and ran under Pinky, throwing the pony into hysterics. This caused Leonora to be hurled into the air against our single support pole. Of course, the tent then collapsed upon performers, audience, and animals and total Pandemonium broke forth. In the scramble that followed, the little bunny, now completely forgotten, managed to escape, unnoticed and unharmed. Our circus days had been ended.

Searching for some new adventures to replace our abandoned circus careers, we next became passionately interested in the Gypsies that encamped near our home each spring. Mammy, endowed with all the superstitions of the black race, delighted in having her fortune told and retold and encouraged our visits with them. About three o'clock each day, when our mother had retired to her room for her afternoon's nap, Mammy, Leonora, and I would start out for their encampment, loaded down with baskets filled with vegetables that we had sneaked from our garden. Once there, we would sit with them beside their gaudily painted wagons, singing songs and dancing the afternoons away. Of course, each time we were with the Gypsies, Mammy would have to have her fortune told, and each time the old Gypsy seer would somehow uncover a new husband for her. At first, all these romantic conquests were most pleasing to Mammy until she began to worry about the ever-increasing quantity of husbands that had been predicted over the course of several weeks.

"Looka here, Miss Gyps'y Queen, Ise done had sever'l matromuny 'speriances. What for you all gonna gib me more?"

My curiosity had been aroused. Not waiting for the Gypsy's reply, I asked hurriedly, "Mammy, what's a matrimony experience?"

"Honey Chile, that's gittin' married."

That answer only left me more puzzled than before. Getting married to me meant having a wedding and staying with that person forever and ever. That's what my parents and my grandparents had done. "But, Mammy, how many times have you been married," I probed further, trying to make some sense of it all.

She chuckled as she answered, "I've done been lawful'y married four times, but Gawd knows how many man I'se done tuck up wid."

Being too young at the time to fully comprehend the meaning of her answer, her explanation only served to mystify me more. It did, however, make an indelible impression upon my young mind and maturity brought with it an understanding of the real meaning of her response and an admiration for her light-hearted philosophy on love and marriage.

It was not too long before our mother discovered the destination of our afternoon jaunts and, much to our surprise, she failed to raise any objections. In fact, she surprised us all and even decided to join us one afternoon. Once there, Mammy insisted that my mother have her fortune told and, upon hearing this, I could not be satisfied until my palm was read, too. It wasn't until several years later that my mother expressed to me her great concern over the future the Gypsy had predicted for me.

"Tom, sometimes the Gypsies are right. I believe some of them do possess strange powers to see into the future and, for some reason or other, I believed the one that read your palm that afternoon. In part, at least. She said that you would travel many seas, that you would never bring happiness to anyone who loved you, or will anyone you love bring you happiness. Then she went on to say that, in spite of it all, you would always have a song in your heart, a song filled with love for humanity. Do try and do that, Tom. Fill your heart with love and keep it singing throughout your life." She hesitated a moment, and then continued with her lyrical voice choking a trifle. "And, always retain the courage of a gentleman."

I have often pondered over the powers of that simple Gypsy woman and her vision to see so clearly and to predict so far into my future.

At the age of ten, like all true thespians, I went violently Shakespearean. I must have inherited this love as both of my parents were inveterate readers of the classics. The complete works of the great "Bard" lined our library's shelves, their leather covers worn and pages wrinkled from many readings. It was just as my own theatrical passion was beginning to grow and consume me that my mother, who was president of a charity organization, conceived of the idea of giving a Shakespearean carnival, using all local talent. From the moment that I learned of her plan, I yearned for the opportunity to emote. I pleaded with my mother so earnestly and so often that I finally broke down all her resistance and was assigned the role of Prince Arthur in "King John."

Rehearsals lasted for several weeks, and I attended every one. Gradually, I began to live the life of Prince Arthur, acting it out throughout the days and even dreaming of it at night. My family was continually encountering me in hallways, descending stairs and rounding corners, all the while reciting my lines with as much dramatic flair as I could muster.

The evening of the actual performance is still vivid in my memory. I smile when I think of how comical my skinny legs, encased in a pair of my mother's white silk stockings in lieu of tights, must have looked. I can still recall the fervor and agony with which I delivered my lines. On that important night, the evening of my dramatic debut, my success seemed tremendous. The light praise I received from family and friends for my small part in the production became the thunderous applause of all the world in my ears. I felt sure I was destined to become the greatest Shakespearean actor of all times. I began to act every moment that I was awake. I read his other plays, learned other roles, and soon became dramatic to my fingertips!

But this new endeavor, too, came to an unhappy ending. One afternoon, during a period in which I was especially intrigued with *Othello*, I was asked to mind my little sister, Natalie, for a short time. An audience was all that I needed, so I seized this as an opportunity to exhibit my best acting capabilities.

I began my performance most dramatically, with Othello's speech "Tis the cause. Tis the cause." My enunciation was none too perfect and, in retrospect, my "cause" probably sounded more like "cars." Natalie's big eyes widened and I knew that I had made an impression. Thus encouraged, I grabbed a pillow and with the deepest and most blood-curdling voice I could produce, pounced upon my little sister crying, "Desdemona! Desdemona!"

Natalie nearly had a spasm and screamed at the top of her very capable little lungs, "Save me! Save me!" Instantly, Mammy came rushing into the room and Natalie flew into the protective embrace of her arms, frightened into an avalanche of tears.

I stood there, hands on my hips, most pleased and satisfied with the results I had managed to obtain and feeling completely assured of my future dramatic success. However, when my mother learned of this little escapade, she expressed a different view on the matter and proceeded to whale the ecstasy completely out of me. I was promised an even greater punishment if I dared ever to repeat such an offense. I was crushed. I could not continue. For years, I was absolutely convinced that my mother had deprived the world of its greatest tragedian.

It was about this time that I was sent to a public school, and I must say that I did not like it at all. I had never been very fond of school, and now that I was separated from Leonora for the first time, I liked it even less. I had never been considered a particularly good student as I had no interest in the subjects considered to be the practical necessities in life, especially arithmetic. Being somewhat recalcitrant, I simply refused to study it. However, history, poetry, and the languages were much more to my liking, and I would spend hours pouring over historical accounts, writing prose, and learning new phrases in perfect French. There was no compromise for me then and there has been none since. The things I like I put my whole soul into. The other things, I make not the slightest effort to master.

Shortly after I had celebrated my tenth birthday, the Cavalier approached me one morning saying, "Sonnybuck, you're a man now." Actually, I don't think that he had ever thought of me as being anything else since that day on the train, eight years earlier. "I think that it's time you join some of the men on one of our fox hunts."

I went absolutely wild with excitement. Leaping up and down, I exclaimed, "Father, do you really mean it? How soon can I go?"

"We'll arrange to take you on the very next one. Some of the men are planning a hunt for next week. I'll let you know in time."

The anticipation was unbearable. I could hardly wait until the day came. We were to start out on the horses at three o'clock in the morning. I was so excited that I didn't sleep a wink, but was up, dressed, and waiting for the others in the stables before I was called. The Cavalier gave me Old Nellie to ride. She was an aged, flea-bitten, sure-footed white mare who could be trusted to find her way anywhere. Although I had ridden almost every day since I was a small boy, The Cavalier knew that riding over hills, fording rivers, jumping fences, and hunting foxes was going to be quite a different story. Old Nellie was to be my protector for the day, my father trusting her to take care of me. Somehow I managed to hang on throughout the chase, and she delivered me home safe and sound, exhausted but oh so happy.

The summer of 1892, we spent at a resort in Virginia and there, on my birthday in July, I had the greatest thrill of my life. Nothing has quite equalled it since. I simply do not have sufficient command of the English language to describe my feelings when the Cavalier presented me with Headlight, a beautiful thoroughbred bay mare with four white socks and a white-blazed face. This great joy was further enhanced by a white leather bridle, an English racing saddle, and a red blanket bound in white leather. My happiness was something beyond expression. Headlight instantly seemed to sense the depth of my emotions, and we rapidly became fast friends. I shared all of my thoughts with her, and she gave me a loyalty that very few humans are capable of equalling.

At this resort, one morning a little before noon, I met my first celebrity. Although many more celebrities have come into my life since then, I always look back at that time, still retaining some of my boyish wonder and innocence at the encounter. Headlight and I had just returned from a glorious morning outing, which had been finished off with a gallop along a sandy beach. The stable boy was rubbing her down, and we were engrossed in one of our usual intimate conversations. Headlight was resting her head upon my shoulder when suddenly she jerked her head away and, with feminine intuition, threw back her ears and flared her nostrils. I turned around and beheld the most beautiful lady I had ever seen in my life. She stood framed by the stable doorway with the sun behind her shining and glistening in her hair. I can see her as clearly today as then, so very stately and elegant, her golden hair and pink cheeks complimented by a flowing pink summer dress, her smile so friendly.

She took a few steps closer and spoke to me. "Young man, that's a beautiful mare you have. You must be very fond of riding. I am, too. I've done a very great deal of it in my time."

"Yes! Yes, indeed!" I exclaimed in a stammering fashion, not taking my eyes off of this lovely vision. Her apparent appreciation of Headlight pleased me greatly. She had won me over easily, and we chatted freely for quite some time.

"I must return to my hotel now," she said, then hesitated a moment as though thinking. "I wonder if you'd like to come with me? I received a very large box from New York today. I haven't opened it yet, but I'm sure it's candy. Suppose we do a bit of exploring together?"

It turned out to be the largest box of candy I had ever seen, and I believe that I consumed almost half of it. My mother never allowed me to have more than a few pieces at a time and, since she was not there to stop me, I took full advantage of the opportunity. All the time I nibbled, we talked. Or rather, she talked and I listened. She told me of the horses she had owned and how she had ridden all over the South, both by day and night, seemingly knowing all the roads and paths. I thought that she must be the most wonderful woman in the whole world.

I was late for luncheon that day and, quite naturally, arrived with no appetite. Under fire of questioning, I told my father and mother about the beautiful lady and the box of candy. The Cavalier smiled.

"Sonnybuck, I know your beautiful lady. I saw her myself this morning. Her name is Belle Boyd[1] and she was probably the most daring and brave of all the Confederate women in the espionage service. She had such charm, personality, and beauty that she could always outwit men in hazardous circumstances. Many times during the war she would make trips to Washington by horseback and cleverly collect thousands of bags of quinine and morphia. She would then sew them onto the hoops of her dresses and deliver them to the Confederate hospitals behind the lines. She was a humanitarian and probably did more good by relieving the suffering of the wounded than any other single person on the Confederate side.. Today you met a truly great woman."

Although I never saw Miss Boyd again, I have never forgotten her. She still remains, in my mind's eye, the most beautiful woman I have ever seen. She must have been close to fifty at the time, but she gave the impression of being young. It is hard to understand how she was able to have performed such a great service during such a dangerous time.

We returned to Vicksburg in the fall, and I spent the winter going to school and riding Headlight. On one of our earlier trips across the countryside, we came across an Indian mound. This burial ground of braves—which I learned included not only their bones, but all their belongings, even cooking utensils—stirred my imagination. I shared my archaeological finding with Leonora, and together we made many visits there, digging for pieces of copper utensils, arrow heads, bones, and the like. With all of these collected items, we then started a museum in a shed on our property for the edification of our small group of fans and followers. While this was indeed fun, it just did not seem to have the allure or the tragic ending of our circus days.

The following spring, a real disaster visited the Deep South. The Mississippi River began to rise, and I was an eyewitness to one of the greatest floods of that time. While our own house was never in imminent danger from the rising waters as it crowned a very high hill, we could stand in our yard and see other families marooned on the roofs of their floating houses. They would scream for rescue, all the while clinging to chimneys and roof peaks while the muddy, turbulent waters carried their homes further downstream. It was this disaster that made me begin to realize that life also held real tragedies and not just those found on the pages of my beloved authors.

One morning during the flood, only a short distance from our home, the nude body of a young woman was found. She had been dead but a short time when she was discovered. No one locally seemed able to identify her and the advertisements placed in all the river towns around us brought no positive responses either. She was finally laid to rest beside the Indian mound and on a small, marble tombstone was inscribed:

"The Fair Unknown,
Found Floating
In the River."

This event made a great impression upon my mind. Leonora and I would often visit her grave and place flowers there, always wondering who she was and weaving fanciful stories about her life.

Years later, I had the pleasure of meeting Mr. and Mrs. George Barr McCutcheon[2] and Miss Clara Laughlin. Mr. McCutcheon's *Graustark* and other bestsellers had made him famous. Miss Laughlin, who was still a prolific writer at the time, had become known the world over for her guidebooks for travelers. I related this tragedy to them and suggested that one of them might write a very interesting story around it. Miss Laughlin's reply seemed very strange to me at that time.

"I think it would be much more interesting to write about the little boy who dreamed of this fair unknown."

When I was fourteen an even greater tragedy visited our community. This time it was the yellow fever. The calamitous epidemic of 1878 was still so fresh in the minds of the older people that the mere mention of yellow fever was enough to throw them into a panic. In August of 1895, when a few cases were reported in New Orleans, pandemonium broke out. Every city and village quarantined itself against the others. Volunteer guards with shotguns were positioned at every crossroad. No one was allowed to either come in or go out, but the fever managed to defy them all and spread anyway. Within a week of the first reports, numerous localities reported cases.

The Cavalier, having considerable influence in the area, managed to complete all the necessary arrangements needed to transport his entire family to the safety of St. Louis. Train tickets were purchased and trunks were hastily packed, but on the morning we were to leave my little sister, Natalie, broke out with a rash. The doctor was summoned and pronounced the rash to be scarlet fever. My parents became frantic. New arrangements were hastily made for us to occupy a farm that was about twenty miles distant from Vicksburg and completely isolated and out of the danger zone of the yellow fever. Carriages and wagons were assembled, and the family left at once. I was to remain behind to superintend the closing of the house, the packing and storing of the valuables, and to arrange for the care of the livestock. Headlight and I were to follow as quickly as all of this had been accomplished.

It was almost dark before all of my responsibilities were completed and I felt free to leave. I had never been to this farm before and, although I had been given directions by my father, I had only a general idea of how to get there. So, somewhat nervously, Headlight and I started out on our journey. Every road we came to was guarded by grim-faced, determined men who stopped and interrogated us. However, while we were still close to home, the men knew me and we were allowed to pass. Dusk came and we got further from home. With the darkness, I became frightened, so I started to sing at the top of my lungs to keep up my courage, but Headlight—like the thoroughbred she was—knew the truth behind the song. She held her head a little higher and lifted her feet daintily as though she were on parade. She knew what her job was and was going to carry it through gallantly.

At about ten o'clock in the evening, we reached a big crossroad, which I assumed was where I had been told to turn off. Ten or twelve men were on guard duty with double-barrel shotguns, and we were told to halt. One burly, unshaven man of more than six feet in stature approached me and held a lantern up to my face. "Well, I'll be damned. It's a kid. What in hell are you doing out in this country at this time of night?" The men all gathered around me in amazement.

In a trembling voice I tried to explain that I was joining my family who had, that same day, moved to a farm. They seemed to doubt my story. "Sorry kid. You may be telling the truth, but no one passes this way tonight. You'll have to turn around and go back."

"But," I cried, "I have no place to go. My family are all at this farm. You must believe me and let me pass." I was panicky. I thought of the dark night and the guarded roads behind me. I could envision Headlight and myself riding around and around without food or water. "Surely someone of you men knows my father, George Rector," I pleaded with them.

One of the older men who had been standing off to one side, stepped forward at the mention of the Cavalier's name and looked me over carefully.

"I know George Rector," he said, turning to the men. "I've been fox hunting with him several times. He has a son, too, about this boy's age, although I've never seen him. Let's take a chance on the kid's story and let him through."

"No way." "We can't take the risk." "Nothin' doin'," they all replied in unison.

"Hell, men, we can't run the kid back. It's dangerous. Let's be sensible about this thing. I'll take all the responsibility."

But his pleas met with further responses of disapproval.

It was at this point that Headlight, seeming to sense the seriousness of the whole situation, leaped forward in a mad gallop, which did not slow down until we were well out of reach of a shotgun. The men hollered and yelled and even fired several shots into the air, but I could not have stopped Headlight, even if I had tried. I have only Headlight to thank for my rescue, for I am sure that the other men would never have given in to my defender and let me pass.

By this time, I was too scared even to sing. On and on we went into the black night. Hardly a star was visible and the road became difficult to follow. It suddenly took a sharp turn, and I could hear a stream of water running along side it. Faintly, I could see the glow of a light ahead and, as we cautiously approached it, I was able to discern more guards around the entrance to a small bridge. New fears began to envelop me. What was I to do now? I dared not take a chance of being turned back by them. Of that, I was sure. I quickly and quietly turned Headlight around and, before they could spy us, we proceeded to carefully pick our way down the banks of the stream. After traveling for about a quarter of a mile, I found a place I that I felt was shallow enough to ford ,so Headlight and I plunged in and swam across to the other side. As we could find no road on the other side, we were forced to strike out across the countryside. The ground became somewhat swampy and new fears of snakes and who knows what began to present themselves to me, but we had no choice but to go on. It was a sparsely settled area and what few Negroes lived there had long since gone to bed, with all the lights out and the doors bolted. There was not a single sign of life anywhere.

I began to feel that we were completely lost and my courage was practically gone. After what seemed to be many hours of riding, I began to consider the idea of stopping for the balance of the night, praying that daylight would bring, at the very least, encouragement. Suddenly, without any warning, Headlight lifted her head, neighed, and broke into a canter. I saw a tiny light ahead. As we drew closer, Headlight slowed down and I was able to distinguish the outlines of a farm house. We approached it cautiously, not knowing just what new danger might be awaiting us. Yes, there was a figure in the doorway. Yes, it was a man. Once again, Headlight assumed control of the situation and broke into a gallop. You can imagine my exultation when I recognized the figure standing in the doorway as that of the Cavalier. Headlight had somehow managed to recognize him long before I had.

The relief upon my father's face was unmistakable. He seemed to sense what I had been through, but, with true generalship, managed to control his emotions, not wanting to upset me any more than I was already.

"Did you enjoy the ride?" was the Cavalier's greeting, trying to sound casual about it all.

"Wonderful," I answered rather weakly.

"That's just fine. Why don't you go on in? I'll stable Headlight for you. Your mother has some fried chicken, hot biscuits, and fig preserves waiting for you. We thought you would be here about this time and knew that you would be hungry after the long ride."

I ate and slept that night with the joy that comes to one who realizes after a great danger that he is, at last, safe. That same feeling has returned since, but never with as deep a feeling of thankfulness.

My little sister, fortunately, had only a mild attack of scarlet fever, and within a few weeks the doctor allowed us to pack and leave the farm. This time, we boarded a train and arrived safely in St. Louis. It was the very last train that went through from Vicksburg to St. Louis until after the epidemic had subsided.

There, in St. Louis, I had my first romance. I fell desperately in love with none other than Miss Maxine Elliott[3]. She was playing in St. Louis at the old Olympic Theatre with her husband, Nat. C. Goodwin, in *American Citizen and Nathan Hale*. Miss Elliot's beauty was then being acclaimed all over the world. She was tall, with a magnificent figure (when women really had figures and men liked them), very dark hair, and eyes of rich tenderness. She was the daughter of Thomas Dermot, a Maine sea captain. Her beauty had led her to the stage at an early age, an event that gave to the American stage one of its most outstanding characters and actresses.

Although I never met Miss Elliott in person, I could not have given any woman greater adoration. We were living quite far out on Olive Street, at a boarding house that many Southern families patronized at that time. I was allowed a dollar a week for pocket money, which gave me just enough funds for a seat in the theatre gallery for two matinees a week, but no carfare. I walked the forty blocks each way, twice a week, with winged feet. The distance did not seem to dampen my ardor. The scene at dawn, just before Mr. Hale was to be hanged, with its heart-wrenching farewell, always left me quite inconsolable.

We were able to return to our home in Vicksburg in the middle of November. Sadness and sorrow seemed to be everywhere. While not as virulent as the former epidemics, the yellow fever had taken its toll on the state. Farmers, merchants, and all the businesses had been deeply affected. The overflowing river and the following disease had brought devastation everywhere and to everyone. The crops were a total loss; the property damage was enormous. The scourge had left that portion of the South in desperate financial straits.

The Cavalier, who had left the banking business years before and established a wholesale provision company, suffered large financial losses. He was forced to sell most of his hounds, horses, and other personal property, but he decided to keep Headlight at all costs. Her loyalty in a time of need had been too great. For several years we lived most simply, and there were times when our table held little food, but the indomitable courage and the gay spirits inherited by all true Southerners managed to keep us going. We smiled in the face of adversity and planned our march forward. In other words, we took it on the chin and didn't bellyache. I'm grateful I learned this lesson early in life as it fortified me for the years to come.

The next few years were rather uneventful. I was too old for childish pranks and to young for grown-up escapades. Somehow my parents managed to provide the funds needed to send me through preparatory school and then on for two years in college. It must have been a real financial struggle for them, but they held fast to their high principles and ideals and gave their children all the necessary advantages possible.

My parents were ardent lovers of the theatre, and I was taken to see the greatest artists of that day who toured the South. I saw such famous people as Joseph Jefferson, Madame Modjeska, Sarah Bernhardt, Olga Nethersole, Mary Mannering, Viola Allen, James K. Hackett and many others, but the greatest of all theses artists, to me, was Madame Nellie Melba. I still believe her voice to be the most divine that I have ever heard.

I was also deeply interested in reading. During these few years, I made the acquaintance of such writers as Victor Hugo, Sir Walter Scott, Thackery, Bulwer-Lytton, Tennyson, Edgar Allen Poe, Tolstoy, DuMaupassant, Balzac, D'Annunzio, and countless others. I look back now and greatly appreciate the fact that my family never made any restrictions upon my choices of literature. I was allowed to read what they, as adults, read. I was so serious minded and derived considerable pleasure from my literary associations and the doors to the new worlds that they opened.

And then I came face to face with my first great grief. In the fall of 1905, my mother died suddenly after an illness of only one day. My sorrow was deep rooted. I just could not grasp the fact that anyone so vibrant, so warm, and so giving could be taken with such little warning. Shortly after my mother's death, my father's health broke down, and he was taken to a sanitarium. At the age of twenty-four, I was faced with the full responsibility of my two sisters and what was left of a once-thriving business.

For two years I was forced to keep my nose to the grindstone. My family depended totally upon me, and I could not disappoint them. My only outside interest was singing. I had always had a naturally good voice, and so I was easily persuaded to begin taking lessons from an excellent local teacher. In singing, I found a distraction from the monotony of the daily grind of the business world. I became intensely interested in my studies and put my whole soul into them. My vision for my future began to grow and change with each lesson I took.

In a few years my financial and family responsibilities were adjusted. My father was back at his business, and we began going forward at an even pace. I could, at last, think about what I wanted for a future. I wanted fame. I wanted adventure. I wanted wealth. I wanted love. One evening, about dusk, I mounted Headlight and rode up into the Blue Ridge Mountains. The air was crisp and the golden crimson autumn foliage seemed brazen against the background of the soft blue velvet of the mountains. I thought of the old Indian legend that weaved the story of the beautiful mist, which surrounds these mountains with its mystical glory, filled with the spirits of the departed warriors who have come back to their happy hunting grounds. I felt the urge to become a warrior—to conquer the world and gather the fame, fortune, and love that I was dreaming of. Somewhere beyond those mountains was the answer to my dreams. I knew that only by leaving would I find what I was seeking. I must go forth.

I put my arms around Headlight's neck and gently stroked her mane. "Headlight, I'm going to have to leave you. You've been the most perfect friend a boy could have, but I must go now. I have things I must accomplish. I'm going to New York where opportunities are awaiting me. Goodbye, old pal. I shall never forget you or the great love that you've given me."

Headlight seemed to know and understand. As we rode back, her head was drooped and her gait slow. Her heart was filled with sadness, but I looked on and dreamed. I had made up my mind and chosen the path I would follow. Had I known of what was to come, what sorrows fame can bring, what prices one has to pay, what crises one has to face when years outlive fame, what struggles one has to endure in a fast-moving and changing world, I don't know that I would have had the courage to follow that path.

Leonora Rector, George Pickett Harrison Rector, Natalie Rector, Thomas Allen Rector

Chapter Two

At last! I had arrived in the city of my dreams. A writer once compared New York to a great Bengal tiger, coiled and ready to pounce and devour everything that crossed its path. Well, I was certainly ready and willing to be devoured. With very little money in my pockets, but fortified with youth's glorious and eternal optimism, I was ready to brave this wondrous new world and prepared to fight for what I had dreamed of for so long. Curiously, I never once felt that loneliness which so often grips people who arrive in a new place for the first time. On the contrary, I felt exhilarated, uplifted, and most friendly. I liked New York, and I certainly wanted New York to like me.

I went to live at a boarding house in the West Fifties, which had a considerable reputation among the gentry of the South. The establishment was run by three sisters from Georgia and was frequented chiefly by young people from that section of the country. I shared a room with two other young men and delighted in three substantial, nourishing meals a day. For this I paid the enormous sum of seven dollars and fifty cents a week!

Once I was settled in my new lodgings, my thoughts immediately turned to my longed-for career in music, hoping that with the proper training I might be able to achieve something worthwhile with my voice. One of the few letters of introduction that I have ever presented in my life, was to a well-known New York vocal teacher. Upon acceptance of my credentials by this respected instructor, arrangements were made for me to take three lessons a week. I immediately began practicing my vocal exercises almost every minute of the day, irritating my roommates somewhat, but wanting to advance quickly in my course of study.

All too quickly my money supply began to run very low, and I was forced to realize that I would have to find some sort of gainful employment to cover my current living expenses, yet would still allow me the time necessary to pursue my musical career. This became quite a problem as I seemed to have no experience or talents of the kind that were being sought out by New York businesses, but I did possess a fairly good, if still untrained, voice. I scurried around and, after much searching, was able to make a connection with a well-known philanthropic organization which furnished free concerts to the laboring men and women of Manhattan. I was assigned to sing during lunch hours each working day, between eleven and one, first to the men digging the subway at Columbus Circle and second, to a large factory employing mostly women. For this I was to receive the sum of one dollar and twenty-five cents a concert.

Never have I sung to such enthusiastic audiences. I was accompanied to these midday concerts by a musician who carried a portable organ. We would both descend ladders into a huge hole in the ground, which is now the subway station at Columbus Circle, and join the large group of working men, mostly Italians, who were anxiously awaiting us. While they munched away on their sandwiches made from thick slabs of crusty bread and filled with pungent meats and cheeses, I would express my whole soul in *Traviata, Rigoletto, Boheme,* and other standard Italian operas. Their applause after each number was always gratifying to me, and their appreciation most sincere. What lovers of music those men were! Often they would join me in the more popular operatic pieces, their rich voices filling the underground cavern with beautiful harmony. It was always difficult to pull myself away from them, as eager as they were for more.

Leaving there, my accompanist and I would then rush down to the women's factory where I usually arranged to perform a group of sentimental love songs. The favorite ballad of that time was *Forgotten*, and I would pour all the pathos my romantic soul could muster into the rendition of that song. These pathetic, work-worn women appeared to have been touched by romance in only a sordid kind of way. Many of them had been left alone at young ages, struggling to feed several children and to pay the rent in grimy, run-down tenements. During the concerts, tears would form in their eyes, spilling over and running down their hollowed-out cheeks. Possibly they were remembering the romances that had once been or dreaming of those which might still be. It was so touching to see the expressions on their sad faces, and I always came away feeling a bit depressed, wanting to do more for them and knowing that I could not.

Due to the timing of these concerts, I would miss the lunch provided at my boarding house, so I began to patronize the free-lunch counters which abounded in New York in those days. What a lifesaver they were! My favorite places were Pabst on Columbus Circle and the Hotel Imperial on Broadway. For five cents, I could buy a glass of beer and eat all the cheese, ham, pickles, pretzels, and other delicacies I could devour. I never really cared for beer in those days, as it always seemed to make me lethargic, but, oh how those free lunches helped me make it through those long, lean times.

I had always been very much interested in the French language, having started my studies while still a young boy and continuing on with them while in College. My vocal teacher quickly discovered my linguistic talents and presented me with some delightful French songs to perform. I then decided that, in order to do the songs the justice truly deserved them, I needed to master the language as well as I possibly could. Since I could not possibly afford a French teacher on the meager earnings from my noontime concerts, I concluded that the next best thing would be to live with a French family. As fate would have it, just such a family resided in the same block as my rooming house and, as there just happened to be a sign advertising "Room for Rent," I immediately went to investigate. I was quickly deemed acceptable by them and moved in on the very same day. This was a most fortunate step because the associations and friendships I made there were delightful and enduring. Their home seemed to have an attraction for success and I became intimately acquainted with men who have since made their marks in this world. They were and are friends who paid the price of fame, but were ultimately victorious.

These French people were aristocrats who were waiting for the settlement of a family estate in Russia. (The settlement was made, timely enough, just a few days before the outbreak of the great World War.) They were a charming and delightful couple and blessed with two very beautiful daughters—one their own and one adopted. These daughters, of course, were the main reason why the house eventually filled with young men. When I moved in, the house was still comparatively empty of boarders as the family had just recently settled there. However, as soon as my companions and their friends discovered these charming and attractive young ladies, the house rapidly filled to overflowing.

I shared a room with another chap on the second floor in the rear of the house. We boasted of having a private bath with our room which, although billed as a luxury, we actually found to be an economy for us. We would do most of our laundry in the big, claw-foot bathtub. Our socks, underclothing, pajamas, and such we did not have to iron, and our handkerchiefs were plastered on the windowpanes to dry stiff and smooth. Our keen sense of humor and our youth made all these struggles seem like fun, rather than drudgery.

I became quite friendly with the young man who occupied the front room on the second floor. His name was Victor Chenais, and he was blessed with a God-given baritone voice. Instinctively, our musical interests brought us very close together. He had a delightful, sparkling personality. Everyone he met he liked and if he saw them a second time, they were considered his friends. His friendships transcended all economic and social bounds. He was made godfather to the Italian fruit peddler's child and was intimate with the socially prominent of the times. His closest friend was one of America's great millionaires.

One afternoon, as I was heading home after my lunch hour recitals, I couldn't help but notice that our entire block was lined with the most expensive limousines I had ever seen. Liveried chauffeurs and footmen stood around in groups, talking. It certainly was a most unusual event for our humble neighborhood. As soon as I entered the front door, I discovered that it was our house that was the recipient of all these lovely guests. As I climbed the stairs, the rumble of voices seemed to be coming from everywhere. Much to my amusement, I found a great many of New York's fashionable set perched upon beds, floors, furniture and any place they could find. Our entire floor was crowded to capacity. Victor was singing in his most engaging manner, and his audience was absolutely entranced. Refreshments for the group consisted of a case of beer, a wheel of cheese, and crackers. Since then, I have attended many musicals at the homes of some of these socially elite people. Great stars would sing, liveried butlers served sumptuous repasts, and everything was carried through with delightful precision, but never have I seen them radiating such pure enjoyment as they did that afternoon, sitting just anywhere, dropping crumbs on the floor, and drinking beer out of the bottle.

Another intimate friend I made at this rooming house was Stuart Walker[4], who already was well on his way to success. He was, at the time I met him, stage manager for David Balasco[5]. Through his generous courtesy, I was able to enjoy the very finest in dramatics that New York had to offer, and many scenes from these performances are still vivid in my memory. One of the things that I have always admired in Stuart was his great love for his mother and his continuous expression of it. I rejoice in the great success he has made. He most certainly is deserving of it.

Probably the most colorful person in our house was a young French nobleman who was on his uppers. For the sake of the story I am about to tell, I will have to call him Count de L. He was a great sportsman and a lover of horses, so naturally we became friends immediately. I still remember the day he burst into my room with a most anxious look on his face.

"You know," he said quite nervously, "I'm in a frightful mess. I am completely out of funds. The remittances from my estate in France have not arrived. They are long overdue and I do not know what to do."

I laughed as I had become quite used to such shortages, their having become a routine part of my life. "Oh, that's not so serious. Why don't you pawn that diamond ring you're wearing?"

I could see that I had absolutely horrified the Count with my suggestion.

Fumbling for words, he muttered, "I, ah, I simply could not do that. It is a family heirloom. I ah, ah ..."

"It's quite all right" I quickly interrupted, trying to reassure him. "Look here, I know Uncle Ike around the corner very well. I've been taking my watch, cigarette case, scarf pins, and the like to him regularly. It's all perfectly safe. You can get it out as soon as your money arrives."

"I couldn't do that. Why, I wouldn't even go into the place. It's a disgraceful thing to do."

"Oh, not at all. It's just an old American custom. Come on. Let's go through your things and see what we can hock. Look, I'll even take them over for you. No one need ever know. You've got to eat, and right now this seems to be the only way."

With some further argument, I finally convinced him of the practicality of my plan. We went through his affects and collected all the jewelry in his possession. In a very short time, I had visited Uncle Ike's shop and was back with three hundred dollars of cold cash.

The Count fairly beamed at my success. "I shall always be indebted to you for helping me in this way. Surely this has caused you considerable trouble and embarrassment."

"Absolutely none, my dear friend. My only trouble was in convincing Uncle Ike that I hadn't stolen the jewelry. I had to do some fast thinking and strong talking and even though he finally gave me the money, I'm sure he's still quite doubtful as to where I actually got the jewelry."

For this simple act of kindness, the Count became my life-long friend. Since then, I have met him in all parts of the world, and at each meeting he has entertained me lavishly, usually presenting me with some sort of handsome gift. He vows, to this day, that I saved his life in a time of desperate need.

Griffin Barry[6] also lived in our house. He is the brother of Richard Barry, the writer. Although we were close friends there, our lives have not crossed often since the old days. He was a fine type of a boy and was having a hard struggle to survive, but fighting with his chin up. I'm glad of the success he has made.

All of us at the house had very little at that time, but we always shared what we had with each other. I have the greatest warmth and affection for my days there. When one of us was broke, the whole crowd would rush forward to assist. Each one did what he could to further the career of the others. I am sure that it was the unselfishness and willingness to help each other that, in a way, attracted the later successes of all these men

In the immediate vicinity of our boarding house, there was a little tearoom known as "The Students' Inn," which was endowed by a wealthy New York woman. I have often wondered if she ever knew what joy and aid she gave to the struggling young artists of that time. Mrs. Sayre, the tearoom's manager, was a most efficient woman who supervised the preparation of delicious foods which were then sold to us at cost. It was all sold "a la carte" and, with the exception of the meat courses, none of the items were ever priced at more than five cents.

As our group ate there frequently, I conceived of the idea of forming what we called "The Spangled Set." Just why I came up with this name, I haven't the faintest idea. Anyone who paid more than thirty-five cents for his or her dinner immediately became a member. We did have an awful lot of fun there, although we were considered to be rather wild and fast by the few prim maiden ladies who dined there. Each day they would sit down, eating their twenty-five cent dinners after having struggled all day teaching music, painting, and other arts to grimy-handed youths. Often they would stare at us through the wire-rimmed glasses perched low on their noses, their tired faces registering both wonderment and disapproval at the hilarity of our antics. The number of "The Spangled Set" members grew quickly. We made more friends, met more people, and went more places. Life, to me, was kind and gay, and everyone I met seemed to be offering a helping hand.

One of the livelier members of this group was Frances Foster, the daughter of Judge and Mrs. Foster of Canada, and known to us as "Daisy." She was a very fine pianist at that time and has since made excellent strides in the musical world. David Howell Lindley, a young actor, was also quite active and the first of our group to achieve success. Fred Zubriskie ran around with this crowd a lot, however he was not an active member of the set. He was really the plutocrat of the group, coming from a very prominent family and being well endowed with the world's goods. He was a boy with a great capacity for both giving and enjoying fun. Many times, when our pocketbooks were low, it was Fred who would take us out for a grand dinner. He also introduced us to a drink at the old café Martin called the "Amier Pican." It was quite a potent concoction and could make a jackrabbit spit in a bulldog's face!

Through a member of this set I met a fascinating woman, who, for many reasons, I will call "Sally." She seemed to know absolutely everyone of importance of that day and delighted in throwing interesting and innovative parties. Sally was especially kind to me and did many things to further my aspiring ambitions in the music world. Through her I met such people as Alexander Woollcott[7], who had just come to New York. His brilliance and superlative wit were already attracting the attention of the world. In those days, he was quite slim and rather good-looking, and he was always the most brilliant of any group he joined. I also remember Billy Armstrong[8] very well; at that time he was one of the greatest musical critics in America. He had such a gentle, charming manner and a keen sense of humor.

I must tell you about one particular party Sally gave. She had just moved into a new flat on lower Fifth Avenue and had issued invitations to a large crowd for a fancy dress party as a housewarming. Being young and still rather foolish, I succumbed to the romantic side of my nature and gave into my weakness for tights that I had cherished since my youthful debut in *King John*, many years back. After pawing through racks of stage costumes in several shops, I finally found and rented a costume of Romeo, which consisted chiefly of blatant silk tights of an off-shade of pink that fit none too well. After viewing myself in full regalia and not daring to make such a bold appearance alone, I arranged to dress at the home of some friends who lived on Forty-fourth Street, just off Fifth Avenue, and to return with them after the party and spend the night. I was definitely in need of their moral support if I was to carry off the wearing of such a flamboyant costume.

Well, the party was a huge success, as all of Sally's parties were. The flat was literally jammed with personable people the world already knew or would soon know. Shortly after our arrival, I discovered that Sally had decreed it was to be the order of the evening that everyone must perform for the other guests in some manner or other. A smile still comes to my face when I remember the comments—both pro and con—that Romeo caused when he performed an exhibition dance with the most famous Spanish dancer of that time. At its conclusion, I was quite embarrassed at the brazenness of my action, as well as plenty warm from the strenuous dancing, so I slipped out into the hall in an attempt to regain my composure and to cool off.

While standing out there, I began to notice that I could hear other music, laughter, and gaiety drifting up through an open stairwell. I must admit that I have always had a rather inquisitive nature, and that evening it seemed to be somewhat sharpened by the quantity of wine I had consumed. After a deliberation of only a few seconds, I decided to fling conventions to the winds and, appointing myself as a committee of one, went off to investigate this jollity. Two floors below I found an apartment door wide open and what appeared to be a most exciting party in full progress. The sight of a pseudo-Romeo appearing suddenly at the door created something of an uproar within, and I was immediately dragged in by the revelers and offered the choicest of everything. Plied with more wine, I was flung into almost an orgy of excitement. Time lost all meaning, and it was four o'clock in the morning before I realized it. Dashing back upstairs, all the while practicing apologies for my hostess, I arrived at her door only to find Sally's party broken up long ago; the lights were out and the door was bolted. Behind that door and out of my reach were my overcoat and hat.

There was nothing left for me to do at this point but to go back to my friend's home on Forty-fourth Street. Without the price of a cab, for my purse was in my coat pocket, all I could do was walk, so I started the chilly journey homeward—a bedraggled, forlorn spectacle in disheveled pink tights. What a commotion I caused as I walked. Some latecomers, coming from equally merry parties, shouted all sorts of greetings to me, including a few nonprintable remarks. Others must have thought they were delirious, the way they rushed by me pretending not to notice my ridiculous garb. But with a haughty air, I managed to get to Forty-second Street without any physical interference. There I encountered my first policeman.

When he saw me he blinked and rubbed his eyes in astonishment. He roughly grabbed me by the shoulders and blurted out, "What th' hell! In all th' years I've been on th' force, I ain't never seen anthin' like this before. Where in th' hell are you goin' at this time of the night in them pink tights?"

I hastily stammered my plight—bemoaning the sneers and taunts I had endured thus far. He surprisingly proved to be quite understanding and insisted upon escorting me the remaining two blocks home. My irate hosts, who had been quite anxious about me during my disappearance, quickly forgave me in their howls of laughter as I stumbled through the door and related my experience.

The next day, I meekly called for my overcoat and hat, expressed my apologies for having been so thoughtless, and described what had transpired the evening before to a very understanding Sally. She had heard of the party below and explained that my second hostess of the evening was none other than one of the original girls of the *Florodora* sextette[9]. I understand that shortly after this party, her particular gentleman friend at that time had the floors of that flat made soundproof in order not to disturb the neighbors too much during future parties. I was never invited back there, so I cannot say just how effective it was.

It was only a few mornings after this festive occasion that my friend, Victor, came rushing into my room, awakening me at an unusually early hour. He had a newspaper in his hand which he was waving about in the air as he excitedly cried, "Look! Look here, Tom! The Metropolitan Opera Company is advertising an audition to select a hundred promising vocalists for a free scholarship. I've decided that I'm going to try for it. Why don't you join me and audition, too?"

I sat up quickly, running a hand through my pillow-tossled hair and trying to pull my thoughts together. "That's wonderful, Victor. Of course you must try. You have a wonderful voice and should be able to win a position easily."

"But, you. What about you? Aren't you going to try out with me?"

"Oh! That's shooting way too high for me. My voice isn't that good. I wouldn't have the ghost of a show of making it."

"Sure you would. You have a good voice. Besides you dance well. And ... and, well, you're good looking and you have the perfect personality for the stage. Come with me and try. I'll bet you're accepted. Think about it for a while, and I'll be back later to talk about it."

I thought about Victor's proposal constantly throughout the day. In my wildest fantasies I had never dared to dream of becoming a member of the world-renown Metropolitan Opera Company. But what was there to lose in trying? After all, the audition experience itself would be good for me. Yes, maybe I would give it a try. Here was opportunity knocking at my door, and I had better be ready and willing to open it or it might pass me by, never to return again.

In talking with Victor, I discovered that the audition was but a week off so during that time I put my nose to the grindstone and nearly sang my head off practicing the scales. I was absolutely determined to put everything I had into this trial. At last the day of the auditions arrived and, with a copy of Tosti's *La Serenata* under my arm and mentally armed with an infinite amount of nerve, I accompanied Victor to the most famous opera house in the world. We were not alone in desiring this opportunity of a lifetime as, upon our arrival, we discovered that there were about three hundred aspirants ahead of us. Once inside, I began to feel a little nervousness creeping up on me. As time went by, I grew tired and anxious, but slowly I began to realize that this waiting was just the beginning. If I was accepted by the Metropolitan, I would surely be required to rehearse for hours and hours, for days and days, even weeks and probably months. I would have to withstand incredible physical and mental strain to attain success. All artists had to go through this. Contemplating these thoughts seemed to stimulate and reinvigorate me. I straightened my back and once again directed my attention to the performers going on before me.

One of the assistant conductors was holding the audition. He was German, small of stature, and certainly the possessor of a rather unusual personality. Throughout the proceedings he seemed to have a case of the jumps, constantly sitting down and then popping up to pace a bit and then sitting down again.

Our turn was getting nearer. I grew even more nervous and fear began to take its grip me. Fight it as I could, I had to recognize its presence and attempt to regain control. Victor was in line just before me, and when his turn came he walked to the piano in a confident manner and sang as I had never heard him sing before. A certain fire shown forth in his voice that was of rare quality. Everyone in the room knew instantly that he had been accepted, even before he had finished his number.

My turn was next. I tried to grab hold of myself, to steady my nerves. I closed my eyes in hopes of finding calmness. As I thus turned within myself, I seemed to hear a small voice saying, "Success is within the knowledge that you will succeed." I was instantly inspired. Yes, that was true. I would succeed. I had come here with only one goal in mind and that would be fulfilled. I felt lifted on air and my whole being became vibrant with this electrical thought. Just then I was called forward, and I walked toward the piano with seemingly no physical effort. Giving my music to the accompanist, I stood beside the piano and began to sing. My thoughts were so filled with my new revelation of success that I almost forgot that I was standing before a great conductor, the man who held my future in his hands. I must have been in some sort of trance for, when I finished, he startled me with his deep broken voice.

"Too black at de top. Too white at de bottom. But you vill do. We vill make an artist out of you. I vill take you. Leave your name and address. Next, please."

I was too stunned to even thank him. A joyousness burst through me that must have fairly beamed upon my face. I had to be the happiest person in the whole world. I had managed to withstand my first real career test and had emerged victorious. I was a success!

From that day on, until the opera school opened in the fall, I lived in the clouds. I mentally acted and sang all the leading lyric tenor rolls such as Faust, Romeo, and Rodolfo. Daily, I envisioned myself upon the Metropolitan stage, acknowledging the applause and adoration of the multitudes who had come to see me. It was all reminiscent of my youthful Shakespearean acting days, except that this time the reality was that I truly was to act and sing upon a world-famous stage. I could imagine nothing but the greatest achievements. I would be a great star. I was definitely on my way.

Chapter Three

I was the first student to report on the day that the Metropolitan Opera School opened. Arriving considerably before the designated starting hour of nine o'clock in the morning, I worked hard throughout that first day and each succeeding day thereafter, having definitely made up my mind to put all I had into this work. Classes were held in Italian, French, German, sight-singing, ballet, and stage deportment. In addition to these classes, we immediately began to stage the choruses of the great operas. It should not take any imagination to realize that such an extensive course of study was a strenuous one for the students involved.

I had entered this school, blindly hoping that something would happen to furnish me with money enough to continue to pay for my room and buy my food as I had no capital left whatsoever. The scheduling at the Metropolitan had forced me to give up my lunchtime concerts, so my income came to end with the first day of classes. Again, fate intervened and was indeed kind to me. One morning, shortly after the term had started and before I was completely destitute, I was called in to the office of the little German conductor and informed that I was one of ten young men who had been selected to be what they called a super-super. That meant that I was to learn certain routines such as carrying a spear, leading the other supers on and off stage, and doing small bits—not real parts. My financial problem had been solved. Victor was also among the chosen ten which assisted in creating a comfortable companionship between us throughout our school years.

For all of this extra work, we were paid the grand sum of ten dollars a week. The management certainly got their money's worth as the additional work was by no means easy. We were all required to remain in the opera house until twelve o'clock every night, but I did not object. The fact that I was a mere super-super bothered me not in the least. I was thoroughly enjoying the glorious experience of being on the greatest stage in world, day and night, and becoming intimately associated with the greatest aggregation of singers living. I needed no spare time and I desired no outside amusement. Everything I could possibly desire was there in the opera school.

It was but a short time after instruction commenced until I met Miss Jessie Baskerville, a brilliant and gifted woman who enjoyed the reputation of being the greatest operatic coach of that time. She spoke twelve languages fluently and, having traveled all over the world, knew anyone and everyone of any interest. She, too, was a loyal Southerner, and it was not long before the two of us had formed a strong bond of friendship. You know, we rebels must always stick together. She was extremely kind to me, and it is to that kindness I owe the opportunity of knowing so many of the great stars in a more personal way.

Miss Jessie lived at the Metropolitan Opera Studios, and it had become her custom to entertain by give interesting breakfast parties. Her kitchen was presided over by a real southern colored mammy, whom she had brought with her from the South. Aunt Mary was known to everyone in the musical world and all had, at one time or another, either enjoyed her beaten biscuits, fried chicken, corn bread, or other Southern delicacies. Having tasted her delicacies once, they were sure to want to come again for more. Most of them made it a point to be on intimate terms with Aunt Mary, and her kitchen was often visited by the greatest stars. I was most fortunate to be included in many of those intimate parties.

It was at one of these breakfasts that I met Miss Alice Neilson[10], who had recently joined the Metropolitan, originally coming from Kansas City where she had sung in a church choir. Alice had found success with the famous Bostonians, then America's leading light-opera company, singing the leading soprano roles. At the height of her success, she went abroad, studied, made her debut in grand opera, and quickly became the toast of the Continent. She had been an ideal of mine for quite some time. Two years before, when she was touring the South, I had had the pleasure of hearing her several times and had, since that time, felt a strong desire to know her. I related all of this to Miss Jessie, so she arranged that I sit next to her at this particular breakfast party.

After the usual formalities, I turned to my idol and said, "I think that you should know, Miss Neilson, that this is a very big moment for me."

"Indeed? Would you mind telling me why?" Oh, what a delightful smile she gave me with that reply.

"Well, two years ago, when you were singing in Vicksburg, I became one of your staunchest admirers. You made such an impression upon me that I've had, since that time, a great desire to know you. I hung around the theatre where you were singing; I sat in the lobby of your hotel; I walked the streets, hoping that I might get a glimpse of you at close range."

"A stage door Johnny and so young!" She laughed and asked, "Well, now that you are sitting next to me, do I still look good to you?"

"You sure do," I hastily replied.

"That, indeed, is a compliment. I was afraid that the competition had become too keen!"

I looked around the table and realized just what she meant. There with us sat Caruso[11], the gorgeous Lina Cavalieri[12], the regal Madame Emma Calvé[13], and other international stars. With an understanding smile I replied, "You see, you did make a lasting impression on me."

It was a few moments before she spoke to me again. "Such admiration and devotion must be rewarded. I'm planning a small Christmas party and I would very much like for you to come. I do need help in getting ready, though. Would you like to come by Christmas Eve and help me decorate the tree?"

"That is a great reward. I would love to attend and most certainly accept."

And accept I did, for Christmas Eve found me there with several others, including her accompanist, filling bags, pinning stars on the tree, arranging gifts, and many other odd jobs that needed doing. Everyone was filled with the holiday spirit, and we were having a wonderful time working and singing Christmas carols until her maid came into the room and interrupted us by saying:

"Miss Neilson, you're wanted on the telephone."

Excusing herself, she left the room, returning in about five minutes with a determined look upon her face. Turning to her accompanist she said, "I've just been informed that I must sing 'Rosina' in *The Barber of Seville* tomorrow night!" The last time I sang that role was Covent Garden, four years ago. We have lots of work to do if I'm to be ready."

Immediately the apartment became a beehive of activity, with everyone scattering in all directions, new job lists in hand. Drawers were torn apart and closets pawed through until the music for the score was finally located. With her accompanist seated at the piano, Miss Neilson began to rehearse violently. The maid was sent scurrying to dig out the Rosina costume which needed to be pressed and freshened. I was sent to the kitchen to make black coffee. Hour after hour she worked, and I plied the crowd with black coffee regularly. All activity and all thoughts were turned toward the rendition of a perfect role in true artistic style.

It was five o'clock in the morning before Miss Neilson finally became aware of time. She gave us all a very tired smile and said, "I am about dead. I had forgotten that this is Christmas. Merry Christmas to all of you, and thank you so much for helping me. Suppose we stop now. I think I can get through tonight all right. You all run along and get a good sleep and remember that you have a date with me after the performance tonight for a real Christmas celebration."

The performance Miss Neilson gave that night was truly wonderful. Her singing was splendid. No one in the audience could have possibly been aware that she had not sung that role for four years.

I have never forgotten that Christmas Eve. While I had seen the operatic stars rehearse on the stage for hours on end, it was not until that particular evening that I fully appreciated just what actual work was behind a true performance. What sacrifices a true star must make. What a slave they must become to their profession. I was learning fast the requirements essential for success. First you must catch the vision, and then you must put your whole heart and soul into that vision. You must work unceasingly and make countless sacrifices to attain your goal. It is a tremendous price for one to pay, and few have the willpower and determination that is necessary to make the dreamed-of success a reality.

It was through these breakfast parties of Miss Jessie's that I also began to get to know Caruso off the stage. He was a very sociable person and enjoyed these morning diversions immensely. I have read, in recent years, that he was always seized with stage fright before each performance, but this is hard for me to believe. It may have been that he diverted this supposed nervousness into practical jokes for he was really quite a prankster. He delighted in such stunts as mingling among the chorus women during the kermesse scene in *Faust* and untying their apron strings or doing little things to the men's costumes what would cause them embarrassment upon the stage. I remember one occasion during a performance of *Manon*. I was standing in the wings, waiting for my cue to carry a platter of sandwiches to a group of chorus men on the stage. The great Caruso approached me, a sly grin on his face, and took the platter from my hands. Chuckling all over, he then proceeded to sprinkle red pepper generously on all the sandwiches. Nervous, knowing full well what would happen next, I proceeded on stage and the sandwiches were taken by the unsuspecting cast members. The red pepper immediately caused an uncontrollable sputtering and coughing among the men on stage and almost broke up the scene. The great tenor sat in the wings, convulsed with laughter, enjoying the prank immensely.

What a hard worker Caruso was, seemingly having the energy of ten men. I never once knew him to be late. At dress rehearsals, he was always on the stage promptly at ten o'clock in the morning, dressed in costume, fully made-up, and ready to work. He seemed never to tire and willingly worked until the last minute to make sure that everything was perfect.

One morning he approached me backstage with a small package. "This is something for you." He smiled broadly. "Please do not open it until you get home."

I could hardly wait to see what the present was, yet was quite aware that it might just be another one of his practical jokes. That evening I carefully unwrapped the package, expecting almost anything to come flying out at me. To my great surprise and joy, I found an autographed copy of one of his books. I was thrilled beyond expression, and it has always remained one of my most cherished possessions.

Of course, I worked daily with such other great artists as Emmy Destin, Emma Eames[14], Madame Sembrich, Louise Homer[15], Amate, Plancon, Scotti, Ricardo Martin, and many others. Geraldine Farrar[16] was at the height of her career and the entire company was deeply infatuated with her great magnetism and personal charm. Gustave Mahler and Arturo Toscanini[17] were the two outstanding directors of the time. The world knows these two geniuses only too well and there is little here that I can add to what has already been written or said concerning these two great men except my own great appreciation of them.

Victor and I continued our close companionship throughout these rehearsals and performances. We usually walked back and forth to the Metropolitan together, talking and laughing about the incidents that had taken place during the day. I think we enjoyed working in *Tannheuser* and *Carmen* the most because we could wear romantic costumes in these productions and not have to be lowly waiters or carry spears. In *Tannheuser,* we were dressed as Thuringin noblemen with magnificent robes and golden crowns, marching to the rhythm of the bridal chorus. In *Carmen,* we dressed as picadors with equally appealing, eye-catching costumes. Victor was always more partial to *Carmen* than to any other opera as the story and music seemed to release something in his soul. Only a few years later, he was to be singing all over the world the role of Escamillo.

An unusual incident took place at one of the performances of *Carmen*. I tell it only to illustrate the depth of the emotional feelings and jealousies that these great artists sometimes gave vent to. The occurrence took place one evening during the scene in the last set of *Carmen*. One particular prima donna disliked very much a certain baritone with whom she often had to sing. Escamillo, turning his back to the audience, took Carmen in his arms and sang a few very beautiful and touching notes to her before entering the arena for the bullfight. The entire ensemble was horrified when, during the embrace, they saw the baritone's face writhe in pain and then become livid with anger. The prima donna had secretly stuck a dozen large straight pins in the bosom of her dress, and when he embraced her they had gone through his costume and pierced his chest. Somehow he managed to finish the scene but, needless to say, the tempers displayed after the final curtain came down were quite a show to watch.

The general public seldom knows of nor understands the trials of artists, their petty jealousies, or the tragedies that they occasionally must face. One particular tragedy took place during my first year with the company and has always remained most vivid in my memory. The new Academy of Music in Brooklyn had just been completed and the Metropolitan Opera Company was scheduled to give as the opening performance, *Faust,* with Caruso and Farrar singing the leading roles. It was a gala opening, and every box and seat in the theatre was occupied by one or other of the most socially prominent Brooklynites. Immediately after the opening scene, the entire cast had assembled on the stage, awaiting the rising of the curtain for the kermesse scene, when suddenly there was a terrific thud, which was followed by piercing screams from the chorus women. A young electrician had been perched high in the wings and, in his eagerness to catch a glimpse of those two great artists, had somehow lost his balance, fallen onto the stage, and was instantly killed. Naturally, this horrible accident had a very distressing effect upon the members of the company. The Italian choristers immediately began crossing themselves and muttering under their breaths, "This is a bad omen." Caruso and Miss Farrar were as deeply affected by the accident as the rest of the cast, but, with true showmanship, the remainder of the performance was completed. The audience never knew what had happened backstage until they read about it in the newspapers the following day. Both Caruso and Farrar sent handsome checks to the young man's family in an attempt to express their sorrow over the young man's death. Personally, I have never believed in signs or omens, but the fact remains that some sort of a hoodoo still hangs over the annual visits of the Metropolitan Opera Company to the Academy of Music. Something usually happens on these occasions, although nothing as catastrophic as during that first performance.

But, of course we also had fun, and amusing things were always going on during rehearsals and actual performances. To me, the ballet in the Venusberg scene in *Tannheuser* had quite a humorous side. In it I was dressed as a faun with little horns. It was my business to cavort all over the stage, as fauns are prone to do, finally grabbing one of the nymphs, throwing her over my shoulder, and rushing off stage in a most excited manner for, according to the librette, "no good purpose." The nymph I had been assigned to carry off was a very plump little German girl. I suppose that I must have looked rather ferocious every time I grabbed her or, more likely, I tended to indulge in a bit of overacting. Anyway, the fraulein always appeared to be truly frightened of me and would actually squeal and wiggle like a little pig as I rushed off stage with her. When I put the plump nymph down in the wing, she would give me a relieved smile and breathlessly say, "Danke," scurrying away as fast as her short little legs would take her. I never got to know her any better than this.

Of all the great artists, Emma Destinn[18] was one of most charming and gracious to the boys and girls who were struggling to gain recognition in the chorus. She often went out of her way to be nice and assist us. I was particularly grateful to her one afternoon when I was not in the best of spirits. We had been rehearsing *The Bartered Bride* since ten o'clock that morning, and it was now late in the afternoon. I had carried the spear across the stage for seemed to me a million times, and it had actually begun to drag as I walked. Miss Destin noticed me as I sat on the corner of the stage and recognized that I was not acting my usual, cheerful self. She walked over to me and putting her hand on my shoulder said, "Why don't you go home? You look very tired."

"I can't," I replied. "How can the rehearsal go on without me?"

She laughed at this rather exaggerated view of my own importance and, turning to the stage director, asked, " Don't you think we could get along without this spear carrier for the balance of the rehearsal? He really seems quite tired. Why don't you let him go home and rest?"

With a curt nod from the stage director, I scurried out with quite an inward feeling of thankfulness knowing that she, too, must be very tired and would undoubtedly have to remain for hours more, going over and over the same business and arias. Actually, if the truth were known, my moodiness that day came from a date that I hoped to keep and not from overwork. Thanks to Miss Destin, I kept that memorable date. I only wish that I could tell you about it, but my Southern manners and courtesy to the young lady prevent me from doing so.

I did not know the great Feodor Chaliapin[19] as well as the Metropolitan stars; however, I cannot help but relate an incident that happened during Beite's *Mefistefele* which, in retrospect, amused him greatly. In the Brocken scene, electric wires were suspended from the ceiling with tiny sparks on the ends. These wires swayed across the stage in an attempt to make hell look more realistic. On the night in question, one of the electrically charged wires swayed and gently but firmly flipped Chaliapin on the hip. At this, he gave out one loud yelp and leaped into the air, falling into the scenery and knocking the entire background of hell to hell, or rather, to the floor. The stage crew was forced to bring down the curtain and repair the damage to both pride and scenery before continuing.

This first year I spent with the opera company was the year Madame Marcella Sembrich[20] announced that she would retire from the operatic stage at the end of the season. Her exquisite coloratura voice and perfect artistry were still unimpaired, but everyone realized that her career was drawing to a close. She was greatly loved and admired by the entire organization, and the news of her retirement brought a great sadness to each and every one of us. An elaborate farewell performance was arranged to present one act each from three of the operas in which she had scored her greatest triumphs. They were the first act of *La Traviata*, the second act of *The Barber of Seville*, and the first act of *Don Pasquale*. All the great stars of the day assisted in the various accompanying roles and filled the ranks of the chorus. It was a wonderful tribute to a truly great artist. Never in my life have I ever heard such an outpouring of song. It was a most fitting finale to one of the greatest operatic star of all times. The applause was thunderous, the flowers magnificent.

Madame Emma Eames also made her farewell appearance that year. However, in accordance with her wishes, it was staged in a manner which was in direct contrast to that of Madame Sembrich's. Madame Eames was a woman of stateliness and charm with a voice that filled the air like a golden flute. She selected the opera *La Tosca* for her farewell performance, and I shall never forget her beauty as she made her final entrance bedecked in the resplendent costume of the Empire Period. Her ovation was equally as great as that of Madame

Sembrich's, although the evening lacked the ceremoniousness.

My studies and work proceeded smoothly and happily until about the middle of my second year at the opera school. As Victor and I were walking home one evening, I noticed that his mood seemed a bit more serious than was usual. He had been called into the director's office earlier that afternoon, and I began to wonder just what had transpired during the interview. Determined to find out just what had happened, I began to probe.

"What did the director want with you this afternoon?" I asked, trying to make my question sound casual.

"Oh, not too much. I'm to be given a more intensive course of study. They think my voice has real possibilities, but they gave me the dickens about taking my work more seriously. They want me to work harder."

"That's splendid, Victor. You know that I'm glad for you. You have a wonderful voice, and you must take full advantage of this opportunity. As for taking your work more seriously, well, you know I've jumped on you for that. After all, you do have nice friends, but you let them use you, and they distract you from your work too much. You're much too generous with your time."

He made no reply. We strolled on for quite a few minutes before he finally broke the silence. "While I was waiting for my interview this afternoon, I overheard a conversation about you. They seem to have taken a special notice of your dancing. I rather gathered that they expected to give you some individualized instruction and then possibly feature you in some way or another. Have you ever thought of dancing?"

"No, not especially, although you know that I'm fond of dancing." I pondered this new thought for a little while. "What do you suppose they are going to do?"

"Oh, I don't know. I just heard part of a conversation. But, I'll bet you're called into the office soon."

What did this new idea mean? Dancing? Yes, I could do that. It had always seemed a very necessary part of me, but I had never given it much serious thought. Certainly, I would like to receive special instructions. Indeed, I would like to be a featured dancer.

So, once again, I began to dream on and on ...

Chapter Four

When I worked, I put my whole heart and soul into it, and when I played I did so with the same intenseness and dedication. Despite the long hours and hard work at the Metropolitan, I always seemed able to find plenty of time to play. The opera school lasted from the first part of October until the middle of April, which afforded me the opportunity to spend the entire summer in which making new friends and enjoying new experiences was my focus.

I was very fortunate in the variety of people I met. Everyone was always exceedingly friendly and more than willing to help me succeed in my endeavors. I want to emphasize the fact that, no matter what the rest of the world thinks, I know New York offers greater opportunities than any other city in the world for the young person who is ambitious and willing to work hard—willing to struggle and to adapt himself to any and all situations. One thing that he cannot do is to live in New York according to the standards of the old hometown. It is a city of self-expression, through and through. Some of the self-expressions may seem a bit weird and eccentric, but one must live and let live in accordance with definite moods. The soundest advice to the struggling newcomer is to work hard, take advantage of every opportunity, mind your own business, and remember that self-preservation is the first law of life.

I continued to attend the parties given by Sally, though never again appearing in fancy dress attire. For the time being, at least, I had lost my ardor for tights. It was at Sally's home that I was fortunate enough to meet such outstanding artists in the theatrical world as Katherine Emmet, Katherine Grey, Guy Bates Post and his wife Jane Peyton, Shelley and Josephine Hull, and others. These people, too, invited me into their homes and offered me their intelligent and insightful suggestions, as well as provided me with many advantageous introductions to others who might be instrumental in furthering my ambitions.

I soon became quite friendly with an engaging couple who lived on Fifth Avenue. They were very jolly and entertained extensively, often including me as a guest. It was through them that I met the matchless artist, Richard Bennett[21], and his gracious wife, Adrianne Morrision, and, of course, their three very young daughters, Constance, Joan, and Barbara. These three young ladies were certainly as captivating a trio as my eyes had ever beheld and even at their young ages they were already highly individualized, giving you the feeling that each would leave her distinctive mark in this world. Adrianne was a charming mother who lavished great care and devotion upon her daughters. I am deeply amused as I recall one particular evening spent with them. The Bennetts lived in New Jersey, just a short distance outside of New York. Often Adrianne and the three little girls would spend the evening at this young couple's home, waiting for Mr. Bennett to join them after the theatre. On several occasions I was present, and it was one of these evenings that I recall so well. Mr. Bennett had not yet returned and one of the little girls, who was quite tired and sleepy, had begun to express her annoyance to all of us in no uncertain terms. Just why, I still do not know, but I felt duty bound to quiet and soothe this young lady. Despite a very vocal protest on her part, I took her into my arms and began to pace the floor, singing in my most dulcet tones, Brahms' *Lullaby*. I had sung only a few notes when this little girl rolled her big eyes and looked up at me in a most perplexed manner. She then proceeded to double up her little fist and then placed it squarely over my mouth, saying, "You win. I can't make a noise as bad as that. If you will shut up, I'll go to sleep." She was my first negative critic.

I have always greatly admired Miss Laurette Taylor[22]. Naturally her artistry appealed to me, but I believe the main reason for my admiration was the fact that I knew, firsthand, her kind and generous heart. Miss Taylor had just scored her success in *Alias Jimmy Valentine*. Meanwhile, at the opera school, there was a very gentle young girl who was trying desperately to carve out a career for herself. She had an appealing voice, but nature had given her a physical handicap that was a great barrier to her future success. Miss Taylor soon took a special interest in this struggling young lady, taking her under her protective wing and helping her, professionally and socially, in many different ways. Often she would invite this girl to various entertainments, even including her friends in the invitations. I was invited to a birthday party that winter where this young protégée was in attendance, which turned out to be musical evening interpreted with enrapturing recitations by Miss Taylor. I felt quite honored in meeting that evening, Mr. Hartley Manners, whom Miss Taylor later married. These two created history on stage with "Peg O' My Heart" and other plays written by Mr. Manners in which Miss Taylor starred.

It was at about this time that I received my first invitation to a large, fashionable debutante ball. I was very excited and quite anxious to go, but how was I to manage it all? My wardrobe certainly held no suitable raiment for such a resplendent occasion, and my pocketbook offered me with no means to solve my problem. I became convinced that I was going to miss an absolutely wonderful evening, all for the lack of formal attire.

Fortunately, my old friend, Count de L. came to my rescue. He just happened to be passing by my room and overheard my distress as I was relating it all to Victor. In his most suave manner, he threw open the door, swept into the room and, looking my figure over carefully, said, " I am sure that we are about the same size. I shall be most delighted to lend you my evening clothes. I had them tailored in London just last season. Come into my room and try them on, and we'll see if they'll do."

I protested Count L's generosity, but most weakly. Following him to his room, as I had been ordered, I shed my own clothes and donned his formal wear. Standing in front of the Count's full-length mirror, I could see that they fit me perfectly, even to the top hat, and that I looked like a million dollars. Fortune had smiled upon me, and now I would be able to make my own debut in fashionable New York society.

Upon the night of the dance, I dressed carefully and was about to set forth upon this great adventure when a terrific thunderstorm broke out. The lightening, thunder, and generous outpouring of the clouds seemed to have joined in a conspiracy to keep me at home but I refused to be defeated. Even though I had but one dollar to my name, I nonchalantly hailed a taxi, trusting to my luck, which was usually good, to take care of me. We had proceeded but halfway to my destination when his motor stalled in water which was now hub deep. I could not possibly walk through the downpour, so there was nothing left to do but hail another cab. After paying the first fare, my capital had been greatly diminished and was, in fact, half gone. I hoped I could reach my destination on the remaining funds in my pocket, and as the blocks flew past I began to pray. The meter was reading fifty cents when the hotel entrance finally came into sight. Good, I was saved. I would rush in and leave the cabbie to curse the winds for his tip. As we drew up to the entrance, I breathed a sigh of relief. Then, that damn meter very unobligingly clicked—sixty cents. I was in a panic. What could I do?

"Rotten night" I said stalling for time to think.

"Ugh!" was the deep-throated reply. He pulled down the flag and muttered, "Sixty cents."

"That's not much for a trip a night like this. I'll match you. Dollar and a half or nothing."

He turned quickly in his seat and looked me over. I could see his dark, squinty eyes deeply set in a large face blink as he pondered my suggestion. I felt that he instantly recognized I would be an easy prey and nothing but putty in his hands. "All right," he growled, reaching into his pocket for a coin. "You're matching me."

I fished out my lonesome half dollar, nonchalantly flipped it into the air, and slapped it upon the back of my hand, moving forward under the light. He stretched two long arms forward. My heart was pounding a mile a minute. I took my hand off. Heads! He took his hand off. Heads! I had won. Hurrah! Luck was still with me. "Sorry old man. Better luck next time," I said, climbing out of the cab. I gave him the fifty cents as a tip and rushed into the hotel as he growled some kind of unrepeatable retort.

The party was one of the most lavish of the season. I soon forgot my embarrassment over the cab fare and relaxed into having the time of my life. I loved to dance, and dance I did. The room grew a trifle warm as it filled with people and activity and I soon began to notice a most unusual odor. Much to my horror, I discovered that the odor was emanating from me! The Count, like a great many foreigners, went in very strongly for perfumes. The heavier they were, the better he liked them, and now the combined heat of the room and my body was bringing out the powerful aroma of seemingly all the perfumes of Arabia. He must have had a strong preference for the "Night of Passion" or "Kiss Me Quick" varieties. To say that I was horrified is putting it mildly. I had never used perfume nor would I ever consider doing so!

Despite the perfume, I was having a wonderful time at the party and whirling around the dance floor, I resolved not to let this odorous problem defeat me. As I danced with each new partner, I would attempt to cover my embarrassment by saying, "Don't you hate practical jokes? Just as I was leaving, several of my friends threw a bottle of perfume all over my clothes."

The young ladies all took my story differently. Some, being gullible, believed me while others I knew did not. I have never forgotten one girl's reply. She was petite, very attractive, and quite sophisticated. I particularly remember that her patrician nose was tilted just a little bit higher than the others. Maybe it was the perfume. Anyway, in a most knowing manner she replied to my often repeated excuse with, "Yes. I wondered just what you stepped in on your way over."

From Victor, I learned the priceless lesson that friends can be found in all walks of life. Quite in contrast to the people I have already mentioned, I became entranced with a group of circus people. In looking around for inexpensive places to eat, I had come across a quaint little restaurant which was run by an ex-circus man and his wife. For the paltry sum of fifty cents, I could come away from the establishment completely satisfied, my stomach filled with well-cooked food. It was a small, cozy place. One large table ran the length of the dining room, and it fairly groaned with the weight of huge platters of beef, chicken, numerous vegetables, several kinds of pie, and other tempting dishes. All of this was washed down with a never-ending supply of red wine. You served yourself to as many helpings as you could eat, and it was strictly family style, including all who ate there.

This restaurant was chiefly patronized by people who had been associated with the circus or who were still in that profession and in the city between engagements. There I made the acquaintance of lion tamers, trapeze artists, bareback riders, clowns, and all types that follow the ring. It was a new world to me and quite a revelation. I soon became fast friends with many of them. They gave me a kindness and companionship that I will never forget. Here was a group of people living entirely in a world of their own with ideas, thoughts, and mannerisms completely different from the rest of the world. Their English was even of a special variety. The one thing I found they had in common with artists in other fields was their jealousy of one another. They shared that same feeling of invidiousness that is so characteristic of the opera singer, the theatre, or the social set.

I became very friendly with Madame Z who, I was told, had once been a famous bareback rider of electrifying beauty in her days. When I met her, it was very difficult for me to conceive of her in that role as, at the age of sixty, she weighed around two hundred and fifty pounds. She had a distinctly individual sense of humor, and when she laughed she seemed to shake all over, and you could actually hear her for blocks. I always called it "enthusiasm of the bosomism." Like most circus people I have met, she was the possessor of an exaggerated sense of values. The moment I met her she considered me a Metropolitan star, and so I became to all of the others, despite my insisting otherwise.

Upon learning of my operatic background, Madame Z. conceived the idea of giving a brilliant musical at which I was to be the star attraction. Parties were a great event to these people, and this one was to be the crowning event of their social season. A great Metropolitan star was to attend and entertain them. Of course this all amused me greatly, but I thoroughly enjoyed these people and was more than willing to oblige. Besides, I was quite anxious to attend one of their parties of which they talked about so often.

When I arrived on the appointed night after the opera, I found about twenty-five guests assembled. I knew most of them, but had never seen them so expressive of their individual natures. They had dug deep into their trunks and extravagantly dressed themselves in their old costumes or in assembled bits of time-worn finery of a past generation. I have never seen so many spangles in all my life. Ornaments were everywhere, and it appeared that the more glitter, the better. One ex-lion tamer wore a home-fashioned dress made from the skin of her pet lion, grotesquely trimmed with glass pendants, which probably came from a chandelier long since retired from use. The strong man's costume seemed to be little more than tattoo marks and a balloon-like chest, which he seemed to have trouble holding up. My hostess was arrayed in a combination of costumes that suggested a continuous reminiscence of past circus splendor, becoming vividly more regal as the years slipped by. Upon her buxom bosom there was reclining, in a lackadaisical fashion, the most enormous sunburst of imitation diamonds this world has yet to gaze upon. I felt as though I had, in some magical manner, been suddenly hurled backward through several decades. I was in a world of dreaming, an intense reliving of the past, a world filled with fantastic souls who had forgotten all hardships and heartaches and were inwardly responding to the echoes of melodic applause.

I must admit I had a bit of difficulty acclimating myself to my surrounding. These were not the same people with whom I had so often eaten. I sang many songs, with most of the selections being ballads with tender love lyrics to attune with their romantic and visionary natures. My obese hostess delighted in Roger Quilter's *Now Sleeps the Crimson Petal*, and at Madame's Z's insistence I sang it. She became wrapped in reverie, and as I came to the lines, "So slip into my bosom and be lost, be lost in me," I poured forth my most heartbreaking pianissimo. As I sang these lines, I noticed that the eyes of the entire audience were focused upon her abnormal sunburst that was now rising and falling in a very dramatic manner, apparently objecting to being disturbed from such a comfortable resting place by such deep breathing. When I finished, the applause brought Madame Z. to with a start. In her most dignified manner, she rose and, in somewhat embarrassed tones, more commanded than suggested. ""Now that our great tenor has finished singing, we will proceed to enjoy ourselves."

Whether this was intended as a compliment or as an insult, I still am not quite sure.

Toward the close of the second year of opera school I was, at last, summoned to the office of the little German director. Naturally I was nervous, as I knew then that he held my entire future in the palm of his hands.

"Sit down. I vant to talk vit you," he said, greeting me rather abruptly. "You are a nice boy. I like you. You work very hard. Your voice has a good quality, too, but, vell, not enough. You do not have the power for opera work. You are not big enough in size to make a success in opera. What would you like to do? Have you thought?"

What I had long expected was finally coming. I suddenly realized that Victor had not told me all that he had overheard that afternoon.

In a very weak and nervous voice I answered, "Yes, I know. I have been expecting this. I would like to be an operatic star, but I do realize that I cannot be. I do appreciate all of that. You have been very helpful to me. I feel that this school has been a marvelous education to me. I have enjoyed every moment of it, and I am grateful for the experience. I cannot thank you enough for all you have done for me. If I have failed—well, it certainly is neither of our faults."

"It is nice to hear you say dat. Ve try to help everybody. But, you have not failed. I have a plan for you. Maybe you vill like it."

"I am sure that I will," I interrupted, regaining some of my hope.

"Vell, you have a nice voice. You dance beautifully. You are young and good looking. Vhy don't you try light opera?"

I was much surprised. "Why, I had never thought of that. Do you really think that I have a chance there?"

"I am so sure dat I have spoken to Mr. Charles Dillingham[23] about you. I told him many nice things. He is interested and he vants to meet you. I vill make an appointment for you to see him if you would like? Yes?"

"Yes. Of course. I would be more than glad to see him."

"All right den. I vill let you know. Goodbye."

I left the room in a confused state of mind and went straight home, speaking with no one. I knew that what had happened was inevitable. My voice was not big enough for grand opera. I knew that, but still I had hoped and hoped. Well, I must become accustomed to such disappointments. I must learn to square my shoulders and to look life in the face again, this time from a new perspective.

Somewhere inside of me there was a small voice trying to say, "This is good. This is good." The more I thought over the possibilities of a career in light opera the louder the little voice became. By morning I was quite willing to make the change. By the following night I was very eager to meet Mr. Dillingham. By the next day, I was filled with enthusiasm. Yes, of course—light opera. I would love it. That is where I would be a big success. I could see it all clearly now. Why had I not thought of that before? My old powers of imagination took full sway. I dreamed of delightful roles, beautiful scenes, large audiences, and victory. Yes, that was exactly what I wanted. I was exceedingly happy with this new turn in my career.

Several days later I was notified that I was to have an audition with Mr. Dillingham at the Globe Theatre the following morning. I was ready. I arose on the appointed morning and dressed carefully. The sun was shining gloriously as I walked to the theatre and I was feeling in fine fettle. I walked upon the stage with the complete assurance that victory was soon to be mine. I gave the accompanist my score and with a calm determination to do my best, I lifted my voice in a light, laughing song. I had sung only three bars when my eyes fell upon a middle-aged woman who was scrubbing the floor of the theatre. She had momentarily stopped her work and was listening to me intently. In her face I recognized the expression so familiar to me in the days when I sang to the factory women. I knew I had won.

I was immediately escorted into Mr. Dillingham's office and presented with a contract. I was to receive seventy-five dollars a week for the first year, one hundred and twenty-five dollars the second year, and one hundred and fifty dollars the third year. It sounded like a fortune to me, and it had all happened so fast that I was stunned. A great joy surged through me. The feeling that I had had when I won the scholarship at the Metropolitan was nothing compared to the elation I felt now. I had finally found my niche in life.

After going over all the contractual details, I was informed that I would be called late in the summer to begin rehearsing the role of Little Billy in "Trilby." Louise Gunning was mentioned as the prima donna.

That morning, when I stepped out into the Great White Way with a duplicate contract in my pocket, success seemed to be pouring from every point of my being. At last I had found my career. I was definitely on my way. I was determined to let nothing whatsoever come between me and success.

Chapter Five

Throughout all history it is ingeniously woven that before every great war the people go dance mad. In the early days of Greece and Rome, great dance festivals were always held before the outbreak of one of their numerous battles. Just before the French Revolution, arrogant aristocrats nightly danced the stately minuet while the hungry masses reveled in the Carmagnole. On the night preceding the historic battle of Waterloo, prolific writers have devoted paragraphs to the magnificence of the ball given by the Duchess of Richmond in Brussels. In their best dramatic style, they describe how officers were torn away from their partners, wives, and sweethearts to meet the onrush of Napoleon's army. Previous to the outbreak of the Franco-Prussian War, all of Europe was madly waltzing to the strains of the immortal music of Strauss. Before our own Civil War, the aristocratic Southerners traveled from plantation to plantation, attending balls of a most elaborate nature. Meanwhile, the Darkies were nightly gathering in groups, singing their spirituals and nimbly dancing in a manner reminiscent of the exotic dances of their homelands.

Now, once again, Europe had gone dance mad. Emanating originally from Russia, this dance madness quickly spread throughout the Continent and across the Atlantic, into our own America. The Russian aristocracy was then living in an era of splendor and extravagance never before known in modern civilization. The Imperial Ballet was at the height of its supreme glory, having within its ranks such great artists as Pavlova, Nijinsky, Karsavina, Fokine, and Mordkin. Excessive and elaborate preparations, never before dreamed of, preceded their nights of revelry. Every small café had its own Gypsy dancers and was crowded into the early morning hours with the nobility, relaxing and unwinding from the pompous splendor of their own ballrooms.

Down in the Argentine Republic, the public halls were filled with the Latins dancing what they called the "Tango." It was a dance of seduction with the sinuousness of a snake, which had originated in the jungles of Africa. It had migrated to the Moors and then passed on to the Spanish before invading Argentina in such a wholesale fashion. In the process of its travel, it had gradually lost its primitiveness and crudity and the Latins, with their superb sense of rhythm, had, in the recreation process, filled it with a new, sensuous beauty. The French dancing masters quickly seized this tango and, in their own masterly fashion, toned the movements down to be presentable in a ballroom.

Out in San Francisco, raucous sailors were wiggling and twisting to blaring trumpets in what was called the "Turkey Trot." Originating on the Barbary Coast in the lowest of dives, this dance was destined to revolutionize the dancing of the entire world. Again, the descendants of Terpsichors gently polished and refined this almost savage chorea into what the whole world grew to know as the turkey trot. Thus, with the evolution of the tango and the turkey trot into their new, more socially acceptable forms, the jazz dance age was born.

Of course, there had been dance halls in all the cities in America since the early settlement days, but now they were becoming more numerous and more crowded. Places like the Haymarket in New York City, where everything was sold except hay, were springing up everywhere. However, the "better class" of Americans still seemed to suffer from a strong streak of Puritanism and found it vulgar to be found dancing in public places. However, it took only a short time for an extremely enterprising woman, named Mrs. R. W. K. Hawkesworth, to conceive of a brilliant idea which effectively countered the heretofore immovable Puritan resistance.

Mrs. Hawkesworth had just returned from Paris where the tea dance was fast becoming popular. She was well known in the New York social set at that time, having made quite a name for herself in planning and arranging entertainments for great social leaders such as Mrs. E. T. Stokesbury, Mrs. Stuyvesant Fish, Mrs. Arthur Curtis James, and others. Why shouldn't the more refined persons of the younger sets find favor in a thoroughly respectable hotel during the late afternoons? There they could enjoy a cocktail or two with sandwiches and other delicacies and, at the same time, occasionally dance to properly censored music.

The McAlpin Hotel[24] had just recently been completed and was considered to be the most up-to-date hotel in the world at that time. Mr. Boomer, The McAlpin's manager, was one of the most brilliant and highly regarded hotel men in the world. Mrs. Hawkesworth immediately approached him with her idea of introducing the tea dance to America and, with his marvelous foresight, he instantly recognized the possibilities and profit which would come from the creation of an entirely new type of entertainment for the New York social set. With the aid and guidance of Mrs. Hawkesworth, plans were cautiously drawn up and dignified, engraved invitations were mailed to a carefully chosen list. Society was immediately thrown into an uproar. The Puritanical old-timers bitterly denounced the very idea that their young daughters were expected to dance in public, subjected to the gaze of the common herd. Others received the news a little less hysterically, deciding either to completely stay away or, seeing no special harm in such a place if properly chaperoned, to attend and view the procedings quietly from the sidelines. The younger set received the announcement with great exaltation and enthusiasm. Life-long conventions were to be thrown to the wind, so their plans to attend were completed with a great deal of consideration. At last, the much-anticipated day arrived.

The ballroom on the roof of the McAlpin had been beautifully decorated and arranged for the occasion. Flowers cascaded from arrangements in every corner and small, linen-draped tables, each with a small bud vase and candle, ringed a large dance floor. Jim Europe, the outstanding orchestra leader of that time, had been engaged to furnish the music. To insure success, Mrs. Hawkesworth intentionally invited a few of her personal friends as guests, choosing those with a slightly more daring nature to assist in the launching of this new venture. I was among these favored few. The guests began to arrive, some exhibiting rather nervous, self-conscious looks and others reveling in the spirit of the adventure. Europe's orchestra struck up a somewhat wild tune and we, at Mrs. Hawkesbury's table, immediately got up and began to dance the one-step. Soon, a few timid couples joined us and then a few more. Within only half an hour, the dance floor was crowded. Jim Europe let his orchestra out with all the primitive rhythm of darkest Africa. The floor was absolutely packed, giving the impression of a great mob moving in a premeditated rhythm. And thus, the Dansant[25] was born in America.

Before the week was over, it became necessary to rope off the entrance to the McAlpin and hundreds were turned away daily. Within a month, all the leading hotels in the city had instituted similar entertainment and even the smaller cafés took up the craze. The Dansant was an instantaneous success and was there to stay.

With the Dansant receiving a favored status in polite society, transformations soon began to take place. Maiden ladies became a bit more bold. Their lives were becoming monotonous and boring. Why should they have to wait for some man to invite them out? Why shouldn't they give a small party? And they did, but they began to ask the younger men to be their partners. After all, the few older men who could dance at all were very slow, and who wanted to dance with them anyway? So these prim ladies curled their hair, painted their faces, loosened up old ironsides, and with girlish glee invaded the dance floors, forgetting they ever had any inhibitions. The days of the "Fermented Virgins" were gone.

The envious, married women, who were so extremely misunderstood by their husbands, quickly followed suit. They entertained at afternoon teas, inviting the most attractive bachelors they knew. The idea became almost malignant and, thus, the gigolo was introduced to the waiting world.

Tired businessmen from nearby stuffy offices and from hectic Wall Street, began to drop in the Dansant for relaxation. Bored husbands joined groups of friends. All whirled away on the dance floors at every opportunity. Very soon they asked their pretty blonde stenographers to join them in a cocktail and a dance on their way home. The idea became contagious and, thus, was paved the way for the office wife.

Mrs. Hawkesworth arranged the most delightful entertainment for these tea dances. The greatest ballroom dancers of the age were invited to appear. The Vernon Castles[26], fresh from their triumphs in Europe, immediately became popular. Joan Sawyer, the most beautiful waltzer I have ever seen, won new acclaim. Carlos Sebastion and many others enthralled these afternoon crowds.

New York had definitely gone dance mad, and it was a madness that was continually gaining momentum. The dinner dance was introduced and was followed shortly afterwards by the supper dance. Dancing became continuous throughout the day, from late afternoon until two in the morning.

There was only one serious drawback to this dance madness. Only a very few people really knew how to dance these new dances correctly. Dancing teachers and schools sprang up over night, filled with mostly inexperienced instructors. The supply was simply not equal to the demand. New York was enjoying the greatest prosperity in the history of the world and everyone was paying enormous prices to these various pseudo-professionals for instructions. They would then rush to some public place and do their practicing. Upon entering almost any private home during the day or night, you could hear a phonograph and see someone practicing steps. Steps. Steps. Rhythm seemed to mean nothing. Poise and grace were not essential elements. They only wanted steps—new steps!

Fortunately, I was among the few who had previously learned these new dances. My special training at the ballet school had been excellent, and I very quickly learned the tango, the one-step, and the most beautiful of all the ballroom dances, the maxixe breziellene. With my knowledge of the new dances, I quickly found myself in a whirl of popularity. I was invited everywhere and included in all the best parties. Because I knew how to dance well, my invitations were actually voluminous. While I did accept many of them, I still managed to keep my mind focused on the most important thing in my life—my career. I was determined to let nothing interfere—not even this dance madness.

The designated time arrived for my call to rehearsals. When I received no word from the Dillingham offices I called inquiringly. Complications had arisen, they told me, but the production would be starting shortly. I waited patiently, but my funds were now extremely low. Other visits to their offices brought forth further excuses. I was offered a small part in a musical comedy—the part of a country yokel with no singing or dancing. I was totally unsuited for the part and to accept meant the possibility of ruining my future stage career. I refused. Many more weeks passed. Finally, I came to the realization that I would not be appearing in a musical that season. I awakened from my dreaming to a sad reality. Apparently, I had been completely forgotten by Mr. Dillingham.

I was desperate and disconsolate, but I held my head high and kept my own counsel. My heart sang to all I contacted, even though I could but faintly hear it myself. My room rent began to run in the red. I was extremely fortunate in having such fine friends as this unusual French family for they understood my professional struggle, although it was never mentioned, and allowed me to remain in their home, despite my inability to pay them. I was grateful for a place to sleep, but the problem of eating rapidly became a very serious one. I distinctly remember three very gloomy days when I lived off of rice, which I boiled over the gas jet. My invitations to the tea dances became a Godsend. I could walk to the hotels and fill up on all the tea and very thin sandwiches I could snatch between dances. Sometimes I was asked to dinner. These were definitely eventful occasions for my stomach. My courage was at its lowest ebb and my great vision was almost overshadowed, but somehow my pride lingered on. Not even my most intimate friends knew of my dilemma. Only my tremendous vitality and courage had brought me this far, but where to now?

Life had become a complete mockery of all that I had once held important. At last my pocketbook and my stomach forced me to face the situation squarely. The sham acting must stop. My assets were exactly ten cents and my liabilities included six weeks back room rent. Something must be done and done at once. I knew that I must act and act immediately, but just how I could not figure out. Certainly, the first step would be to stop the almost continuous dancing and find a real, paying job.

I decided to attend just one more tea dance. I accepted the invitation as a farewell, but I would refuse all others. I dressed very carefully that afternoon, putting on a white suit that had just come from the cleaners. I had been saving it for a special occasion and my farewell to the Dansant seemed to be just that occasion. The entire time I was dressing, a very strange feeling, a premonition that something was going to happen, seemed to hang over me. Possibly an accident. I might even fall dead from starvation. Hideous ideas presented themselves to me, one after the other, but I dismissed them. I took more pains about my toilet and went out, down to the hotel in my funeral clothes.

Outside the sun was fairly beaming and the air was clear and invigorating, filled with that crispness that incites a faster pace. I began to feel better as I drew closer to the McAlpin. Whatever was coming, good or bad, I would face it with a singing heart. I began to hum one of my favorite tunes and before I had reached my destination I had almost forgotten my woes. If this was to be my last dance, well, I would enjoy it to the fullest extent.

My favorite young hostess of that afternoon was radiant, wearing a gauzy peach dress that swirled around her as she moved. Immediately I walked to her and claimed the first dance. What a majestic figure she seemed as we danced the one-step. In the hesitation waltz that followed, we fairly floated through the air. The floor was not yet too crowded, and we both let ourselves go in wild abandon. She was a perfect dancer and we executed all the steps in excellent timing and rhythm. Somehow she must have felt that "letting go" spirit I was in and followed along willingly.

We returned to our table and, as I was holding her chair while she was being seated, the headwaiter approached me and slipped a card into my hand. He whispered, with a sly wink, "This is from a real lady. I think I would talk with her. I feel positive that this is no flirtation."

I knew Gaston, for that was his name, quite well from my frequent visits to the hotel. He had given me many such cards, and he knew that it was my custom to utterly ignore them out of deference to my host or hostess. Do not think that I am flattering myself. This dance craze had carried with it this new custom. It was not at all unusual in those days for an unescorted woman, in her eagerness to dance, to press a nice tip into a waiter's hand together with a billet doux to some man whose dancing particularly attracted her attention.

That afternoon I was in a reckless mood, so I decided to accept. There certainly was nothing for me to lose. Leaning very close to my companion and whispering in her ear, I said, "Would you excuse me for a few moments? I've just had a message from some old friends and I'd like to speak to them."

"Old friends," was her knowing reply, "or just someone who wishes to become an old friend?"

Gaston piloted me to a table where were seated six well-dressed and apparently well-mannered ladies. I bowed and introduced myself.

"Won't you please sit down," the one at my right said with an apologetic smile. "This is most unconventional, but we're in somewhat of a quandary. We're dancing teachers from the Middle West. We've come to New York to learn the new dances and have visited all the dance schools but have been greatly disappointed in what we've found. We've been watching you dance this afternoon, and we like your style better than anyone else we've seen. Of course, you must be a teacher to dance so well."

"No, not a teacher. I mean by that, I haven't hung out my shingle and opened a studio. I've been quite busy, however, teaching my friends and acquaintances."

"Would you consider taking on the six of us as pupils?"

I could hardly believe my ears. Grasping the chair for support, I finally found a voice to reply. "I'm truly quite flattered. It would be a great pleasure, I'm sure, but I have no studio."

Very eagerly she continued. "That can be arranged. We'll furnish the studio and pay you one hundred and fifty dollars for a series of six lessons. That is, if you can give the lessons at once. Time is quite a factor with us, as we're only remaining in the city for a few more days."

My spirits soared to the skies. In the most suave and assured manner I could muster, I replied, "I, too, am on a sort of vacation." And what a vacation I added to myself. "As I have the time for the balance of this week, I shall be most happy to be of service to you."

Preliminary arrangements were hastily made and I returned to my hostess. She quietly studied me for a few minutes, breaking the silence by saying. "You must have enjoyed meeting your old friends. I don't believe I've ever seen you so radiant. Something wonderful must have happened."

"If you only knew," was all I could find to answer.

I left the hotel that afternoon on winged feet. Stopping at a neighboring restaurant where I was well known, I bought a sumptuous meal, mellowed with red wine, and all on credit. I was fairly bursting with song. I went home, piled into bed and slept like a child. It was my first good night's sleep in weeks.

The next morning I had a studio in Carnegie hall, one hundred and fifty dollars in my pocket, and a greater feeling of optimism than I had, as yet, known. I felt saved from the gallows!

Chapter Six

No matter how modest I try to be, I am forced to say that my dance studio was a great success. The six teachers from the Middle West were just the beginning of an avalanche of students that descended upon me. Within a matter of a week or two, I found myself working from about nine in the morning until eleven at night for the rather give-away sum of twenty-five dollars an hour.

My financial affairs did an abrupt about-face. Very soon all of my obligations were paid in full and I was the proud possessor, for the first time, of a bank account that was steadily growing. Strangely enough, however, I was still faced with my old problem of eating, only the question now was when could I eat? Just a few weeks ago I had had all day to eat, but very little had been available to put on my plate. Now I had plenty of money to buy the choicest of foods, but very little time to devote to the pleasure of consuming them. Fate must have been laughing up her sleeve over the merry little prank she was playing on me this time. I must confess, though, that I definitely preferred the problem of when to eat rather than the how.

Broadway immediately followed the trend of the dance-mad world, and dancing was featured in almost every performance. This addition made it quite difficult for some of the prima donnas and leading men who, heretofore, had just been required to be good looking, to dress elaborately, and to sing well. They were now forced to join the rest of the New Yorkers who were rushing to the dancing teachers. Shortly after I opened my studio, I found many of these professionals among my pupils.

I was greatly perplexed one morning to find my doorway quite filled with a six-foot two young man. He was very fine looking and had a charming manner, and immediately I recognized him to be Wilfred Merkyl, a popular leading man in light opera of that day. He had been rehearsing in "Sari," which was soon to have its premier. The day before, he had been told by the producer, in no uncertain terms, that he must waltz. Yes, waltz, in spite of the fact that he was a singer and not a dancer, so he came to me and placed his burden upon my shoulders. We began to work together for several hours each day. The first few hours went by with me literally dragging him around the floor, but after a few lessons, he finally got the swing of the waltz and made good with his dancing in his part in the show. The show, as everyone knows, turned out to be a big hit and Jack, as we called him, and I became fast friends. His sense of humor permitted us both to laugh over the strenuous efforts I had used in making a man of his size waltz in just a few lessons. I have often told him that it was the hardest money I ever earned.

My enrollment of July pupils fell off considerably. In fact, I had reached a point where I was working just an hour or so a day. With so much time on my hands, I began to feel the definite urge to vacation. I really needed a change as well as a rest, so, with my pockets full of money, my wardrobe completely replenished, and my sporting spirit tingling with excitement, I boarded a train for Saratoga, which was then at the height of its social and racing season.

Actually believing that I had gone to this famous spa for a much-needed rest, I engaged a room at a quiet family hotel. How this quaint little place ever found itself in Saratoga, no one will ever be able to tell. I am quite sure that it actually blushed over the idea of where it was located. The history of why it was built there, instead of rural Maine where it seemingly belonged, would make an interesting story, especially if woven together by that fanciful scribe, Alexander Woollcott.

The guests were as out of place as the little hotel, consisting chiefly of elderly women who, I soon learned, had been strangely coming here for seasons as if they had some duty to perform. They had their own rocking chairs and favorite spots for gossip and were self-appointed unofficial chaperones for this little city during its brief social whirl. I am sure that they were hoping and praying that in some way or other they could so impress the others with their strong Puritan ideas that they would soon reform everyone in a body and turn the resort into a camp meeting.

When a young, unmarried man registered there, the news spread like wildfire. I was pounced upon from all corners, much as a rabbit would be attacked if the dogs ever caught it! I was plied with questions, given motherly advice, warned of wine, women, and song, and watched like a hawk. When they learned I was a dancing teacher, they were absolutely horrified. Dancing was a weapon of the Devil, and I would be doomed to that city of fire and brimstone unless I repented at once, I was told upon every occasion. I was showered with invitations to make peace with my God and offers of prayers for my soul.

All of this was very amusing at first, but it quickly became most annoying. If I was to remain there, something would have to be done about these busybodies. The end of their interfering came more rapidly than I could have hoped. The rigid old ladies were horrified early one morning to find a large sign over the entrance door, which I had hung there during the night. In a most undignified manner, it was screaming to the world, "Antiques Here." I was beyond redemption; I was the cat's paw of the devil; I was completely shunned. The idea had brilliantly flashed into my mind on an early morning drive through the country. I had spied that same sign innocently decrying its message over the door of a small antique shop. I still owe it and the shop owner a large debt of gratitude.

I had been in Saratoga but a short time when I was fortunate to meet Mr. and Mrs. Chauncey Olcott, who were among the leaders of the younger social set. Chauncey Olcott[27], of Irish descent, was gifted with a tenor voice of pure silver. For years he had appeared in New York and toured the United States with his romantic plays. He composed many of the songs he sang, among them *Mother Machree*, which is as popular today as when it was first written. At the close of his tour each summer, he and Mrs. Olcott repaired to Saratoga where they had built a lovely home called "Innesscara." During the summer months, they entered into the social life of the summer colony and were among the leaders of the social set. Mrs. Olcott, with her good looks, tact, and charm, was always the perfect hostess at Innesscara. We found much enjoyment with one another, and they graciously included me in their little circle.

They were interested in dancing and, in fact, they both danced beautifully. I was more than willing to assist them with the latest steps, but soon their friends also insisted upon lessons and, before I knew it, I once again found myself with a small hall and back to the old grind. This time, however, I took it all much more leisurely. Taking my play as seriously as my work, I accepted the invitations tendered me and soon was in good standing with the more exclusive of the younger people—for a while, at least.

Weekly dances were held at the Casino. I had not attended more than two of these when trouble started in a rather amusing manner. As the orchestra began playing the waltz from *The Count of Luxembourg*, I turned to one of my pupils, whom I secretly thought was the best dancer, and suggested we join the couples already upon the floor. That turned out to be just the wrong thing to do. Unbeknownst to me, there was a feminine jealousy between this young lady and another one of my pupils. My action caused a little scene, which was actually of no more importance than a smile or two. However, *Town Topics*, the weekly gossip sheet, did not think so. This little display of jealousy was lengthened into quite an article. I was described as "the handsome, blonde Southerner, here dancing himself into all kinds of trouble. You can't get within a block of his hotel for the automobiles of women delivering invitations in person. Last week, at the Casino dance, all precedent was thrown to the wind, etc." This article was the basis of numerous stories concerning me. It was whispered that I was a waiter from New York, here on vacation; again, that I was a racehorse gambler camouflaged, or a notorious this or that and always ruining the lives of the women I became associated with. All of it was jealousy under another banner. I resorted to my sense of humor and got many laughs out of the entire situation. These stories did not seem to affect my popularity materially, and I continued to be invited to the outstanding events of the season, such as the costume ball given by Mr. and Mrs. R. E. L. Cluett, followed by an elaborate ball given by Mr. and Mrs. Edward Murphy.

Toward the end of the season, Mr. and Mrs. Olcott issued invitations to a large Dansant which was to be held at the Casino. The engagement of Joan

Sawyer and Wallace McCutchen caused quite a stir in the summer colony.

On the morning of the tea dance, I received an unexpected summons from Mrs. Olcott. When I arrived, I found her to be very agitated and frantically waving a telegram she held in her hand. "Oh, Tom, something dreadful had happened. Miss Sawyer and Mr. McCutchen can't come today. I'm awfully upset. You'll simply have to help me out."

"Of course, I'll be more than glad to help. It's much to late to get substitutes, but I'm quite sure that your guests will understand. Don't worry about it. It will all come out alright."

"No, no. You don't understand. That's not what I mean," she continued excitedly. "<u>You</u> must dance. <u>You</u> must take their place."

I laughed at the absurdity of the idea. "Now, you know that's impossible. No one could take their place. I'll be glad to help you in any way, but I will not dance for you."

"But you must. You simply must. You know what plans I've made."

"True, I do know that you've gone to a lot of trouble. But you must realize that I've never given an exhibition dance in my life. You are asking far too much."

She pleaded on and on with me, and I finally succumbed to her arguments. What else could I do to such a charming person? We were able to induce the young lady I had previously asked to dance with me at the Casino to be my partner and as we had only a few hours to rehearse, we immediately rolled up our sleeves and went to work.

We agreed upon a waltz and a brief encore for our exhibition. That was to be all. We stepped upon the floor that afternoon, quite nervous; however, the exquisite grace of my partner was most inspiring and we danced in a perfect rhythm. As we finished our performance, we both felt very proud of ourselves and knew we had "done noble."

As we left the dance floor, I overheard Mrs. William Knickerbocker say, "Never in the history of Saratoga has there been such exquisite dancing in the Casino ballroom." Calling the young lady by name, she continued, "She is actually a second Mrs. Castle. And Tom Rector, why that young man will be world famous."

This exceptional praise from such an esteemed person rather stunned me and put new ideas into my head. I had never thought of dancing as a career, but here was a woman who was making a prophesy. I could not help but recall the prophesy of the Gypsies made years before and vaguely wondered if Mrs. Knickerbocker had not, in this manner, pointed out to me a path for success. Oh, yes, I once again began to dream. I dreamt of a perfect partner, like the young lady of the afternoon, of orchestras like Jim Europe's, of large audiences and thunderous applause. Yes, that was all exactly what I wanted. But, how was

I to get it? Suddenly I remembered having read somewhere, at sometime that "realities are made from dreams." Well, I would just continue to dream on and I would see what sort of a reality it would become.

But my dreams were interrupted, just two days later. Included with my morning mail, I found a poem, ironically entitled "Since Betsy and I are Out." There was an inscription on the side reading, "Do you think that very manly revenge?" I was absolutely stunned. Here was a poem written in the first person, referring to that little spat at the Casino. I was depicted as a young man who did not have a serious thought in his head. I dined with this one and danced with another. The object of my life was to have what was referred to as "a peach of a time." I was livid with anger after reading the poem and quickly tore it up, resolving that no one else would ever see it.

But my malingerer had thought of that, too. In addition to me, he had also carefully mailed this same poem to numerous other people about the town. Its message, now known throughout Saratoga Society, created an uproar. Many of my friends turned quite cool, while others indignantly denounced the cowardly act. I was definitely put "on the spot," and all my emphatic denials could not erase the thoughts from a few that, if I had not written the poem, I most certainly had something to do with it.

I eventually discovered who the real author was, but it was too late to entirely mend the trouble. It had been written by an oafish lawyer who was spending the season there with his social-climbing wife. He was past sixty, short and bald, resembling more than anything else a fried shrimp which was possibly a little sick from too much grease. The poem apparently was an outlet for his imprisoned soul, fancifully outlining the things he passionately desired to do. Mentally, he was quite a ladies' man, but all attempts to such an expression were met with guffaws from the fairer sex. Possibly revenge at nature's cruelty to him incited the circulation of the outrageous piece. What a joy it must have given his warped mentality. I never heard of the lawyer after this season in Saratoga. After all, he was a very little man. and he probably got lost in his own small world.

As the season would soon be drawing to a close, I felt that it would be wise if I left Saratoga and returned to the safety of New York. While my stay there had been joyous in many ways, I had encountered several disturbing outbreaks of jealousy. To say that these things had not affected me or my standing with many of the people would be telling an untruth. To some, even, I was a disgrace, but I thank God for those few that had the courage of their convictions and stuck with me.

Chapter Seven

Upon leaving Saratoga, I decided to make a short visit to my home in the South to catch up with my family, and finally returned to New York in October. Settling back in, I was once again confronted with the question of my career. My attempts at the operatic world and the light comedy field had met with such failure that I decided that I had best study the present situation very thoroughly before taking further steps. My dancing school of the previous winter had been a huge success. Should I continue along that line? The dancing craze was certainly continuing with an ever-increasing enthusiasm. Nightclubs and cabarets were springing up everywhere and, following the example of the leading hotels, they were featuring exhibition dancers. It seemed inevitable that these dancers would achieve some degree of success. I had managed to amass a considerable amount of money, and I was paid much more than the average singer received. And now, since the social world was taking dancers into their set, they were being invited into the nicest homes and to the larger functions. Mrs. Knickerbocker's statement had made quite an impression on me. Should I turn professional now? Well, I still had plenty of time to make the decision, so I decided to await further developments.

I had been back in New York but a short time when I was invited to join a small, select dancing club that was being formed to meet every Friday afternoon at the Plaza Hotel. I felt quite flattered to have received the invitation and accepted most eagerly. It was at the second meeting of this little club that Miss Joan Sawyer[28] appeared as a guest. I was thrilled to have this opportunity to meet her in person. After a couple of fortifying cocktails, I summoned my courage and asked her to dance, and she very graciously accepted. Lady Luck was with me and commanded the orchestra to play a waltz. I only wish I could find the words to describe our dance. It was perfect rhythm, an expression of the soul that I am at a loss to explain. Midway through our dance I noticed, much to my surprise, that we were the only couple on the floor. All the others had withdrawn to the sidelines and stood watching us sweep across the floor. Of course, I realized that it was Miss Sawyer who was the idol of this viewing public and deserving of this admiration, not me. When the orchestra stopped there was considerable applause. Upon returning to our table, the members of our little group were most flattering, insisting that it was the most beautiful ballroom waltzing that they had ever seen. I felt sure that all of these compliments were really directed to Miss Sawyer; however, I was more than happy to bask in their reflected glory.

The next morning I received a telegram from one of the outstanding managers in the city, asking me to come and see him immediately. Naturally, I was quite excited and most curious as to what his interest in me was, so I dressed hurriedly and taxied over to his office. He received me at once and was most cordial.

"Mr. Rector, I was at the Plaza yesterday afternoon and saw you dancing with Miss Sawyer. You are, without a doubt, a very fine male waltzer, and the two of you created a beautiful picture to watch. I'm sure that you could be quite a success if you would consider making dancing your profession. If you agree with me, I'd be more than pleased to manage you."

Fate, again, seemed to have taken the reins of my career into her own hands. Here, apparently, was the answer to all the questions that I had been putting to myself. Here was an outstanding theatrical manager, expressing the same thoughts that Mrs. Knickerbocker had uttered but a few weeks before. It took little time to make up my mind. We discussed the matter over from every angle, and when I left his office I again had a duplicate of a most inviting contract.

My first public appearance as a professional dancer was on December 18th, 1913, at the annual Christmas Fund Society Entertainment, held at the Princess Theatre, boasting of such patronesses as Mrs. Stuyvesant Fish, Mrs. Reginald Vanderbilt, Mrs. George Jay Gould, Mrs. Orme Wilson, Mrs. Harry Payne Whitney, Mrs. T. J. Oakley Rhinelander, Mrs. John R. Drexel, Mrs. Chauncey Depew, Mrs. J. B. Haggin, Mrs. John Jacob Astor, Mrs. Townsend Burden, Jr., Mrs. Reginald deKoven, Mrs. Oliver Harriman, Mrs. William Randolph Hearst, Miss Elsie deWolfe, and many others. I appeared upon a program that included my good friend, Miss Alice Nielsen, as well as Miss Ruth St. Denis, Miss Ethel Barrymore, and concluded with a short comedy called "The Bride" starring Mr. Holbrook Blinn. Miss Margaret Hasbrook had been selected as my dancing partner, and I felt very fortunate and was quite elated over my good fortune.

We were second on the program. My excitement was at a high fever, but I felt quite confident. With the opening bars of *The Melody of Love*, my partner and I stepped upon the stage and began our routine, literally losing ourselves in the moment. It was with quite a start that we came to with the applause that awakened us. There was no question but what they liked us and our dancing. After we had taken several bows, I returned to my dressing room, literally walking upon air. When I opened the door, I was greatly surprised to find my manager there, talking with two very distinguished and important-looking gentlemen.

"Mr. Rector, this is Mr. William Randolph Hearst[29] and Mr. Nahan Franko[30]," I heard him saying. I was so surprised at the identity of my guests that I am sure I did not acknowledge the introduction as courteously as I should have.

Mr. Hearst began speaking in a most authoritative tone. "We're very much impressed with your dancing, Mr. Rector. Mrs. Hearst, who is with me, is especially enthusiastic. I've just been talking over a business proposition with your manager here. Mr. Booster's Club of Los Angeles, in connection with my newspaper out there, is planning a large dance festival. We've been unsuccessful in obtaining Maurice as our star, and we're now here to ask you and your manager to accept the contract."

"I feel greatly honored, Mr. Hearst. I should like for you to express my appreciation to Mrs. Hearst. If it's at all possible, I should very much like to accept your kind offer. My manager has made numerous plans for me, but if it can all be rearranged and if he agrees, you can certainly count upon me."

After an appointment was made for a meeting the following day, the gentlemen departed. Many other people came to my dressing room to express their appreciation of my dancing, most of whom I had never seen before. I was a very happy boy, to say the least, as I left the theatre that afternoon. Fate again had fashioned my life according to its own pattern. My opportunity had come, and I had firmly grasped it. Yes, I was beginning to dream again for, as you must have learned by this time, I was quite a dreamer.

Since my success as a dance instructor, I had been residing in rooms at Two East Thirty-third Street over an English teashop. That evening, my living room and bedroom were filled to capacity with well-wishing friends. I was especially pleased over the personal visit of Mrs. Theodore Dreiser, who was so genuinely happy over my success. I had met both Mr. and Mrs. Dreiser[31] the winter before and had found them both to be quite friendly.

"I always knew that you would succeed," Mrs. Dreiser said to me. I have never forgotten her belief in me.

The next day more people came by. Gifts began to arrive—bouquets of flowers, baskets overflowing with fruits, and other things. The most amusing gift was a large cantaloupe with a note attached from a person I had never heard of, asking for a loan of fifty dollars. My intimate enemies also began to call. I call them that because it was with a certain amount of bitterness that I was learning that all of my contemporaries were not as glad to see me successful as I had hoped they would be. Some of my supposedly good friends did not even call, a hurt that I continue to feel to this day. Success is indeed strange. Few take it gracefully, especially when it comes to another. Success and jealousy are very closely related.

Just a little past noon the next day, my manager phoned me and in a very excited manner said, "Come to my office at once. Your dancing was a sensation, and I must see you at once."

Naturally I dressed as quickly as possible. Within the hour, I was in his office, ready and eager to hear the unfolding of great plans.

"Tom, this is all as I had expected. I'm planning a trip for you across the country. This dancing craze has hit the whole United States and many other cities are anxious to organize the Dansant clubs. I've had telegrams by the dozens concerning available talent. To begin with, I've accepted Mr. Hearst's offer. We had a long conference this morning, and the contract is signed for you to appear at the Carnival of Dance in Los Angeles. I've decided that a trip across the country, stopping at various key cities introducing the new dances, and ending at the Carnival of Dance would be a splendid idea. What do you think?"

"It certainly sounds good to me. Of course, it all rather takes my breath away." We discussed the matter in more detail and I left, agreeing with his plans in every way.

How strangely different from my initial expectations my career was unfolding. Would I find success in this new venture or would I to find it ending as abruptly as my other efforts had? This question, only time could answer. I firmly decided to put my whole self into my work and not resist any change that presented itself.

Chapter Eight

But another surprise was in store for me, a surprise that still thrills me to this day.

Upon one of my frequent visits to my manager's office, I found him bursting with enthusiasm. "You're just the person I wanted to see. Where have you been? I've been phoning your apartment for hours, but there was no answer."

"Well, I'm here now, so what's all the excitement about?" I rather flippantly queried.

"You're to dance at the Metropolitan Opera House! You're to dance with Pavlova! This will be the most sensational event of the season. You'll be a star overnight." He was more than a little excited and waved his arms about as he delivered this surprising news.

I could hardly believe my own ears. Between his raving and my own excitement, it was some time before I was able to get the whole story. There was to be a large Pavlova Carnival at the Metropolitan Opera House, followed by a Russian Dansant to be held in the foyer and rehearsal rooms. Someone had suggested that I should be invited to dance a tango or waltz with Madame Pavlova[32] to start off the Dansant. This all sounded exactly like a fairy tale to me. Just a short time ago I had been a spear carrier at this famous institution, and now I was to return as the dancing partner of one of the greatest artists this world has ever known. It all sounded absolutely fantastic.

This carnival was to be a great social event as it was to be given for the benefit of the Music School Settlement and would be attended by everyone of note in New York at that time. The newspapers were filled with articles about the carnival, and I received more than my share of publicity in all of them. I immediately recognized this as an opportunity of a lifetime and became determined to leave no stone unturned to take full advantage of this piece of good luck. Going to one of the greatest costumers in New York, I had an elaborate Russian outfit especially designed for me.

But I was doomed to a certain disappointment. Madame Pavlova was greatly fatigued from a performance in Syracuse, followed by a night's trip on the train and a subsequent appearance at a "Chanson on Crinoline" at the Plaza Hotel that morning. She felt that her ballet appearance that afternoon would be sufficient for the day and, after seeing it, I was certainly of the same opinion. However, my disappointment was certainly somewhat appeased in that Mlle. Alta Plaskowieczja, Pavlova's premier danseuse, was assigned to take her place.

The Carnival was divided into three parts, throughout which Madame Pavlova held the center of the stage for most of the time. She gave a magnificent performance that was filled with the grace, charm, and technique for which she was world famous. The fire and energy that she released as she danced must have left her completely exhausted.

Immediately after the carnival, the audience moved into a large rehearsal hall and foyer for the Russian Dansant. A large throne had been hastily built, upon which Madame Pavlova was most regally ensconced. She was surrounded entirely by her own company, all in their costumes and forming a veritable rainbow of colors around her. It was before this personally earned royalty that Mlle. Plaskowieczja and I did an exhibition ballroom waltz with classic poses and ending with a most reverent kneeling before her Majesty. It was an ideal setting and a perfect performance, made more so by the fact that we had not had one minute of rehearsal together. I have often looked back at the nerve of my youth to attempt so bold a thing. Certainly, the exuberant confidence of youth is one of its greatest heritages.

The Pavlova exhibition succeeded in making me a full-fledged star in my own right. My publicity became greater and offers began to pour into my manager's office, but the greatest barometer of my success was that my intimate enemies became even more active. However, their two-faced activities, consisting of "We just can't understand it" behind my back and "We knew you would succeed" to my face, were of little menace. I knew all of them for their face value and learned to turn my back upon their futile attempts to manipulate me.

At the same time, I knew I should not to let this success go to my head. I firmly realized that to hold onto success was an even greater job than to attain it. I had seen some horrible examples of success lost, and I was determined that I was not to become one of them. What I needed was balance in my life. Yes, balance, that was the word. I was now treading upon a path as narrow as the edge of a razor blade, and I must not stumble.

Chapter Nine

In the meantime, all the arrangements were being made for my invasion into the Middle and Far West. I was to be a pioneer, but certainly a far different type than the earlier red-blooded Americans that James Truslow Adams[33] so perfectly described in his *Epic of America*.

To promote this ambitious tour, I was very fortunate in securing Beulah Livingston as my press agent. Throughout my career and life, I have never had a stauncher or more loyal friend. Although she was just beginning her career when I hired her, she was already well established as she was handling the publicity of Lou Tellegen, Madame Olga Petrova, and Paul Swan.

Beulah had just organized the club, "The Woman Pays." Besides herself, the original members included Beatrice Fairfax, Rita Wiseman, and several other women whose names I have since forgotten. They would meet for lunch in a quaint little house at Fortieth Street, just off Broadway where Beulah had her offices. Today "The Woman Pays" club has a waiting list of over a thousand people. Evidently the concept of the woman paying contains an element of thrill.

Beulah worked very hard for me in arranging the publicity for this, my first big tour. She cooperated thoroughly with my personal manager and soon my Western itinerary was complete. One morning I found myself on the train and on my way to St. Louis, Missouri.

I was delighted to have the opportunity to return to this distinctive city. The memory of having once lived there for a short time during my love attack for Miss Maxine Elliot, even to this day links me with St. Louis in a most delightful manner. I have never forgotten that first love.

At the invitation of one of my former pupils, Miss Irmagard Biebinger, I was to attend a large dance festival to be given under the auspices of the Sunshine Society, a local charity organization formed by the more socially prominent persons in St. Louis. The festival opened with the Mojinanga at the Planters Hotel in the afternoon. It was there that I met most of these charming people for the first time. This was followed, that evening, by a large benefit ball held at the Palladium, at which I was to give exhibition dances with Miss Biebinger as my partner. She was a tiny young girl, her head hardly reaching my shoulders, and one of the most skillful amateur dancers that I had met.

That evening the Palladium was packed to capacity. Irmagard and I gave exhibitions of the waltz, tango, and maxixe. While the majority of the spectators knew nothing whatsoever about these new dances, most of them were inherently graceful, and it was interesting to see their responses and the aptness with which they soon were dancing with their own individual styles. Of course, there were others there who never would be dancers, and their efforts to mimic the exhibition dances afforded much amusement for all of us. Before the evening was over, the ballroom had become a mass of wiggling, squirming humanity. I remained until the end and danced with many of the ladies present.

The morning that followed began with my sides almost splitting with laughter. Mr. Winsor McCay[34], an ingenious cartoonist for the Globe Democrat, had portrayed the modern dance craze as exhibited by the festival in his inimitable style. The caption was "The Orangoutango" or "How They Did It In the Early Days." He depicted about twelve couples of Orangoutangs, clutching each other in exotic tango style, dancing to the music from the clapping rocks and sticks before an enthusiastic audience huddled in trees or swinging by their tails. With the help of my imagination, I thought I could discern a resemblance to me and some of the more prominent guests of the evening before in the faces of our predecessors. I just hope that the others received as much amusement from the cartoon as I did.

I left that day for Minneapolis where I was to stay a week. A series of dances had been arranged at the Radison Hotel, under the personal management of another one of my former pupils, Mrs. Helen F. Noble, and I was to appear in them as the guest star. Mrs. Noble was a grand person, and I was eagerly looking forward to seeing her again.

I spent that long night on a sleeper, which has never been conducive to making me feel in the very best of spirits the next morning. With bleary, red-rimmed eyes, I checked into the Radison and had hardly been in my room long enough to wash my face when the telephone rang. I was informed by the front desk that a reporter from one of the leading newspapers had come to interview me and was waiting in the lobby. Hastily finishing my toilet and feeling very hungry, I went down to meet this press representative. I was quite surprised to discover that my interviewer was a young woman.

"You people certainly are on the job early here," I said as I approached her with an outstretched hand and my best professional smile.

She greeted me with a definite look of surprise. "Oh! I ... I thought you would be a faun with horns and a tail."

I was somewhat taken aback. "I'm sorry to disappoint you. I have no horns, but ..."

She blushed becomingly, but with natural composure proceeded to ask me all manner of questions about the new dances, the Four Hundred of New York, and many very personal questions. The Eastern reporters certainly had nothing on her in the art of asking questions.

The next morning I was almost astounded to find an entire page devoted to my arrival with the glaring headlines: "Society is not as black as it is painted nor as red as it is rouged." I have always been sure that this headline and a large portion of the article was something she had had in the back of her mind for some time and my arrival seemed to be a good opportunity to get it off her chest. I must admit that the article was interesting, even though I was described as a young icicle that thawed out upon knowing. She certainly should have taken the time to get to know me better.

Minneapolis certainly opened my eyes. The wealth of the people and the magnificence of their homes amazed me. It appeared that almost every person I met was a millionaire several times over. I suppose that there must have been some poor people in that city, but I never saw or heard of them.

I crossed the bridge and spent a second week in the twin city, Saint Paul, where I quickly learned of the great rivalry of these two closely joined Midwestern cities. To me, they were one and the same. I even suggested that they might bury the hatchet and get under one banner, compromising on the name Saint Minny, but somehow or other frozen glances were the only replies I received.

My next stop was Winnipeg, Canada. I was a bit dubious about this engagement. I had never been in the Northwest, and my childish impressions were still paramount. I fancied myself somewhat frighteningly dancing with Indian Squaws to the accompaniment of war whoops and the flashing of tomahawks. My fertile imagination carried me almost to the point of not going.

Imagine my surprise to find myself at the beautiful Hotel Royal Alexandra, talking with a group of sophisticated gentlemen who were prominent in the business of that city and were the sponsors of my engagement. Many times since, I have sat in Eastern drawing rooms and listened to egotistical Southerners or stuffy, staid New Englanders or narrow-minded New Yorkers who have not been much further than the nearest boundary line deride the Middle and Far West. I have always just smiled and thought to myself, what a surprise they have in store for them if they are ever so fortunate as to travel in that direction.

The week I spent in Winnipeg was like a fiesta and was made most enjoyable by Miss Josephine Baulf, who had been chosen as my partner for the dance exhibitions. She was a person with great fire and vivacity, and I have never had a more enjoyable associate in my work. The men of the city were cordial, and the women possessed a culture that was most enviable. They were the sons and daughters of Old England and, in many ways, they reminded me of the hospitality of the South. Their greatest charm was their simplicity. I can safely say that the week spent in Winnipeg was one of the most enjoyable of my life. My only compensation upon leaving was the thought that I was, at last, bound for California.

I spent two long days and nights on the sleeper. On the third morning, when I awoke and looked out of my car window, I was filled with total amazement.

I thought surely I must have died and gone to heaven. Never before or since have I seen anything so beautiful as my first glimpse of California. On one side of the train were the Sierra Madre mountains, whose sides were filled with orange trees, both in blossom and bearing fruit, crawling up miles and miles of slopes in an effort to reach the cap of snow glistening in the sunshine on their majestic peaks. I had never seen trees blooming, bearing fruit, and snow at the same time before, and the sight enthralled me. I literally pulled my eyes away to see what the other side of the train had to offer. Here was the Pacific Ocean, with its marvelous turquoise green and blue, breaking high into the air against rocky cliffs completely covered with flowers of every hue, falling over the sides as though daring the sea to come up higher. I was carried away with this beauty and excitedly exclaimed to a middle-aged lady that occupied the next seat, "This is the most beautiful sight I've ever seen. It's a veritable fairyland. All the things they say about California must be true."

I soon regretted this little speech for I immediately discovered that I had addressed a native Californian, and my compliment brought forth an avalanche of unending praise for her home state. I finally had to excuse myself and retire to the smoking car to escape her.

At breakfast I picked up a copy of the Los Angeles Examiner, only to receive another shock which made me quite self-conscious. Spread across the entire front page were numerous photographs of myself and many columns of write-ups. I realized then that the mighty forces of William Randolph Hearst were already at work. From now on, I knew that I would be living in almost an open showcase.

Just what were these Californians like? Was I so different that they would not like me? What did they think of the new dances? I began to feel a bit nervous in attempting to answer these questions and the famous lines of Rudyard Kipling popped into my mind. "East is East and West is West. Never the twain shall meet." Did this apply to Californians? I knew that I had a staunch supporter in Mr. Hearst and just silently prayed that I could live up to his effusive statements.

Upon my arrival at the station in Los Angeles, I was overwhelmed with the alertness and the bustle of the people. The air was charged with electricity, which invigorated me, and I followed their pace. All along the streets were flower stalls filled with the most astounding blossoms I had ever beheld. Could they be real? I wanted to touch them to reassure myself. Violets, the size of silver dollars, roses of every shade, carnations by the thousands, mimosa, acacia, bougainvillea, poppies, and dozens of blossoms I did not recognize filled the streets with their intoxicating scents and bold colors and a sunshine that went right to my heart. Being a child of the sun, it was like meeting an old friend to caress and welcome me.

Any misgivings that I had held about my reception were soon dispelled by the cordiality of the various newspaper reporters and the Booster's Club Committee that greeted me. They escorted me to a most complete suite of elegantly decorated rooms at the Hotel Alexandria.

Just the minute after they left me to shower, unpack, and dress, I called my valet. "I must have some of those flowers. Take this five-dollar bill and go out and buy some. I don't care what kind you get. They're all beautiful."

Emerging from my shower in about half and hour, I was aghast at the procession that I found wending its way into my room. There must have been ten bellboys bringing in flowers of every description. I smiled at the thought of the few rose buds five dollars would have bought in New York City. The next day, when I bought a dozen oranges almost the size of a grapefruit for a dime, I knew that I was going to like California more than I anticipated.

I had four days before the Booster's Festival was to begin, but they were busy days filled with conferences, planning, rehearsals, etc. An enormous building had been converted into a Palais de Dance, with a seating capacity of several thousand and a dance floor that could accommodate easily a thousand couples. The festival was to be in the nature of a grand fiesta, reminiscent of the early days of California. The program, as outlined to me, included two performances a day—one in the afternoon and the other in the evening—of exhibition dancing as my part of the program, along with other artists such as eccentric dancers, acrobats, vocalists, and artists from the various visiting shows, together with an orchestra of fifty pieces. This was all to be followed by public dancing. I realized that when Californians did something, they liked to do it on a large scale.

In addition to my exhibitions, I was to conduct morning and afternoon classes for the general public who was to be charged fifty cents admission to each class. The committee had selected a most competent partner for me, and a group of about twenty local dancing teachers were to assist us with the public instruction. My first duty was to instruct these teachers in all the new dance styles, so for the few days previous to the opening we all worked very hard. I found these Californians very easy to instruct, and within a short time they grasped these new dances as though they had been teaching them for months.

Opening night of the festival was a very big event in my life. Strangely enough, I had no sense of fear. The California air had given me a feeling of buoyancy that I seemed to retain. As the orchestra struck up our entrance music, my partner and I stepped into that huge arena and faced five thousand people. They were a friendly, happy audience. That night, dance history was made in California. Everyone on the program was loudly acclaimed a success. The Booster's Festival had opened with a bang.

The next morning I began to teach the general public, which turned out to be larger job than I had anticipated. Upon reaching the Palais de Dance, I found about one thousand people waiting for lessons, so I had to think quickly. This was certainly more than I had originally bargained for. Just how I was to handle this mob was a big question. Borrowing a megaphone from the orchestra leader, I stood upon the platform. With the assistance of my teachers, I managed to quickly divide the crowd into squads, putting one teacher as a captain to each squad. I began to explain each step in detail, and then my partner and I would demonstrate it as clearly as possible. After this, each squad passed before me, doing this step under the supervision of their individual teacher. It was not too long before we were all well organized.

The enthusiasm of these Californians is something I have seldom seen equaled. Every age, every class—children to grandparents—were eager to learn. It is only natural that such a large crowd would include some amusing as well as pathetic characters. I remember particularly one rather tired young woman holding a three-month baby in her arms. I approached her and asked, "Do you think you can learn to dance with so young a baby in your arms?"

"I must. I've no one to leave her with. My husband is crazy about these new dances, and I have to learn to keep him."

Then, there was the fat widow with a long black crepe veil, holding her dress above her ankles. I wondered if she was preparing to keep the next husband.

There was a very interesting older couple, apparently in their seventies, who told me they had come to California to spend the last years of their lives in the sunshine. They said they had not danced in thirty years and were eager to learn the new steps. Well, they never missed a lesson and they did exceptionally good.

Offers began to pour in for me from everywhere. Many private dancing classes were formed. In Pasadena, I began to appear at the Dansant and supper dances of a fashionable winter resort hotel, and it soon became nothing for me to give six performances a day besides teaching for about six hours. I began to live like a racehorse.

Madame Pavlova was also appearing in Los Angeles at that time, which only served to stimulate the dance madness that was growing in this city. Actually, all Southern California had gone as dance mad as New York had during the previous winter.

It was at the Booster's Festival that I met John McCormick, his charming wife, and their tiny tots, Gwen and Cyril. We exchanged boxes for our individual performances, and I thoroughly enjoyed the one concert I was privileged to attend.

At the end of the first two weeks of the festival, my partner's health began to give way. She was an exceptionally good dancer, but somewhat frail and just could not stand the physical and mental strain we were under. I was in a complete quandary. I knew of no one to take her place, but again Lady Luck stepped forward and helped me out.

That very afternoon, at the Palais de Dance, a pair of wristwatches was being offered to the two most graceful dancers of the waltz. I was not one of the judges, but certainly a most interested spectator. Almost at once, my eye fell upon a very young couple executing the most difficult steps in quite an easy manner. The boy was very blonde and somewhat amateurish, but the girl, she was the incarnation of rhythm and grace. She was not much more than fifteen years of age, with flashing black eyes and raven hair that hung down her back and was tied with a bright red ribbon. Her face was radiant.

I was rather surprised when the wristwatches were awarded to another couple. However, I kept my eyes upon these two. The young boy took it rather well, but this beautiful young girl wept in childish indignation. I strolled over to the place where they were standing.

"I thought that your dancing was beautiful," I said, trying to be soothing. "Had I been one of the judges, I can assure you that you would be wearing that wristwatch now."

"Thank you very much," she replied, drying her eyes.

"I was wondering if you were too tired to dance with me?"

"Why, yes. Yes, I would like to." She was surprised and showed it in the tone of her voice.

We whirled off in perfect harmony. The more we danced, the more I realized I was right. She was an ideal dancer. Fate had again been kind. I had found my partner. I had to be sure of my choice though, so we ran through all of the most difficult steps I could think of. She followed along easily and gracefully. I was convinced.

"You didn't win the wristwatch," I whispered in her ear, "but would you like to be my dance partner?"

She was so surprised that she stopped in the middle of the next step. "Why, what do you mean?"

"I'm looking for a permanent partner. The young lady I've been dancing with since I've been here cannot continue on account of her health. I need a young lady to take her place, to travel with me, to appear in exhibition dances, to assist me in teaching. Would you be that young lady?"

"Oh, I'd love to. If mother would just let me. What can I do to persuade her?"

"Suppose we go and have a talk with her."

And so we did and mother did consent. The young lady had to make her living and, as she was a gifted dancer, this was apparently the best way. As long as she could be with her daughter as a chaperone, the mother had no serious objections and agreed to all of our plans.

We began rehearsals immediately. The following Monday we made our first appearance together. My new partner was a veritable sensation. I can see her now, dressed in her simple white muslin dress with her long black curls and flashing eyes; I can see that luminous expression of supreme joy; I can feel her extreme youth, her wondrous grace. I was very proud to have found her.

And, thus, Dorothy Smoeller[35] made her debut. An instantaneous success and worthy of it in every way.

Chapter Ten

My social life could have been quite full in Los Angeles, but when I started out on my trip West I made a promise to myself to stick close to business. Just the same, I must admit that I did put my promise aside on certain occasions and managed to have a little bit of fun, but only just a little.

Shortly after arriving in Los Angeles, I was pleasantly surprised to run across Richard Barry, whom I had not seen since our French rooming house days in the West Fifties. In the time that had passed, he had been a brilliant success as a war correspondent in the Japanese-Russian War and had also become quite well known in the literary field, having several books and plays to his credit. It was a joyous reunion for the two of, and we had plenty to talk over.

One evening as we were having dinner, I approached him with an idea that I had been toying around with in the back of my mind for several days. "Dick, why don't you write a book for a musical comedy portraying this dance madness that's so prevalent in the country?"

"That's an idea," he quickly replied. "I'd never thought of that. I've been watching this craze gain momentum. There are possibilities there." He seemed quite pensive for a while. "Would you help me with a few pointers?"

"You know darn well I would. Think it over a few days. We can talk about it again."

Dick did think it over and a few days later he took the idea to Mr. Oliver Morosco[36], whose headquarters were in Los Angeles at that time. Mr. Morosco was quite interested in our idea, and his interest was of great value since he was, without question, the outstanding producer at that time, having to his credit two big successes in "Peg O' My Heart" and "Bird of Paradise."

The three of us had several lengthy conferences on the subject. We finally agreed that Dick was to write the book of a comedy to be called "The Tangoer," Mr. Morosco was to produce it, and I was to star in it. Immediately after my return from an engagement I had already booked in San Francisco, we would start work on the production.

I was elated over the idea. Would I become the musical comedy star that I had dreamed of so long ago when I signed the contract with Mr. Charles Dillingham? Would I return to my voice—the voice that I had worked so hard with for so long? Would my dancing, singing, and acting now be joined together in an opportunity secretly hoped for?

At that time, the leading dancers were the darlings of the public. They were receiving the adoration and hero worship that had previously been reserved for the great prima donnas, tenors, and matinee idols. This same adoration has since been lavished upon movie stars, aviators, and prizefighters. What was more important, though, was that these new idols were receiving much more money and publicity than had ever been the case in the past.

An old adage suddenly came to my mind, "Do not cross the bridge until you come to it." I had allowed my dreaming to get the best of me, and I had been ready to cross the bridge too quickly. I had planned and dreamed before, and Fate had waved her magic wand and changed the whole picture. This time I would leave it all to her and put the entire plan out of my mind. She would have it all her way in the end, anyway.

It was about this time that I had a serious domestic problem. No, it didn't involve any family members or female friends, but my Chinese cook, who was excellent in every respect but one—his great weakness for "the cup of cheers." On one particular afternoon, I was going to be giving an interview that was very important to me. In an attempt to create the very best impression possible, I had invited all the reporters to lunch, leaving instructions for a repast par excellence. I returned to my apartment shortly before the time for them to arrive and to my complete disgust found my cook in a dead stupor and not a hand turned toward starting my so carefully planned lunch. I was literally tearing my hair out when the doorbell rang. Trying to collect myself, I opened the door to discover it was my landlord who was in the building and had just stopped in to inquire if everything was perfectly satisfactory—not to dun me for my rent for I was most ably prepared to meet such necessities, thank God. It had been a long time since I was frightened of the ringing of the doorbell.

"Tom, you look distressed. I just stopped by to see if I could by of any service to you," he most pleasantly greeted me.

"I'm in a hell of a mess, but I'm afraid that this time you can be of little help. Look here," I said and led him into the other room where my cook had passed out completely.

"Just leave him alone. He'll be all right soon."

"Soon," I cried in despair. "I have a dozen people coming to lunch within an hour. This is an important press conference. I'll be ruined. Damn that little bastard's hide." I'm afraid that I lost control of myself again as I related my problem and viewed the sodden cause of it all.

"There now. It's not that serious. Can't you take them out to a hotel? Or, better still—I'll cook lunch for you. No, don't worry. I'm a good cook. I'll stake my reputation on it. Cooking is a hobby with me. You can get your valet to serve, and no one will ever know the difference."

It seemed an inane idea at first, but he seemed so willing and so confident that I finally agreed. We scurried about with the details, and within a very short time he had prepared one of the finest luncheons I have ever sat down to in my life. Each one of my guests particularly remarked upon it. Oh, if they had but known that there, right under their very noses was a big story—one even bigger than the one I had given them. Their cook that day was one of the wealthiest men in California and a recognized force in the real estate business, probably one of the largest holders in the state. What a story they could have written!

The Los Angeles Examiner was a very progressive newspaper, and all of my dealings with Mr. Hearst and his staff were very pleasant. During this time I was writing a series of articles for this paper, giving instructions in the art of dancing. With each article, there appeared a series of pictures showing the correct steps and posture. I always tried to stress the fact that dancing was an expression of freedom of the mind and body and a joyousness of the soul. All dancers should thoroughly relax and enter into the spirit of gaiety. Nothing is so sad as to see a couple on a ballroom floor with woe-begone expressions upon their faces. Strangely enough, this expression is most commonly seen upon the faces of married people. I really do not think that husbands and wives should dance together. The song Joe Cauthorne made so popular at this time explains it well—*I can dance with everyone but my wife*. Why should two people who spend so much time together, when they are out for an evening of complete relaxation, dance together? There is a bit of flirtation in everyone's makeup. Dancing with the other man's wife or girl is such a wonderful method of giving vent to such pent-up emotions.

It is strange how one learns to read characters by dancing with people. In my teaching, I suppose that I averaged dancing with fifty different women a day. Soon I began to sense their individual characteristics, and it was not long before I had them all classified according to types.

First there was the joyous type. These were the ones whose spirits were uplifted by the rhythm of music, whose feet scarcely hit the floor before they were wafted on the wings of romance. While dancing they were expressing freedom, joy, and love. What a pleasure they were to have as partners. This type was usually in their late teens or early twenties.

Another was the amorous type. Apparently unsatisfied with their love life, they would grab their partners in a death clutch and dance as closely as possible. They fairly breathed with passion, panting like a thirsty doe. They were seldom good dancers, possibly because their minds were not upon the music or the execution of the proper steps. To me, "earthbound" seems to describe their condition.

I found the stubborn type, too. She was usually a small, thin woman who stepped out onto the dance floor and planted her feet squarely upon the floor with a defiant "I dare you to move me" look in her eyes. They always gave me the shivers. You make an effort, you grab her and finally you get started. Then she is off. Once started, she tries to take things into her own hands and insists upon leading. Usually a tough battle ensued. If a man is determined, he will win out, but when he finishes, it is ten to one that he feels like a tamed bronco. I can usually picture the home life of such a woman. Love is not the basic element in her home. She will rule with an iron hand or bust in the attempt. God forbid that I ever dance with that type again.

Another type is the lackadaisical dancer. Generally she feels inwardly that she is a great mystic and probably writes poetry. She will start by throwing her stomach right into yours, fling her head back, and gaze soulfully into your eyes. Her clothes float with the breeze as she whirls about. She is the one that feels that a little light lovemaking, administered during the dance, helps her rhythm. Well, maybe it does. I have often wondered what the rhythm would be like in a correct posture.

Then we have the "respectable married woman" type, who is usually the wife of the backbone of the community. That is, the husband supplies the backbone and she the whalebone. You can read her life like a book. She is now in her late forties or early fifties: She and her husband started life early in a modest way, working hard, saving and educating the children. Now they belonged to the Country Club, which had become their only outlet for fun since the "Strawberry Festival" days. The dance floor had suddenly become their playground—always dancing with just the right people in just the right manner. They have never heard of the word relax.

Strangely enough, the average man is a much better dancer than the average woman. I believe the reason is that a man is not as self-conscious as the woman. Then, too, most women try to dramatize themselves. Often, some of the largest, fattest women are the easiest to dance with. Although heavy in body, they are light on their feet. Probably this is because so many fat people are jolly and content with who they are, rather than who they might be.

If you do not believe that freedom and love or stubbornness and unselfishness or any other definite qualities of nature do not show up in dancing, well, just turn professional and see how quickly you learn to read people's characters by the way they dance. It is a revelation.

Chapter Eleven

At the end of six weeks, our entire company left for San Diego where we were to appear in a similar dance festival to be held at the Hotel Grant. I am still in doubt as to whether my arrival at this hotel was the occasion of a practical joke or just bad taste upon the part of the management. Anyway, much to my consternation, when I was ushered into my rooms I found that I had been given the bridal suite. It was done all in white, and even the furniture was upholstered in white silk. I will admit that my experience with bridal suites had been rather limited, but I felt that this must be the bridiest bridal suite in existence. I had no bride, not even an illegitimate one. Most certainly, living in such quarters would throw my mind into channels other than dancing, and I could not risk that. Remember, I had made a promise to myself to stick to my work. It simply would not do, and I told the manager so in a very positive way. I insisted that my suite must be changed for one more suitable for a bachelor—something that would keep his mind upon his work—and I got it.

We proceeded in the same manner with our work as we had in Los Angeles, except on a much smaller scale. Dorothy Smoeller was tasting success in a big way, and she was taking it like a veteran. Newspaper reporters used all the superlatives in their possession when describing her dancing. Admirers showered her with gifts, and she had a string of suitors a mile long. To her, each day became more beautiful than the preceding one. She accepted all the attention most graciously and remained true to her art.

As for myself, I was tasting the bitter side of success. There is a quirk in human nature that causes men and women to want to harass those who have achieved some degree of success while they themselves have failed. Parasites I suppose they should be called. I began to receive threatening letters. I was followed. I was spied upon. Stories began to circulate in which I was described as being the Pied Piper of Hamlin, breaking hearts, destroying homes, and corrupting the innocent. Fortunately for me, Mr. Hearst controlled the newspapers in these cities and not one of these stories ever reached the printed page, but they did manage to annoy me to no end. I hired detectives and used every precaution I could think of to protect myself, but still they pursued me.

I finally decided that it would be best to have my youngest sister, Natalie, join me. She had just graduated from a school in Washington, D.C. and I felt that her presence with me would be the protection that I needed from the scaremongers that were following me. I sent her a wire and within two hours I received the following reply.

"Taking first train. Will make good chaperone for big brother."

Meanwhile, the Hotel Del Coronado had made Dorothy and me a

most lucrative and flattering offer. We accepted with no hesitation and at the conclusion of our San Diego contract, we left for that veritable fairyland. The big, rambling hotel was built upon an island just off the coast of San Diego. It was fairly new then and was attracting probably the richest and most select group of all the California resorts. We arrived in February at the height of the season.

The hotel is an irregular, roving-frame structure, built around a large, beautiful court or patio about the size of a city block and filled with luxuriant tropical flowers, shrubs, and trees. The rooms or suites that faced the patio each had balconies with vines and flowers cascading from their railings. Scattered here and there among this rainbow of foliage and blossoms were bubbling fountains that assisted in making this scene a picture from the Arabian Nights.

The morning after my own arrival, I was more than happy to greet my sister, Natalie, at the train station. Upon reaching the hotel, I welcomed her with a sumptuous California breakfast served upon our balcony. She, too, was visiting California for the first time and was experiencing many of the same thrills I had had. That morning, she walked out upon our balcony and stood as though spellbound for quite some time. Turning to me, in a soft breathy voice she said, "This must be the most beautiful place upon this earth. I feel like I never want to leave."

Our breakfast that morning was interrupted by the manager of the hotel who, in a most courtly manner, joined us for another cup of coffee. After a few pleasantries were exchanged, he quickly got down to business. "Our plans for the opening ball are all arranged for this evening, and I'm sure that you'll approve of our efforts. I know that our guests will enjoy your dancing as certainly the newspapers all over California have heralded you in great fashion."

Laughingly, I replied, "I sincerely hope that we can live up to their expectations. You mustn't take the newspapers too seriously though. Remember, I was actually working for one. A cheer for me is, in reality, a plug for them."

My frank statement appeared to take the manger off guard for a moment, but whatever his thoughts were, he quickly brought the subject back to the real object of his visit. "I've a surprise for you," he continued. "Probably you've read in the papers that we have a very distinguished guest here in the hotel."

"No, I haven't seen the papers this morning. The arrival of my sister has been a little too exciting for me."

He fairly beamed at being allowed to break the great news. "Mary Pickford[37] has just arrived here with her mother and brother. We have asked her to lead the grand march with you this evening and she has consented. I hope that this arrangement will be satisfactory to you."

"Will it?" I answered in a most excited tone. "I couldn't think of anything more thrilling."

I could hardly believe that all of this possible. In the East at this time, we all looked upon movie stars as being a part of another world. Mary Pickford, the shining star of them all, was almost a myth.

That afternoon, I caught a glimpse of this famous personage in the hotel lobby. I saw a little, frail girl appear with a heavy black veil shrouding her features. She was followed by several hundred children and grown people who were hounding her for her autograph. I truly admired the sweet and gentle way she gave her signature to almost every one of them and the affectionate manner in which she greeted each one. I knew that she had been on location all that day and must have been exhausted. I knew, too, what a strain this trailing public was. I realized then, why she was so deservedly called "America's Sweetheart." From that day on, she was mine, too, and remains so to this day.

The ballroom of the Hotel Del Coronado, at that time, was one of the largest and most magnificent I had ever seen. It was circular in form, with large plate glass windows looking out upon the Pacific Ocean. True to California style, it was literally overflowing with flowers. From the balconies hung magnificent Oriental rugs. Thousands of well-grouped electric lights cast their joyous and gay effect upon this scene.

As this was the height of their winter season, the hotel was filled to capacity. I was told that there were two hundred and sixty-five private railroad cars in the yards close by which had arrived during the week. Millionaires and their families from everywhere seemed to be there by the thousands. It was difficult for me to conceive of the vast wealth of the West at that time.

There were nearly five thousand guests in the ballroom that opening evening. The display of gowns and jewels was beyond description. Never, at any place, at any time have I seen it equaled since. The superlatives that in the past decade have become associated with California were casting their shadows that evening at the Coronado. The color and dignity of the evening were furnished by the Naval men and their wives from the station at San Diego.

I must confess, for the first time in my life I actually felt the pangs of stage fright. Mary Pickford seemed to be the chief cause of this. I kept asking myself, "What shall I say to her?" I was so afraid that I would seem an awful dud to such a personage as Miss Pickford. Here, among all of these people of such great wealth and social standing was I, me, poor little me, probably stumbling around the floor in a very embarrassed manner with the dress girl of the nation. I anxiously paced the floor of my dressing room.

But nothing stays the hand of Father Time in his inevitable march. A knock upon my dressing room door announced that the time had finally arrived. I came out nervously, and the suave manager of the hotel escorted me across the ballroom to Mary Pickford. Whatever feelings I had had before left me instantly. Such beauty, such charm, coupled with her simple, even shy manner immediately put me at ease. Her radiant smile thawed my haunting fears and, offering her my arm, we proceeded to open the grand march. Without exaggeration, it was the most exciting moment of my life.

After the grand march, I escorted Miss Pickford to her box and was presented to her mother and her brother, Jack. Feeling a bit daring and yet hopeful, I said, "This has been most delightful, Miss Pickford. It would be even more so if I may have the pleasure of a dance with you later this evening."

"I would be very happy to if you can put up with my dancing. I'm afraid that you'll not find it as perfect as you are accustomed to."

This I found to be just another form of her shyness. She was a superb dancer, with the ability to follow my steps easily and gracefully. I was happy to be able to claim more than one dance with her that evening. Later in the evening, it took all the courage I could muster to suggest, "I should be very happy to have you, your mother, and brother join my sister, my partner, and myself for supper after the dance."

To my joy her reply was, "We will be delighted to."

True to her promise, we did have supper in the grill afterward and I, like all who have known her, fell very much in love with her. Mary Pickford replaced Maxine Elliot in my dreams.

Chapter Twelve

San Francisco was the next stop on our itinerary. I had heard many interesting stories of its quaint charm, but I was doomed not to be able to enjoy any of these this time. I came down with a very bad cold on the train and ended up spending most of the time there in bed, trying to save my strength for my performances. A heavy fog settled over the city shortly after our arrival and did nothing to assist in my recovery. I was in San Francisco for a week and saw practically nothing but the theatre and the walls of my hotel room. I managed to conserve strength enough to give nine performances at a theatre and several appearances at a local hotel, all of which were not examples of my best work.

We made several appearances at the Liberty Theatre across the bay in Oakland, where the Bishop Players were producing Henry Miller's famous comedy success, "The Rainbow." In this production, they were using a revolving stage, which, at that time had not yet made its appearance on Broadway. In later years, I was greatly amused with the publicity and excitement that was generated when the revolving stage was introduced in New York City. The stage was heralded as an entirely new invention and received with considerable applause. The old adage, "there is nothing new under the sun," must be more true than we realize.

I must say that I was glad to leave San Francisco, chiefly because I was then going to have the luxury of seventeen days of complete rest, which I knew I needed very badly. Dorothy and I were on our way to Japan to begin a dance tour of the Orient. It was an idea that was filled with thrill from the moment it was presented to me.

The fog over San Francisco lifted in a farewell salute and on a bright, sunny day, my manager, my sister, my partner, and I set sail on the good old ship, Manchuria, with much joy in our hearts. Our staterooms were quite comfortable and displayed the usual assortment of bon voyage packages. One gift in particular amused me considerably. It was a case of champagne with a simple card reading:

"When rape seems inevitable, relax and enjoy thyself." Confucious

I have always known Confucious to be a very wise, old man, but such subtle wisdom I had never attributed to him. To this day, I do not know whether this was a true statement of his, but Confucious or not, it certainly was most sound advice. Accompanying the case of champagne was a smaller box containing a gold wristwatch, but still no sign of identification of the sender. I never did find out who the giver of these gifts was and would still like to know who was so thoughtfully wise. Undoubtedly, it was sent by someone who was very familiar with the Orient and wanted to offer some philosophical advice to a young, green man going to that strange, fascinating land for the first time.

The wristwatch I presented to my sister. The champagne I enjoyed thoroughly. Should the sender read these lines, I would like to express my sincere thanks for both the gift and the advice. I found the latter to be priceless.

The first few days aboard the Manchuria, I remained much to myself, resting, getting rid of my cold, and generally taking stock of my life. Events had been following in such rapid succession that I had never found time to really think. For the past year I had been dancing or teaching for about twelve hours a day, and it was a tremendous relief to just stretch out in a steamer chair and let the world drift by. Late at night, when most of the passengers had retired, I would go to the stern of the boat and sit by the hour in the patch of the moon and relax into my favorite pastime—dreaming. I forgot all the sadness in my life and relived the happy moments. I found great joy in anticipating the adventures that were ahead of me.

We did meet many charming steamer acquaintances, among them Colonel Sam Parker[38] and his son, both natives of Hawaii. Colonel Parker was quite an elderly man at that time and had been prime minister of this island during the reign of Queen Liloukalani. He charmed me with stories of its history and customs, and I began to look forward to spending a day there while the steamer refueled and obtained provisions.

Colonel Parker introduced me to a very fascinating young Hawaiian Princess who, widely traveled and educated, was returning to her home which she loved and respected above all other places in the world. She told me fascinating tales of her people and their enchanting lives. When she discovered I was interested in music and dancing, she related a history of Hawaiian music I have never forgotten.

"Hawaiian music is different. Yes, very different from any other country or nation." Her voice was low, just above a whisper, as though out of respect. "The very early missionaries soon found that the only way to reach this strange tribe of people was through music. At that time their songs and dances were primitive ceremonies. They had their dances and music, as well as ceremonies for marriage, death, sickness, and other rites, all based upon a joint rhythm of sound and motion. These missionaries began to teach these people their hymns, but it was only natural that the natives should play, sing, and dance them according to their own interpretations. The result you will hear tomorrow. It is a strange, pathetic languor that seems to dominate their souls, but it is beautiful—more beautiful than you can realize."

"I certainly hope that I can hear them tomorrow. And their dancing—will they dance for me?" I suppose my question seemed almost childish to her. She smiled as she replied.

"Singing and dancing are their lives. Tomorrow you will see hardly anything else."

"Dancing is my profession, as you know. I'll be extremely interested in seeing them."

"Their dance is something more than a dance. It is a physical and emotional expression of their soul. A volcanic eruption of an inner emotion. I shall not try to explain it to you as it would be most difficult. You shall see for yourself."

We stood for some time in silence. The Princess was so lost in reverie that I felt hesitant in disturbing her. It was she who finally broke the silence.

"So few people really understand or enjoy music. They just accept it without reaching into its depths. To me it has three qualities. First, appreciation, which most people have in some degree or other. Second, understanding, a quality that has been reserved for the artists or intense students. The third quality is realization, which only a few great souls have touched. Music releases some quality of the soul. Often it is a cry for freedom, other times a battle of the inner forces, but more often an expression of unforgettable beauty, a soul expression of luminous harmony." She paused for some minutes and then continued, talking as though only to herself, seemingly in another world. "Music carries qualities that this world has never dreamed of, hidden values of multitudinous worth to all humanity. Music is capable of performing miracles, but we have not reached that stage as yet. Some day the world will understand music. Today, only a few are attempting to."

Such philosophy, I had never heard before. It was a philosophy offering solace to starved souls. I was more than impressed. We stood for some time in silence. I felt called upon to say something and made some sort of meaningless remark, which I immediately regretted. The Princess moved quickly, as though suddenly returning from another world—a world where dreams are realities. With a casual remark, she excused herself and I was left alone with her philosophy.

Very early the next morning we docked in the picturesque harbor of Honolulu. If I thought California was paradise, then this surely must be Seventh Heaven. Hundreds of brown skinned boys and girls were circling the ship in the water, diving for the coins the passengers were throwing overboard. Natives were playing and singing their plaintive melodies upon the docks. It was a music, when heard for the first time, that tugged at your heart strings. Majestic palm trees, growing almost to the water's edge, were waving a lazy welcome. The entire city seemed to be out to greet us. The air was filled with song, melodies of a strange, languorous, haunting beauty.

Upon landing, we went immediately to the Royal Moana Hotel upon Waikiki Beach. What an ideal place to spend a vacation! It would be wonderful to stay here for weeks and loll upon the beach, watch the surf riders, and listen to their music. My romantic nature immediately changed the sight before me to a night scene, lighted by a full moon. Romance? Well, if you couldn't have it here, you must be dead!

After luncheon we drove through the city. Such a profusion of flowers I had not even seen in California. There were blossoms of every color, size, and description. Most of the fences were hedged with hibiscus in full bloom. Then there was a tree called the" Jackdaw" that was covered with a delicate blue flower that seemed to blend with the sky.

Everywhere we heard their strange melodies. I was fascinated by the exotic dances, filled with such natural rhythm. I began to feel, in a small degree, that which the Princess had been trying to tell me. Here was something entirely new. It was a supreme releasement of inner joy that the tired businessman, maiden ladies, and youth—especially youth—were looking for, but not finding. Here it was on a small island in the Pacific Ocean. I was inspired. I must take this music and dancing home with me. America must know of it.

I began to study their hands and feet. I even danced with them. They were all most willing to help and teach me. My mind raced with ideas as I dreamed of a ballroom version of this new rhythm. Yes, it could be done, but here I was on my way to the Orient. I wanted to turn back now and carry this new music to the waiting world. Why did I have to go? I asked myself that question a dozen times over without finding the answer.

As we boarded the ship that evening to set sail for Japan, we were greeted by another scene of beauty that cannot be fully appreciated unless actually seen. Thousands of civilians and natives were on the dock and bidding us adieu, all joining in the playing and singing of "Aloha." The natives bore handmade leis which were placed around all of the passengers' necks. We were literally covered with heavily scented flowers of all descriptions. As the golden sun sank into the west, we pulled away to the strains of the immortal "Aloha," intoxicated by the perfume of the flowers, the beauty of the island, and the friendliness of its inhabitants. I felt as if for one day I had lived in a fairyland. I regretted having to leave this enchantment more than anything in my life, before or since.

We were told that we must throw the leis into the water before the sight of land passed from view as it was ill luck for those who did not obey this custom. Very reluctantly and silently I let fall these priceless gifts into the wake of the ship. I felt as though I were laying wreaths upon something very beautiful in my life. Perhaps I was.

Chapter Thirteen

Again I settled back in my deck chair to continue my resting and dreaming. Hawaii had given me something definite to build upon when I returned to New York. Following my decision to introduce this fascinating music and rhythm to America, I was seized with a great desire to study. Yes, I would study. In each foreign country I intended to visit, I would study the people, their arts, their music, and their dance. Here before me was a magnificent opportunity that might never be repeated, and I must not let it go. With close study and constant application, I could return home with an unlimited amount of innovative ideas to bring to the dance world. Here was a golden opportunity to be truly creative. I was radiantly happy over my prospects.

The second day out of Hawaii, I was interrupted in my dreaming by my manager. A number of passengers had approached him and suggested that they organize a dance class, and they wanted me to instruct them in the new dances. I readily agreed to the proposal and found it all most interesting. My pupils were of several nationalities and various social classes and every afternoon, between four and five o'clock, we held class in the ship salon.

I soon noticed a very dignified woman of about forty-five years of age who appeared each afternoon and watched the class with considerable interest. She constantly remained alone and seemed to always shun the company of others. I questioned my pupils, but no one seemed to know anything about her. She was always appeared perfectly gowned in black, her only ornaments being two large diamond earrings, which sparkled with great luminance. I began to call her "the mysterious lady" and, liking mystery, I began to wonder about her.

The day we crossed the equator, she was again a spectator at my expense. It was my first crossing and I received the usual dunking and other ceremonies that were deemed fitting for such an occasion. She stood by and watched the proceedings from the sidelines with a half-amused smile on her face. Somehow or other, I felt there was great wisdom behind that smile or, maybe, it was experience.

The climax of that day was a fancy dress ball held in the main salon in the evening. I appeared in the Russian costume that I had worn at the Pavlova Dansant at the Metropolitan Opera House. The salon was filled to capacity with passengers, all decked out in their finest attire. I began to wonder about my mysterious lady and, although I was on a constant lookout, I could not locate her in the crowd. As the midnight hour neared, a cabin boy approached me saying, "I beg your pardon, sir, but a lady would like to speak to you. Will you go to her cabin?"

"Would I?" What a question to ask. Here, at last, was high adventure in mid-ocean. Possibly even romance. Who knew? I certainly was not averse to encountering either. As I followed the boy, my anticipations and imagination grew wilder with each step. Imagine my great surprise when I found my hostess to be none other than my mysterious lady with the diamond earrings. I could not help but show my surprise when I entered her cabin.

Without being the least bit coy, she introduced herself, giving me a name which I have long since forgotten. I instinctively knew that it did not belong to her anyway. "This is a bit unconventional, I know," she began, "but I'm not always conventional. I was anxious to have a chat with you and thought that his would be the nicest way."

Looking around I noticed a bottle of champagne and two glasses on a silver tray. I knew then that our chat had been well planned and could prove to be very interesting. To say that I was intrigued is putting it mildly. "It's very nice of you," I said, wondering just what it was she expected of me.

Her only reply was a smile—fascinating but retreating into a suggestion of melancholy, even a tragic aspect. As she poured the champagne, I had occasion to study her more carefully. She was of medium height, dressed as usual in black, but that evening more perfectly appointed than I had yet seen her. Her nut-brown hair was drawn, not too severely, over the tips of her ears that held the long diamond earrings in such a graceful manner. Her face was pale, having an almost phosphorescent pallor, with deep-set eyes, small and shrewd like those of an elephant. Her narrow, high forehead assured me of her cleverness. In contrast, her slightly tip-tilted nose suggested a saucy flippancy. Probably a relic from her youth, I thought. But behind her whole expression, I could see an almost haunting look of despair, as though she realized running from some silent sorrows was only an attempt after all. She seemed completely self-possessed and capable of controlling any type of situation.

"You have never been to the Orient before," she more or less stated, rather than queried, as she handed me the glass of champagne.

"No, this is my first trip to any foreign country."

"The Orient is very beautiful. It's equally very ugly. Nowhere else will you find such contrasts. You'll meet the most generous, kind people living in luxurious homes, reveling in cleanliness, virtue, literature, arts, and all forms of higher education. Yet there are also many thieves, rascals, and desperados existing in hovels, filled with drunkenness, ignorance, and all types of vices. Derelicts of the lowest types. There is an underworld in the Orient of greater treachery than in any other country in the world. It is a land of two extremes. A visitor needs to be very cautious. I wanted so very much to warn you." She hesitated a moment. "You are so young."

"Yes, that is one of my faults," I interrupted, "but I unquestionably will outgrow that."

"Youth is a precious heritage. One should guard it with all his strength." She stood looking out the portholes as she said this, but I felt that she was looking into the distant past rather than at the ocean and sea gulls. She turned quickly. "Another glass of champagne?"

"Yes, thank you very much." I felt awkward and must have appeared so.

As she filled my glass, I could not help but notice how pale her hands were, as if in sympathy with her face. She had such graceful, long fingers which were unmarred with rings yet completely regal.

"All that you say interests me very much. Won't you tell me more?" I wanted her to continue, yet I felt that she had complete charge of the conversation. She had that definite quality of domination that so often makes one feel almost ill at ease.

"You'll hear more. Yes, much more, but not now. Youth is always in such a hurry. Americans especially. We must all learn that time is of so little importance. My only desire at this point in time was to warn you of the pitfalls before you. Think over what I have said and be cautious in your actions." She hesitated a moment, her upper lip dropping down over her lower one in a tightening fashion, then continued. "It is inevitable that our paths will cross again. Soon after we land, I'll communicate with you. In the meantime, you are to not mention this little chat to a single person. For the rest of the trip we will continue as we were before. I realize that this all sounds very mysterious but it must be that way. You will understand more clearly later."

"I shall be staying at the Grand Hotel in Yokohama. My name ..."

"Yes, I know," she interrupted smilingly. "You are Tom Rector of New York—a Southerner, in fact a dancer and singer. Oh, I know all about you! Just be careful. Please."

Finding myself in the hall, I realized that her complete mastery had terminated the interview before I had realized it. Awkwardly mumbling some sort of a goodnight, I hurried to my own cabin, filled with this dynamic personality who was so mysterious, yet simple and motherly.

"What did she mean?" I asked myself a dozen times that night, for I could not sleep. I could not find the answer, either.

Chapter Fourteen

The rest of the trip seemed rather uneventful. On the morning of the seventeenth day, I was awakened by the cabin boy informing me that several Japanese gentlemen, who had just come aboard, desired to talk with me. They were reporters from the various newspapers who, in excellent English, welcomed me to Japan on behalf of the Japanese people. From them I learned that the Orientals seemed to be very much interested in the modern dance. These gentlemen of the press made quite an impression upon me. They used extreme courtesy and tact in the asking of their questions. They also seemed more interested in my ideas on dancing, my methods of teaching, and America's reaction to the new dances than in the details of my personal life. Not once did they ask a personal question nor pry into my private life. Neither were they interested in America's so-called social world. Dancing, to them, was a great art and somewhat sacred. What a change from what I had experienced in California!

My first glimpse of Japan excited me tremendously. I was impressed with the smallness of everything—the people, the houses, the rickshaws, everything. I could not help but be amused with the Japanese men walking on the street, all wrapped in their dark kimonos, wearing wooden shoes, a derby hat, and carrying an open umbrella in one hand and a fan in the other. Customs of various countries are all so strangely different, with each nation finding the others amusing and smugly thinking that their own are not.

We were to begin our tour of the Orient with a number of tea and supper dances at the Grand Hotel[39] in Yokohama. The first dance was to be a most festive occasion. The Japanese were very thorough in all their preparations for the evening. The ballroom of the Grand Hotel was transformed into a vast bamboo forest of a jungle with hundreds of bamboo trees planted in pots against the walls. At intervals among the trees were large wooden buckets filled with purple iris, so arranged as to give a wild vine effect to the scene. The guests were a mixture of the French, Russian, German, Belgian, English, Turkish, American, and Japanese communities of Yokohama. All were dressed in various styles and moods, lending every color of the rainbow to the setting. A conglomeration of individuals, characters, backgrounds, and principles in a strange land. Fantastical. Alluring.

Very few of these people had actually seen the new dances, but most of them had heard or read of them and were intensely interested in their execution. It was an interesting group to appear before and their enthusiasm was genuine and gratifying.

The social life in Yokohama I found very delightful. There were many afternoon parties followed by tennis. There were also delightful weekends spent in the seaside port of Kamakura where many of the Yokohama residents maintained their summer places. There one could visit breathtaking Shinto shrines and Buddhist temples, admire the great bronze Buddha, stroll among real bamboo forests, and enjoy a more leisurely paced life.

I quickly made many friends among the young men of my age in the diplomatic and consular service and, also, among the business houses. At their requests, I loaned all of my clothes that were made in New York to their Japanese tailors. These craftsmen had the faculty of being able to copy anything! All they needed were good models, which I was quite willing to supply.

The second week of my visit, the President Samiento, an Argentine training ship, arrived for a week's visit. It was filled with colorful cadets who attended our performances. At that time I was dancing and teaching the tango as it was danced in Paris, London, and New York, having been tamed down by the French dancing masters in which process it had lost most of its primitive color. The Argentine cadets were all excellent dancers, and they invited Natalie, Dorothy, and me to their ship to show us how the tango was really danced in their country. We accepted their invitation with much enthusiasm. That afternoon, the cadets had the training ship decorated with exotic flowers. When the orchestra began to play the strains of a sensuous tango, about forty of these young men appeared upon the floor, dancing in couples as men and women. Now, here was quite a different tango. Their rhythm fascinated me. Dorothy, Natalie, and I were invited to learn them, and for the next hour or so we followed their instructions minutely. I had a very handsome cadet, about six-feet two in height, who was considered the best dancer on the ship, to teach me. Naturally we reciprocated by teaching them the one-step, hesitation waltz, and the Castle walk. It turned out to be a most interesting afternoon; however, I realized that this Argentine tango could never really be danced well by anyone but expert dancers. The average dancer that I had met could not possibly master the peculiar rhythm. I decided to use the Argentine tango only in my exhibition dances, and for the ballroom sessions I would continue to teach the French version.

During the intervals between performances and classes, Natalie and I made many interesting shopping excursions. We would poke around in all sorts of funny little shops, and it was only natural that we should pick up some very rare pieces of satsuma, bronze, and brass and also some interesting pieces of antique tapestries and ivories.

One of our excursions took us up to Miyanoshita[40], a beautiful inn, situated on top of a peak where one had a perfect view of the famous Mount Fujiyama. It was a superb sight. Standing in the garden of this inn, our eyes travelled over a field of purple iris to rest upon this seemingly peaceful mountain peak capped with snow. The visibility was so clear that you felt as though you could reach out and touch it.

But I was more interested in something else than this beauty. This inn was managed by a Japanese gentleman and his wife. She had been educated in France and had acquired all the charm and coquetry of the French women. However, here she wore her native costume and apparently lived a simple life. It was said that every man who visited this garden fell in love with her, and I certainly was no exception. I constantly found my gaze wandering from the mountain peak and iris to her graceful form. I never saw her again after this brief encounter, but I thought of her many times. I have often wondered what life brought to this interesting woman who possessed such rare charm. I most certainly could never picture her spending the balance of her life in such an isolated spot. I can only hope that Fate brought her more romance and adventure than her life was offering her at that moment.

I had organized a private dance class, in addition to the group sessions, and among my pupils I found some of the leading Japanese women and men. Much to my surprise, they were especially interested in learning the seductive tango, which seemed much easier for them than the one-step or waltz. In teaching them, I soon discovered that once they really learned a step, they never forgot.

Two of my pupils in this class were Madame O. and her daughter. We were somehow attracted to each other, and I was quite delighted when they requested my sister, my partner, and me to attend a real Japanese dinner party to be given in the Japanese part of their palace. To us, this invitation was to be quite a novelty.

We arrived on the appointed afternoon at four o'clock. Their palace was a most unusual one, being divided into two sections, one of which was strictly Japanese, retaining the atmosphere and customs that had been handed down by all of their ancestors. The other section was strictly American, part English, with a bit of the Continent thrown in. All of this suggested a duality in their lives which unquestionably existed. While one hundred percent Japanese, this family had traveled widely and learned the ways of the world. They delighted in living in both sections and giving parties and receptions that fitted their surroundings.

As this was strictly a Japanese party, we entered the gate to that section of the palace. We passed through a garden that I will always remember. Profuse in flowers, pergolas, and rustic bridges, you felt the countless romances it must have sheltered throughout the centuries. We were graciously met at the entrance by three servants who helped us exchange our shoes for sandals before being presented to our hostess, her husband, and their daughter. Almost immediately we were served the inevitable cup of tea.

The room or salon in which we were in possessed a simplicity that was fascinating. It was a combination of perfect art, known and appreciated by cultured Japanese families. Instead of the room being cluttered with many objects, it contained only two pieces of furnishings. One was a large screen embroidered with birds in flight, the colors ranging from a deep purple, shading into the palest lavender, against a background of silver-grey. The other object was a priceless bronze vase, tapering to a small neck and holding one single iris whose natural colors were reflected so delicately in the large screen. The walls, or shoji, were of a putty color that enhanced more than distracted from the richness of the two objects. The floors were covered with a fine hard-woven matting. Pillows of soft down and covered with the same material were strewn about for us to sit upon.

At about five o'clock we were ushered into the dining salon, a room as severely simple as the one we had just left. We sat upon the floor on little cushions of a deep blue. Numerous Japanese girls began to serve us, gliding by as noiselessly as phantoms, charming and coquettish in a most unobtrusive manner.

The first four courses were soups brought in on little lacquer trays on stands, quite indescribable yet delicious. Then the fish courses began to arrive. All the bones had been removed—a custom which I wish our American hostesses would adopt. Course after course followed—meats, fowls, etc.—with the seventeenth dish being a lacquered duck which I might have thoroughly enjoyed had it not been preceded by so many tempting dishes.

About midway through dinner, jugglers and dancers began to appear and entertain us. Probably they were there to serve us a breathing spell, giving our stomachs a chance to digest that which we had eaten so that we might consume more.

What we had for the following courses I do not remember. They began to be tasteless, and it was with much effort that I remained at the table. The dinner was excellent, as much for the variety of the dishes as for their judicious preparation. If anything eatable was omitted, I am sure they never heard of it. Definitely a Japanese dinner is too much for an American stomach. After such a meal it is easy to understand why the belch —the more the better—is accepted as a compliment to the meal.

Much to our surprise, the last course consisted of old-fashioned vanilla ice cream with fresh strawberries. Now this had always been my favorite dessert, and my stomach has always felt that it was a special treat, but not this time. After downing only a small portion, I realized that a revolt was in progress. Strange inner gurglings were going on. I am sure that it must have been the several cups of sake—their heated rice wine—that the ice cream resented the most. I knew that I was growing paler by the minute, and I felt the questioning eyes of my host watching me. It was through his courtesy that the meal was finally brought to a close.

We left the palace around nine o'clock, and I promised my stomach never to subject it to another Japanese dinner. It was a promise I have always kept, probably out of fear of a greater revolt.

Shortly afterwards we were invited to a large dinner dance in the American-European section of their palace. It was a typically modern party that you would enjoy at the home of any of the Caucasian races. This section of their palace was comparable to the homes of any of our wealthier families. I never knew whether this second party was given to show their versatility or to make up for the gorging we had been forced into.

True to womanly instincts, after Natalie and Madame O. became friendly, they discussed clothes. Madame had her dressmaker completely outfit Natalie in a Japanese costume, which, while beautiful and colorful, did not suit her style as she was a very Nordic type. Natalie reciprocated by allowing Madame and her daughter to copy her New York gowns. This was apparently quite the thing to do in Japan. It was a custom that I am sure most of our dowagers would greatly resent. The result with Madame was no more satisfactory than with Natalie.

The evening of this second party, our hostess and her daughter appeared in a copied dress, both exactly alike except that one was blue and one the other was pink. They had somehow lost that frail, sweet flower-likeness.

Chapter Fifteen

It was during the earlier part of my visit to Yokohama that I met the most interesting personage of my entire lifetime. One evening I joined a group of young men on a sightseeing expedition of the city. There were six of us—an Englishman, a Spaniard, a Frenchman, a German, another American from Texas, and me. We had covered all the various points of general interest and had become a little bored with it all.

The Englishman, somewhat more travelled than the rest of us, came forth with a suggestion that would reveal considerably more of life to me than I had so far encountered up to that time. "I say, let's go to house Number Nine."

"What's that?" the Texan questioned before any of the rest of us had time to query.

"By jove, haven't you heard of house Number Nine? It's the most famous house of prostitution in the world."

The Spaniard and Frenchman answered simultaneously, "Where is it? Let's go!" This seemed to be the general verdict, so our rickshaws were headed in that direction. It was but a short time until we found ourselves at the front door of a typical, well-kept Japanese house. The entire ground floor was well lighted and apparently quite a few people were already there.

Upon entering, much to my consternation and amazement, I saw about a dozen of my acquaintances scattered throughout the room. Men and women of the most representative social circles were sitting together at tables, eating sandwiches and drinking beer. My face must have expressed my surprise as the suave Englishman turned towards me and laughed heartily.

"By jove, Old Fellow, you look like you've just seen a ghost."

"But, is this the right place?" I stammered. "What are all these people doing here?"

"That's all right. Come on in."

"But ... I ... let's come back another time." I could not conceal my embarrassment.

"There's nothing to be afraid of," the Englishman replied, taking hold of my arm and pulling me forward. "This just happens to be the only restaurant in the vicinity where one can have supper late in the evening. It's quite proper for the foreign element to drop in for a bite before turning in. They never go above the first floor."

My other companions did not seem to have any of the qualms about entering that I entertained, probably because they had not crossed on shipboard with the few that I recognized there. I followed my group hesitantly, mumbling some sort of recognition to those I knew, stumbled into a chair and ordered a ham sandwich and a glass of beer. It struck me as a most bizarre proceeding. However, I noticed that none of them seemed the slightest embarrassed. It all was most casual.

We consumed numerous beers as I refused to budge from our table until all my acquaintances had left. When they finally did, the league of nations, as we jokingly called ourselves, approached a desk in the back, signed a register, and paid for our rooms in advance—much as you do at any hotel in America. We were then ushered upstairs into a luxurious Japanese drawing room. I noticed heavy Japanese brocade drawn across the windows, which accounted for the fact that I had seen no lights in the house but on the ground floor.

Within a few minutes there entered this room the most extraordinary being I have ever encountered—woman, very small in stature, dressed in exquisite Japanese fabrics worn with a decided suggestion of Western influence. She appeared to be ageless with skin wrinkled like brown parchment. Her eyes, slanting toward the temples, were like live seals. As she approached us, she walked with the dignity of an empress, superbly self-possessed.

"Good evening, young men." She spoke in a soft, rich voice that suggested a musical training. "It is a pleasure to have you as my guests. Won't you please sit down?"

We all did so rather clumsily. I am sure that none of us had expected such a charming, gracious lady.

We were in the presence of Mother Jesus, as she was known to the travelled world. She was a woman of great mystery, and many fanciful stories have been woven around her. Some people claimed that she was a Manchu princess who had escaped China and, after leading an adventurous life, had become the madame of this famous house. Others claimed that she was a peasant woman given extraordinary mentality and charm, which had enabled her to lift herself above her humble beginnings.

I have understood (although I have never had it verified) that it was she who was characterized in the famous play, *Shanghai Gesture*, with which the theatre going public is so familiar. This play, which was written by John Colton, who was born and reared in Japan, served as a starring vehicle for Florence Reed.

I have always preferred to believe that her background was even greater than any of these theories. In my whole life I have never seen a more regal, cultivated woman in any part of the world.

Tea was served in rare china with a decided suggestion of continental suaveness. As she poured, I could not help but notice her hands, now tiny, wrinkled, and bony, but still carrying the evidence of the china doll she must have been in her younger days. She began to speak to each one of us, and I was astounded to hear her converse fluently and easily with each one in his own language. I learned afterwards that she had discussed the literature and arts of my companions' countries in a most intelligent manner. They all felt sure that she must have travelled and lived for some time within their own boundaries.

In complete command of the situation, she presently clapped her hands. We immediately heard the fluttering of many small, tiny feet and into the room came about twenty Japanese girls, all giggling and twittering. They stood around the room like so many toy dolls, their bright colored kimonos reminding me of a garden of butterflies. While they were very young, their ages seeming to range from about fourteen to eighteen, their faces wore no expressions whatsoever, for, as I learned later, they had been literally painted upon them—first a layer of white to cover the brown skin and then a coating of red and pink. Their eyes were heavy with mascara and their lips were a brilliant crimson. Somewhat confused, the boys and I began to look them over.

"The young lady of your choice will be glad to entertain you in your private quarters," Mother Jesus was saying, thereby inviting us to choose one to our liking.

The passionate-blooded Spaniard was the first to respond, taking the first one at hand and hurrying off excitedly. The Frenchman was next, choosing the most piquant of the group. The German followed with the plumpest and the Englishman, the shyest. We two Americans were the only ones left.

My Texas friend, displaying a bit of embarrassment, looked at me and said, "Oh, hell! What's the difference in the morning?" He grabbed the first one at hand and beat it.

I was left alone, confused and confronted with fourteen masked dolls. Mother Jesus, seeing my hesitation, smiled. "You are so young and an honored guest in our country. May I suggest that you have the privilege of several companions for the evening?"

Just about daybreak, the league of nations met downstairs for an early pick up. I was the last to arrive and found my companions in a rather solemn mood. Conversation was very sparse and the feeling was mutual that we hurry out of the house.

Outside, the air was fresh. The sun was just coming up and at this early hour we had to wait for rickshaws to appear.

The Englishman was the first to refer to the night just past. "I say, ol' chaps. What did you think of this affair? Rather stiff or what?"

The Frenchman was the only one eager to answer. "Just a mask, a bunch of false faces. In my country the women are beautiful and alluring. But here, no. An interesting experience but very jejune. Just let it go at that."

The Spaniard agreed by remarking, "No passion. In Spain, we make love, we live. The women, they respond with great emotion. But last night, it was no fun—more like a ceremony."

The Englishman, turning to our German companion, asked, "And what did you think?"

"I've had so little experience. I don't know what to say, except that I'm glad its over. I don't want to go back again."

The Texan, feeling it was his turn to add something, grinned boyishly and said, "To me, well, it was just like putting it out the window. I think one should," but the balance of his speech was lost in a round of uproarious laughter. The tenseness had been broken and we all became ourselves once more.

I alone had remained silent. The Englishman turned and said, "Well, we haven't heard from you. You have had an experience, I am sure. What did you think?"

I hesitated to reply, not wanting to go into the details of my evening. I was not sure of my own reactions to what had happened. In the brightness of the summer morning, it did not seem as though it had been fun. "I like reciprocity, and I did not get it," I replied. "Let's grab that rickshaw. I want a bath."

I made several other trips to Mother Jesus' establishment, but only for the purpose of food and a visit with this strange woman. She interested me greatly, and it was an interest that grew with every visit. I will never forget her dissertation on sexual relationships.

"The Oriental," she told me, "looks upon sex as a perfectly natural and normal function, much the same as eating, sleeping, and breathing. Many of the daughters of our poorer classes are put into the houses by their parents, much as an American girl would be put to work in a factory or store. Our girls send part of their earnings home every month to aid in the support of their families. When the time of their apprenticeship is over, they return to their homes and marry."

It all seemed a strange custom to me. I wondered about the exposure to diseases, but I felt hesitant to ask. Here I was in a country that considered it immoral for their women to wear low-cut evening dresses which show their bare arms and bosoms, yet it was their common practice for an entire family to strip themselves and collectively take a bath in a large wooden tub in the front yard, exposed to the view of the passerby.

I thought it all strange and bewildering, even abnormal.

Chapter Sixteen

The next morning, upon the first mail, I received the following note:

Dear Mr. Rector,
    I always believe in keeping promises.
    On Thursday evening next we are having a small informal party here at our home. I should be very happy if you could arrange to join us about nine o'clock.
    I shall be happy to see you again and will arrange for us to continue our conversation started aboard ship.

                                        Sincerely,

While I had made other arrangements for the evening, I knew that I would accept this invitation. I was still very much interested in solving the mystery that seemed to envelop this quiet, glamorous woman whom I had met on shipboard. Then, too, I had always been interested in adventure, and this might prove to be an opportunity.

I broke my date, said nothing to anyone, and prepared to present myself at the appointed hour. Arriving at the address given, I passed through a gate into a small garden, typical of many seen in that part of the country. It was faintly lighted with lanterns, and I could see several couples here and there—Japanese girls in their native costumes and men dressed in Western linens, indicating that they were from overseas. The small house sat at the back wall of the garden, was well lighted, and extended a friendly greeting. I was met at the open door by a petite maiden who curtsied and took my hat.

"I am Tom Rector," I said, not knowing just what was expected of me. "I received an invitation the day before yesterday."

"Yes, Mr. Rector." This reply was made with a knowing smile that spread to her eyes. "Madame has asked that I bring you to her when you arrive."

I followed this maiden and was ushered into a room that was both Eastern and Western in its appointment. A large Chinese rug covered the floor, so soft that I felt as though I was walking upon cotton. A comfortable divan was placed between two open windows and several chairs were scattered about the room at attractive angles. A huge screen of dark, heavy material and embroidered with large gold dragons filled one corner. On a teakwood stand stood a very large Japanese vase, profuse in iris blossoms. The mysterious lady was standing at one of the open windows, looking out into the garden and smoking a cigarette in a long holder. She was dressed in a sapphire blue evening gown of Western design that gave great color to this setting.

"Madame, Mr. Rector."

She turned, advanced a few steps and, extending her hand, gave me a most welcoming smile. "I'm so happy that you could come." Turning to the maiden, she ordered, "Have a bottle of champagne served at once." Seating herself upon the divan, she turned her large eyes toward me. "Won't you please sit here?" motioning to a chair opposite her.

"It was very nice of you to invite me. I'm indeed quite happy to be here." I still felt tremendously awkward in her presence.

She smiled and did not answer for a minute or two. "This all probably appears very strange to you, or doesn't it?"

"Not knowing, I can only suspect."

"In the East, we do things much differently from the way you do in your country." She hesitated a moment. "I hope you don't mind my being quite frank?"

"I was hoping that you would be. I have never cared very much for formalities."

She smiled. "We try to harden our young people. Although we do not always succeed, I do believe our measure of success is greater than any other place." Noticing the maiden bringing in the champagne, she turned to the tray with the glasses and began to pour. "You will join me, won't you?"

"Indeed I will. That just happens to be my favorite tonic."

As she handed me the glass, I noticed that her hands were very white and soft, with long, tapering fingers and highly polished nails. "Frankly, I have under my supervision several houses in various cities of the Orient. They are run openly and with every precaution. Please do not misunderstand. I did not ask you here to gain patronage or in an advertising sense. I felt that you were so young and our ways were so foreign to your ways."

"I can't help but be pleased with your interest." I wanted to ask a definite question, but the proper words would not form in my mind. "I have really wondered just why you pick on me."

"I knew that would puzzle you. Probably it's a mother's instinct. Especially since you are so blonde. Easterners very seldom see anyone as fair as you. I know that for this reason you will attract attention wherever you go. Unfortunately, there are groups that might not be, shall we say, entirely ethical in approaching you. As you can see, I am a Westerner myself, and I felt that a little education in such matters might possibly protect you from any harm."

"I do appreciate your kindness. I ..."

"Thanks are not necessary," she interrupted. "Please do not succumb to the wiles of strangers. If you feel the incentive, there are the proper places to go. Choose a licensed house under the supervision of a doctor. There you will receive the proper attention and are most apt not to contract any disease. I must give you this warning. As I told you on the boat, the Eastern world is two worlds in one. Please stay above the ugly one."

"I do appreciate your advice and I shall adhere to it. However, at the present time, to be very frank with you, I am not suffering from sexual oppression." She laughed with a quizzical look in her eyes.

"Sex is such a normal function. It is quite too bad that the Westerners make such a mystery about it. I do believe the time will eventually come when they will educate their children along that line. I can only hope that it will be soon. It is so much better that way." She began to pour more champagne. "Now, tell me something about yourself. What have you been doing and what have you been seeing?"

At that moment there was only one thing on my mind. I did not know whether I dared mention it or not, so rather cautiously I asked, "Do you know Mother Jesus?"

"Yes, have you met her?"

I told her briefly of the expedition with the league of nations. She smiled at my boyish inexperience. I ended my little talk by saying, "I do think she is the most fascinating woman I have ever met. I've heard many strange tales surrounding her and should very much like to know the real truth about her background."

"The truth will probably never be known. I've heard many of the explanations given and in each one there is a fragment of the truth. I probably know a little more of her background than most people, but even then I know but a little."

"Won't you please tell me what you know about her?" I asked eagerly.

"Should we trespass upon that which is so personal to another?"

I knew then that Mother Jesus' background would always be clouded with fantastic stories. A speck of truth gathered here and there would weirdly gather imaginative notions much as a snowball gathers size in rolling down a long steep hill.

Rising, my hostess broke the chain of my thoughts. "I want you to meet some of the guests and, of course, my girls. Remember that you are strictly a guest tonight. The house is yours. Stay as long as you like and do not hesitate to take advantage of our hospitality in any way that you wish."

"That is very kind of you. I shall most certainly do so."

However, I did not remain there for very long. Madame disappeared and I did not see her again. To me, she had been the chief interest at the party. The others, I knew, would be all very much like my previous experience. I decided to return to my rooms at the hotel rather than linger there any longer. Madame had given me much to think about.

Chapter Seventeen

Completing our engagements in Yokohama, we travelled on to Tokyo where it had been arranged for us to appear at the Yurakoza Theatre in the heart of the city. Naturally, there had been a considerable amount of advance publicity as our manager was a very good businessman. Then, too, our appearances in Japan had created some excitement as we were pioneers in the modern dance. We had become curiosities. Dorothy had so deftly described our situation when she said, "I feel like we are appearing at a side show at Coney Island. They come to see us as though we are freaks, but thank goodness they go away with some appreciation of the beauty."

Upon arriving at the theatre for our first performance, we found a mob of people, literally thousands, blocking the streets. We felt sure that an accident must have occurred or something else to incite the people as they were restless and jabbering continuously.

Our interpreter jumped out quickly, saying, "Wait here. I'll find out just what the trouble is." He was gone but a few minutes when he returned with a wide grin upon his face. "The trouble is that every seat in the theatre is sold out for tonight, and this mob is trying to get in. They hear that the tango is a very immoral dance and want to see it before the police put a stop it."

The explanation amused me, but not for long. It was with considerable effort that we reached the theatre. Although every seat had been filled, a death-like silence hung over the audience. Just what did this silence mean? Give my imagination a little rope and I'll be hung before the first curtain. Here, Dorothy and I were strangers in a strange land, preparing to give a dance that they did not understand. East is east and west is west. What if they were offended? What if they thought the tango vulgar? Just what do the Japanese do to express their disapproval? Would they throw eggs and cabbages like they do in cheaper places in America? What if they expected vulgarity and they did not get it? No one knows the agony of stage fright until they have been through it. No one can possibly realize the lurid things the mind can suggest. Although we know in our hearts that something is highly improbable, our minds can still make it possible. That in itself is enough to unbalance you for the time being. My panic persisted, but I resolved to not let Dorothy know of it. If she knew, she might become too hysterical to give the performance. Then what? I paced the floor.

Just before the performance, I summoned all the courage I had and walked to Dorothy's dressing room. My heart was racing as I knocked on the door. "About ready?" I tried to sound casual.

"Oh, Tom, it's you," she answered, unlocking the door. I knew then that she, too, was frightened. She had never locked her door before. Her voice quivered. "I'm so nervous."

I feigned a little laugh. "Nervous? And what about?" I knew immediately that I had not managed to make this sound too convincing. I felt sure that she now knew that I, too, was nervous.

"I've been imagining the most terrible things," she cried. "Maybe they'll hari-kari us. What is that, anyway? Oh, Tom, I don't believe I can go on!"

"Of course you can. We've got to, that's all. You'll get over your little fright as soon as you're dancing." Just then the sound of the opening bars of music reached our ears. "Come on. Let's go." I grabbed her arm, pulled her out the doorway, and literally shoved her upon the stage, bounding after her. Whatever fate was in store for us, we were going to face it fighting—or should I say dancing?

Silence still reigned in the audience, an almost deathlike silence. We began to dance with a little difficulty at first, but soon we fell into the sheer joy of the movement. The orchestra was excellent and we forgot everything—well, almost everything—but that we were dancing. The audience continued to remain a silent, motionless mass of humanity, and I watched them very closely. Their faces were registering a complete blank and our first number was about to end. I purposely finished the dance close to an exit, dragging Dorothy off stage with more force than I had used in pushing her on stage.

Suddenly, there was thunderous applause. What a relief. They did like us. We had just misunderstood them. To this day, I have not forgotten the fear that enveloped me during the first part of that evening.

But that was not all I was to experience that evening. After the performance was over, we had great difficulty in obtaining rickshaws for the return to the hotel. In all the confusion, I suddenly found myself completely separated from my party and being pushed further and further from them by a surging mob. I somehow managed to grab a rickshaw and ordered, "Imperial Hotel[41], and hurry," hoping that my companions would do the same.

The man, a bit larger than the usual Japanese, began to run. His speed steadily increased as we passed through side streets that were rapidly becoming almost alleys. I suddenly realized that we were not going in the direction of the hotel but away from it. I tried to stop the man, but the more I yelled the faster he seemed to run.

Panic seized hold of me. Where in this strange city was he taking me? He certainly had understood Imperial Hotel. Was he a lunatic? Was he kidnapping me? It was then, with a terrible horror, that I remembered what the mysterious lady had told me about the underworld of Japan, and I knew that I was now in their hands. My recent stage fright was only a mild attack of fear compared with what enveloped me at that moment.

Faster and faster he went—further and further away from the Imperial

Hotel and safety. I stood and started to jump from the rickshaw, but I thought better of it when I realized I could break my leg and that would only make matters worse. We were now in strange, deserted streets and it was pitch black. Windows were shaded and not a soul was in sight.

I realized that I must do something and do it quickly, but what? How? If I could just hit him over the head? But with what? Sitting down again, I untied my shoe and took it off. By holding the toe of the shoe very firmly in my right hand and bracing myself with my left hand, I could almost reach his head. With a terrific swing I hurled the shoe at him. The heel hit him on the temple and he dropped almost immediately, stunned.

The sudden stop of the rickshaw threw me out on my side, bruising me considerably. Despite the pain, I quickly jumped up, retrieved my shoe, and began to run in the direction in from which we had come, turning into one street and then into another. They were all dark and deserted. I ran faster, turning into another street. There was an occasional light now and I was passing a few people who stared at me as I sped by. After several minutes of running at full speed, I was forced to slow down from exhaustion and began to walk in as fast a gait as possible. I turned another corner and found myself upon a major thoroughfare. Hailing a passing rickshaw, I said in a rather squeaky voice, "Imperial Hotel," praying that I would get there this time.

Arriving at the hotel, I rushed directly to my room. I had a definite urge to just lock my door from the outside world and remain in seclusion, but this could not be done. After taking a few minutes to collect myself and brush the dust from my clothes, I found my party gathered in my manager's room, all in an excited state of tension. "Where have you been? What detained you so long? We were just about to notify the police!" These were my greetings. Although I tried to be casual about it all, I was not able to satisfy them with my lame excuses. They knew something was wrong, but it was several days before I could collect myself enough to explain the entire incident to them.

The following week, we attended an exposition being held in Tokyo at that time. The main feature of this exposition was the snow flower and, being a lover of flowers, I spent practically all of my time there. Here, in the homeland of chrysanthemums, I reviewed the elaborate displays of their native blossoms. It certainly was anything but what I expected. Recalling the enormous flowers we had in America, their beautiful coloring and long stems, I was prepared to see almost trees with even larger blossoms and greater coloring. Imagine my surprise to find this not true. The Japanese train the chrysanthemum as a vine, with many small blossoms on each plant forming a cluster. These vines cling to wire fences and are tenderly guided into forming various types of figures. I especially remember the vines that had been ingeniously woven into the figure of a geisha girl, a most artistic representation of the many colors of butterfly over which countless blossoms had been arranged to bring out the proper blending of colors. Of course, there were hundreds of smaller figures lending their beauty, color, and fragrance to this unusual exposition. I could not help but be impressed with the patience it must have required to so arrange and train these vines. I thought, why don't American florists copy this idea? But, remembering our impatience and consciousness of time required, I knew they never would.

That afternoon, we attended a performance of the most famous geisha dancer in Japan at that time. She was appearing at this exposition, assisted by about twenty young girls. It was a beautiful performance, unlike anything I had ever seen. Their use of the fan intrigued me, as did the tilting of the heads, the flirtatious use of their eyes, and the suppressed smiles that changed so infrequently. The quick movement of their tiny feet in such short steps enthralled me. While it was one of the most charming performances I had ever seen, I was disappointed. Disappointed because I realized that I could not transport any part of it to America. I knew that it was too distinctly Japanese and must be done by them in their own inimitable way. Here they had something that could not be copied. Any attempt at adaptation would be suicide.

After the performance, Madame Hatsuka, for that was her name, had requested that our group join her for a cup of tea. We were delighted to accept. Although we had to converse through an interpreter, we managed to carry on a most intelligent discussion on dancing. Madame was well informed on the subject and its history. She took great pride in explaining some of the steps and movements of their dancing, having some of her assistants demonstrate as she did so. We, in turn, reciprocated. As we did so, the young girls sat in groups, watching hardly anything but our feet. In their dancing, they seldom lift their feet from the floor, and our swift movement and lifting of our feet interested them as much as the Hawaiian dance had me.

As we were about to leave, I noticed that all of the geisha girls were in a huddle, looking and giggling at me. I thought I must be loosing my pants to attract such attention. Madame Hatsuka smiled, and through the interpreter, explained that the young girls had never seen a man with blonde hair, blue eyes, and a fair complexion. She turned to them and tried to explain that it was not unusual for a Westerner, but they were not satisfied.

"The young ladies have requested that they be allowed to feel your hair, " the interpreter was saying, increasing my embarrassment. "They think that it is gold. Do you mind?"

I tried to stammer a refusal, but they had already formed into a line and began passing by me, touching my hair with their tiny hands and then running out of the room, giggling hysterically. I had thought that I, at my age, had lost the ability to blush, but during this examination I felt my whole being surging with blood rising to the surface, adding more and more color to this harassing experience. Dorothy took great delight in this embarrassing experience of mine and never missed an opportunity to tell it to all who would listen, each time adding a few more fanciful features. I was forced to take a great amount of kidding from all of my friends and acquaintances for a long time afterward.

We had been in Japan for about ten weeks when we decided to accept an offered engagement in Manila. I was busy packing for the trip when my manager came to my room.

"Better hurry. We don't have much time," he said, flopping himself into an easy chair and opening an English newspaper he had just purchased.

"I'll be ready in ten minutes," I answered, beginning to hurry more. "Any news in the paper this morning?"

"Not much. See where some crazy person shot the Archduke of Austria. They got him. Don't suppose it will amount to anything though."

"Guess not," I replied. "Those countries in Central Europe are always getting into each other's hair." I turned to the bathroom to collect my toilet articles. "Have you checked with Dorothy and Natalie? Are they ready yet?"

"Women are never ready. You know that." Hardly looking up from his paper he continued, "Say, those Castles are certainly going over big at home. Looks like they're cleaning up."

Chapter Eighteen

As we were to sail for Manila from Kobe, our manager, who always kept his eye on business, booked an appearance for us at a theatre in that seaport. Arriving in the morning, we found that the furnace-like heat of the tropics had set in. All of the elements were conspiring to make it as uncomfortable to move as possible. It was such an effort to breathe that you began to wonder just how you could stop.

We had accommodations in an old, picturesque hotel overlooking the harbor, and I felt as though I had reached my room using the last bit of manpower that I had. I stumbled, more than stepped, into a cold shower, determined to cool off if it was at all possible and to rest for the balance of the day. I hurried through the shower in order to get to the bed, hoping to catch a nap. Rushing from my bath into the bedroom in my birthday suit, much to my consternation I found my manager filling the one comfortable chair by the window, mopping his brow in a rather exhausted manner.

"Damn, but it's hot. Don't suppose by any chance we've died and gone to hell, do you? Sure couldn't be worse there than it is here."

"Is it always like this here? I knew it was to be hot, but this is unbearable." I was trying to find a pongee robe in my trunk to put on, but of course I had packed it in some obscure corner.

"They say that this is unusual, but that's what people always say about the weather when it's uncomfortable. They claim it's the forerunner of a storm. Wish it would hurry and break. I could stand anything but this."

"So could I. Listen, I hope that you don't think I'm being rude, but I do wish you would go to your own room," I asked of him, still being in a state of complete undress and unable to find my robe. "All I want to do is rest here until tonight. I don't even want to eat. Just call me in time to get to the theatre."

"That's what you think," he smiled sardonically. "Wait till I tell you the latest news." He began mopping himself all over again, and I noticed that his face had taken on a peculiar pallor. "You've got to dance now, whether you like it or not."

"Like hell!" I stopped short. "What in the devil are you talking about? I'm going to bed, and I hope to able to get at least a little bit of sleep."

"Oh, no! The mayor of this furnace of a city has heard that your dances are immoral. Particularly the tango. Says you can't go on. He forbids it." He grunted more and louder. "And every seat is sold out in the house."

"That suits me just fine! I'm going to bed. Call me in time to catch the boat." I could not help but feel a twinge of rejoicing in hearing this news.

"Oh no you don't. The theatre had put up a squawk. They're not passing up a capacity house when they're usually begging for patrons in this kind of weather. They've reached a compromise with the mayor. You and Dorothy are to go to the mayor's office right now and show him this satanic dance, the tango. If it's not as bad as he thinks it is, he'll let the show go on."

"What? Dance now? In this heat?" I exclaimed. "You must be crazy. I won't do it!"

"It's got to be done, Tom." He was pleading now, his voice having taken on a whining quality. "We just can't buck these foreigners. It's all arranged. I swear I've done my best."

We argued some more, but to no avail. I reluctantly agreed to go, quite dubious as to the final outcome. I slowly began putting on my clothes, and he left to break the news to Dorothy.

So, one half hour later, Dorothy and I accompanied our manager, laden down with phonograph and records, to the office of the mayor to demonstrate the supposedly wicked dance. We were escorted into a stifling office. His honor, a small man with deep eyes and a grotesque black, stubby beard, sat in a large chair surrounded by four of his officials. He spoke English slightly and greeted us stiffly.

The phonograph was set up, and Dorothy and I began to demonstrate our dancing in this ridiculous setting. If we ever, at any time, infused sex into our dance, we certainly did not that afternoon. The weather certainly was conducive to anything but sensuousness. The sweat literally poured from our bodies. We stumbled through the steps in about as amateurish a manner as beginners. The five men sat there with absolutely blank expressions, displaying not a single emotion. After we finished, we were asked to wait outside in a smaller and, if possible, stuffier room while they held a conference. It seemed hours before our manager was called back into the other office for their verdict.

"Oh, I hope they say no," Dorothy said weakly. "I wish we'd made the dance a bit more wicked so that we could have gotten out of it."

I smiled, feeling the same way about the whole situation, but I wanted to wait until we heard their verdict. I knew if we had to go on, I would have to be more encouraging to Dorothy than I felt at the present moment.

After about ten minutes, our manager returned, smiling. "Well, it's alright. They say that you can give the dance this evening." He saw the look of despair upon both of our faces. "Oh, come on, it's only for one evening. Tomorrow we sail for Manila. The ship will be cool and you can relax."

So back to the hotel and into another cold tub I went, with the comforting thought that I could, at last, sleep for a few hours. Finishing the quick shower, I sank onto the bed with the first sigh of comfort that day. I had just dozed off when a knock came upon my door. I resolved not to answer but it only became louder and more persistent.

"Tom!" I recognized the voice of my manager and groaned inwardly. "Tom, you've got to let me in. It's important."

Grumbling, I stumbled out of bed and opened the door. "Can't you let me rest for a while?" My voice must have betrayed my annoyance.

"I'm sorry, but I can't help it. I want to let you alone as much as you do." He flopped again in the comfortable chair but did not mop his brow, apparently having given up the job as an impossible one. "I've got bad news for you."

"If you tell me that we can't dance tonight, that will be the best news that I've heard today." My tone indicated that I meant it.

"No, it's not that." He hesitated as though hating to go on. "They have the damndest custom here I've ever heard of. Wait until I tell you what you have to do now."

"Oh, please do," I exclaimed, "but I won't do anything more and still dance tonight. Forget the damned custom! We're leaving tomorrow and not coming back!"

"It's not as easy as all that. This happens to be a courtesy due the editors of the local papers, and you know what the press is like."

"Well, what is it?" I asked disgustedly.

"Apparently it is quite the proper thing here for visiting artists to call upon each editor in person and present him with a fan and a towel." He looked at me in a quizzical manner, as though not knowing what to expect.

I stood there, absolutely dumbfounded. Immediately I thought that the heat had gone to his head and must have addled his brain "You're not feeling well. I'll call a doctor." I moved toward the house phone.

He jumped up and grabbed me. "Honest, Tom. It's true. You've got to go with a fan and a towel."

"Well, why not give them a bath, too? I bet they need one!" I was wondering what to do. Was this man out of his head?

"Tom, be serious. I'm only giving you the facts."

We argued on and on. I was finally convinced that it truly was the custom, but just why I have never figured out to this day. So, out into the stifling sun the three of us went, laden this time with fans and towels, to visit the eight editors of the city in succession. After much bowing and scraping over the course of several hours, I again reached my cold shower, hoping for a rest.

"I wonder what could possibly happen now?" I asked myself audibly as I fell upon the bed. It was not long until I found out.

It was a funeral. Just outside of my windows was a large graveyard. Some local personage, with a host of friends and relatives, had apparently fallen over with the heat, and they were putting him away with much ceremony. I am absolutely sure that they must have used every Japanese ritual ever invented that afternoon. I finally gave up all ideas of getting any rest and sat by my window, watching the almost pagan ceremonies drone on and on.

Yes, we gave the performance that night, such as it was. Dorothy and I went through our numbers in a dull, lifeless manner. Every costume we used was wringing wet when we finished. Through some power greater than our own, we got back to our hotel and finally slept from sheer exhaustion. It would have taken more than a Kobe furnace to keep us awake that night. Our sleep was more like a stupor.

Chapter Nineteen

The next day, July 26th, 1914, we boarded the old boat, China, for our trip to Manila. The heat had grown even more intense and not a breath of air was stirring. You felt as though you were moving about in a huge oven and a death-like stillness pervaded the atmosphere.

Out manager was extremely glum, which was very apparent as he usually was a very jovial, outgoing person. I noticed this and watched him carefully while we were boarding the ship. After getting settled in, I went to his stateroom in an attempt to solve the situation.

"What's troubling you this beautiful summer day?" I asked, trying to sound casual.

"Heat. This damn heat." His voice lacked its usual spontaneity, and I waited for him to speak further, watching him closely. "I was talking to an Englishman. He's a foreign correspondent. Swell fellow, too. He says we shouldn't sail today. That this extreme heat is the forerunner of a big storm. Claims they have storms that are storms like we've never seen on this China sea." He hesitated. "Guess we'll be alright, though. What do you think?"

"I don't particularly relish the idea of a big storm, but even that would be welcome if it just broke this heat spell."

"He's probably being an alarmist. Maybe it won't be as bad as he says." Apparently not wanting to scare me, he pointed to the paper on his bunk. "Take that paper and read it. The slaying of the Archduke in Austria has created quite a rumpus in Europe. War is threatening. That Englishman was deeply concerned over it. Thinks there might possibly be a war. Can't last long or be much, he claims. Six weeks at the most, he says.

"Well, I'm not going to worry about those central European countries. Whatever they do won't affect us much, anyway. I'll take the paper, though, if you're through with it."

"Go ahead."

As I returned to my own stateroom, I noticed that the ship had left the dock. The sea was very calm and there was little movement of the ship as we glided out. Everyone and everything was unusually quiet.

At dinner that evening, only about half of the two hundred and fifty passengers made an appearance. Everywhere was heard the remark that, "Its too hot to eat."

Like everyone else on board, I expected that nightfall would break this intense heat, but it did not. The moon came out in all its glory, forming a huge, silvery path across a motionless sea, but the air refused to stir. When bedtime arrived, a few brave souls brought their mattresses up from their staterooms and placed them in the salon or on the deck and tried to gain some sort of rest or comfort. Others soon followed their example, and it was not long before the entire passenger list could be found seeking relaxation in the moonlight. The Captain did not offer the slightest objection.

Toward the morning, a breeze began to spring up and very quickly developed into a wind. Clouds appeared in the sky, moving rapidly and becoming darker, uglier, and increasingly heavy. Waves began to lash the aged ship, and it began to rock roughly. Everyone grabbed their belongings and rushed to their cabins. The heat spell had been broken and a storm was well on its way. Everyone was expressing a sigh of relief.

I dressed, as did many others, and went back out on deck. I noticed that the seamen were all working feverishly, fastening down all movable objects. The Captain was rushing about, stern-faced and grim, issuing orders to his hands.

The clouds had now joined together and spread across the horizon as though trying to hide the lightening that was flashing behind them. The thunder roared deep and made loud reports across the waves. The passengers began to grow seasick and clustered together in groups at the rail. Suddenly a terrific wind hit us broadside as though all hell had broken loose.

"A typhoon!" someone yelled. "Typhoon! Typhoon!" The cry was quickly taken up and resounded throughout all the ship. Terror was expressed in all eyes. Some of the women began to scream hysterically. The men's faces took on somber, worried looks.

The wind rapidly increased its velocity. The clouds burst, as if in great anger, and an avalanche of water poured down upon us. Great waves that were mountain high, suddenly dropped upon us, moving with terrific speed. The old ship, scarred by many storms at sea, would rise with the waves, balance upon the crest, and then fall into the trough behind, creaking and groaning with every movement. Another and another. Many and more, greater and longer. Each time it felt as though we were going to crack in half and sink right down to the bottom of the ocean.

The cargo in the hole below, tumbled and rattled. Crashes were heard everywhere. Objects that time had not permitted fastening were washed overboard. The passengers, most of whom were now deathly sick, clung to what they hoped were stationary objects.

The rain increased in volume, coming down in torrents. It was a regular deluge with the speed and size of bullets. The wind increased its velocity, reaching one hundred and twenty-five miles an hour. Midnight darkness was everywhere, and there was not a light on the ship. Occasionally, lightening would flash through the heavy clouds, revealing grotesquely distorted faces and ghastly sights.

The wireless was completely broken. Disabled. When this news reached the passengers, pandemonium broke loose, as if the wireless would be of any help to us now when we were so completely at the mercy of the elements. No other ship could possibly reach us in time to help. We had to fight this battle alone. We had but to hope.

All of the passengers but ten were very sick and I was one of that ten. We became unofficial members of the crew, rushing about, taking orders, and doing what we could to help, working with every ounce of strength we had.

The dining salon was turned into an emergency hospital. Groans, cries, and screams were heard everywhere. We tried to administer to our patients as often and as best as was possible, but mostly they had to care for themselves.

During the darkness, a new passenger stole noiselessly on board. Fear. You could see him mirrored in the faces of all. He shone in the eyes of everyone. You felt him hidden in every spoken word. He was everywhere, behind the doors, in the salon, in the halls, everywhere. Even the Captain unknowingly expressed his presence.

A middle-aged woman screamed, "Let's pray!" Others screamed, "Yes, oh, God!" Other similar cries echoed around the salon. Passengers began to mumble prayers everywhere, their voices becoming louder in their petitioning. People, who in all probability had not thought of God in many months, were now on their knees, begging, beseeching, and imploring Him, whom they did not know, to reach down and lift them bodily out of this stern.

I could not bring myself to join them. It all seemed so hypocritical. Their God was too personal. I turned from such mockery. I must work. Yes, work. That was the answer, not this groveling and pleading. I must not think of this disaster. I must serve, give, and trust. With renewed strength, I turned to help the crew, assisting the stewards, comforting the sick, anything and everywhere that I could think of. I became automatic.

In spite of their prayers, the storm only grew worse. The sea surged like boiling pitch, leaping hungrily upon the deck. The petitioning and the storm continued on and on. Time was lost. Hope was about gone.

Suddenly, I heard a wild scream. Turning, I saw a frantic woman, wringing her hands in the air and crying at the top of her voice, rush past me and head out of the salon for the deck. A man yelled, "Stop her! For God's sake, stop her!" A member of the crew rushed forward just as she reached the railing and grabbed her before she could leap.

"Let me go!" she screamed, writhing to get away from the restraining hands around her waist. "I can't stand this anymore. Just let me go!"

Three crew members dragged her away to a cabin, and the ship's doctor followed. The woman had lost her mind and had to be given an opiate to sedate her. Her husband sat at her side, glassy eyed, with their cabin door locked.

The storm continued on and on in its fury. For three full, horrible days and nights the old ship rocked, plunged, and surged. With each ferocious attack of the bursting sea, we felt that the end was here. It seemed impossible for her not to collapse. Those who had been so violently sick for days did not care anymore. Death would be a relief from this unending terror. Those of us who were able to be about, were about ready to give in. We thought we could hear the "counting to ten."

Without any warning, the wind loosened, the waves subsided, and the rain stopped. Within four hours, the typhoon had left us as quickly as it had come. The sun, which we all felt we would never see again, shone brilliantly as though nothing had ever happened. The ship, barely holding together, glided over perfectly calm waters, continuing its groans from its pain. A miracle had happened. There was no doubt about that.

I was exhausted. I had not slept for three days and had eaten but little as nothing could be prepared. I dragged myself to my cabin and sank down upon the bed, not moving for twelve hours.

When I came out upon the deck again, I found most of the passengers stretched out in steamer chairs. The strain under which they had been was etched upon all their faces. I searched for my party and found my sister, Natalie, and my partner in chairs in the stern. They both looked like pale ghosts. Natalie had lost twelve pounds and Dorothy was almost too weak to feed herself. I fed them hot broth almost continuously, then stronger foods. Their strength came back, slowly but surely.

Upon the fifth day after the subsiding of the typhoon, upon a calm, opalescent sea, we gracefully glided into the peaceful, welcoming harbor of Manila. A real prayer was on the tongue of everyone. A prayer of gratitude.

What joy it was to see land again. How would it feel to walk upon terra firma? Could we ever leave it again?

The gangplank was lowered. Suddenly everyone stood aside. A stretcher passed by us, carrying the frail, limp body of a woman. Her face was expressionless, a frozen mask. Following closely behind was a stooped man, seeing no one as he passed. A grim reminder of the past.

Chapter Twenty

Manila, the Vienna of the Orient, I salute you! What a haven it proved to be for the tired, broken-spirited group of China passengers. I shall never forget the joy expressed upon all their faces when we landed at the wharf and set foot upon firm soil once more.

My group went immediately to the Hotel Manila, which had very recently been completed and was modern to the last word. I was assigned to a suite of rooms overlooking the Manila Bay, as beautiful a view as I have ever seen.

I hastily began to unpack my bags with the idea that a good, old-fashioned American shower would be the first item on my day's agenda, but I was interrupted by a knock upon the door. Upon opening it, I was greeted with the smiling countenance of a distinguished and neatly dressed man of about forty.

"Mr. Rector, I am the hotel manager," he said, coming into the room. "I hope that everything is quite satisfactory and to your liking."

"Indeed it is," showing my enthusiasm in my voice. "I must compliment you upon your magnificent hotel. I'm quite sure that I will be very happy here."

"Thank you very much," the manager replied, walking to one of the windows and looking out, more into space than at the beautiful bay.

I waited a few minutes for him to continue the conversation, but he did not, continuing his gaze into nothing in total silence. I felt obliged to break the silence, saying, "I presume that we should discuss the arrangements for the dances, or would you prefer to do that a little later?" I hoped that was the correct thing to say.

"Yes, we must discuss our plans." He turned from the window and I could see from his expression that he was disturbed about something. "I'm not at all sure that it is wise to have the exhibitions. This war has done a lot to all of our plans."

"What war?" I exclaimed, completely shocked at his statement.

"What war? Why, what do you mean? Surely you know that all of Europe is at war." His voice was stern and crisp, almost a rebuke.

"No, I didn't. I can't believe it." My head was in a whirl, trying to grasp this startling news. "Surely this couldn't have happened. I ..."

"It's only too true," he interrupted me. "The fighting is very serious just at the present, although I do not think it will last long."

"Our wireless was disabled by the storm at sea, and we've been entirely out of touch with the world until we landed. All of this has happened and we didn't know a thing about it."

"I didn't know that you were so completely out of touch. Germany has invaded Belgium. England, France, Russia, Austria, and all Europe are mobilizing their armies. Of course, it will not last long. Just as soon as England can convey her troops and join the French, they will force the Germans back into their own country and peace will be declared, but it may take weeks, possibly months. In the meantime, I'm at a loss as to what to do about the plans I have made for you."

"I just can't believe what you've told me." Cold chills swept over my being as he recited the incidents of the past ten days. "Surely the slaying of the Archduke and his wife didn't cause all of this."

"No, I don't think so. Central Europe has been at a boiling point for quite some time. Jealousies, hatred, and conquest have been running rampant. This killing has loosened the cap and violence has exploded. It's a deplorable situation."

"I'm stunned. I just can't believe that all this has happened while we were at sea. I'll be glad to cancel the engagement if you desire." My own voice startled me. I felt as though I had suddenly been dropped into the lion's den.

"I want to talk with a few people before deciding just what to do. This is an unusual city as we have large representatives of all the important nations here. I want to seek the advice of some of the consuls and the newspaper representatives. Naturally, geographically we won't be affected, but so many of the residents are vitally interested in the outcome of these events. I don't want to offend them in any way by appearing to take this situation too lightly."

"No, no, of course not. I'm so glad that I'm an American. This war shouldn't affect us except in a roundabout way."

"No, America is quite safe from the ravages of war." The manager stood silently thinking for a minute or two. "Mr. Rector, I'll meet with the gentlemen I referred to right away, and I'll be back to see you in the morning and we will decide then. Will that be perfectly satisfactory?"

"Yes, perfectly."

"In the meantime," he continued, moving toward the door, "I'll send you some newspapers so that you can read about the war yourself." Opening the door, he turned to leave. "I want you to feel that we are happy to have you with us. It is just most unfortunate that all of this has occurred. I ..."

He was interrupted at this point by the sound of several reports of large guns coming in through the window. We both rushed to see what was happening. Several merchant marine ships, flying the German flag, were sailing at full speed into the harbor. Behind them were three English war vessels who had been firing upon them, hoping to capture or sink the boats before they crossed the international three-mile limit. They were unsuccessful. The manager and I stood there silently watching these merchant vessels sail into safety and anchor in the harbor below.

During the ten weeks that I remained at the hotel, these ships stayed at anchor just outside of my windows, silent and grim reminders of the conflict on the other side of the globe. I have often wondered just how long they kept their solemn vigil and what was their eventual fate.

The news I had just heard had quite a disquieting affect upon me. Everywhere I went the rest of the day—in the dining room, in the lobby, on the streets—there was but one topic of conversation—WAR. I felt hurled back through the ages. War to me was something medieval and completely alien to our modern times.

Early the next morning, the manager of the hotel again came to my room. He appeared much less tense than upon his previous visit.

"I have spoken with numerous people," he began telling me. "Chiefly General Thomas H. Barry[42] commander-in-chief of the American forces, Major George Holmes, Mrs. Thomas Carey Welch, and many other men and women of military and press prestige. They all felt that we should not abandon out plans, assuring me that, in their opinion, everyone needs some outside interests to take their minds off the present situation in Europe. I think that we can safely go ahead with our plans."

"I'll be more than glad to follow whatever decision you make. I've certainly felt the tension in the city since I arrived here. Possibly our dance exhibitions can help relieve it somewhat."

"I hope so," he replied with emphasis.

"For music, we've been offered the use of the constabulary band. It's the one that took first prize at the St. Louis Exposition in 1904. Captain Loving is their very gifted leader and he has kept the band in splendid condition. Can you meet with them this afternoon, select the musicians you need, and go over the music?"

"Gladly," I replied, feeling not quite as enthused about all the arrangements as I had expected to be.

The dances were held on the roof of the Hotel Manila, overlooking the bay. Great care had been spent in the decorating, turning the roof into a veritable flower garden, profuse in gardenias, orchids, cadena de amor (a fascinating little white wine that I had never seen before) and the ylang-ylang, a parasitic growth which filled the night air with pungent perfume.

On our opening night, the sky graciously conspired with the sponsors and offered a full moon, millions of twinkling stars, and an atmosphere that was absolutely enchanting. About five hundred people were present. Americans in their beautiful evening gowns were vying with the Spanish women in their lace mantillas and flashing black eyes. The army and navy men, in resplendent uniforms, added dignity and color to the scene. I do not believe I have ever seen a crowd so picturesque.

The constabulary band proved to be excellent. Upon the strains of our first number—a slow, dreamy waltz—we felt that we were living a moment of beauty. The typhoon and its horrors and the war and its threatening tragedies were completely forgotten as Dorothy and I floated across the floor.

Classes were immediately arranged and almost all of the social element (army, navy, Spanish, American, and civilians) were learning the tango, maxixe, waltz, and one-step in the approved modern methods. The atmosphere of the hotel assumed a gay, almost holiday air, and only the faces of its guests betrayed the strain everyone was under.

As the weeks passed by, the war news only became more alarming. Hopes of an early settlement had been extended from a few weeks to a few months or longer. Our dances continued, each one a miniature Duchess of Richmond Ball. Once again, the world had gone dance mad before the war. Once more people were hiding their nervousness and strain under the mask of joviality. The couples dancing knew not just what minute they would receive a call to arms. All realizing that, we stood at the open door of activity.

While in the Philippines I met a most interesting man, known to all who visited Manila as Mayor Brown. He was the most enormous person I had ever seen and endowed with all the wit and humor of the proverbial fat man. He had amassed quite a large fortune in the commercial field and, although remaining a bachelor, he took great pleasure in entertaining. It was said that he first came to Manila as a cabin boy on Admiral Dewey's flagship, Olympia, and liking the place so much, he decided to stay. Due to some sort of glandular trouble, he began to gain weight,, and it was but a short time before he had reached gargantuan proportions. His greatest wish was to be able to return to America but he had grown so stout that he was unable to get through a cabin door! I spent many pleasant evenings at his home and listened to his fascinating tales of the Chinese pirates and the vast wealth that had passed in and out of the city.

"Rector," he said to me one evening, "I've met people from all over the world right here in Manila, but, believe me, of them all, the Americans are the finest." He laughed, literally shaking all over. "I've had many propositions made me, too. Some good, some bad, and others a bit on the interesting side." He paused a moment, turning in his huge chair that he was outgrowing. "Even considered going to Japan and starting a harem once. Ever been in one?"

"Not a real one, I suppose," I replied. "The thought of having one has occurred to me, though, but I suppose that's natural. Every red-blooded fellow dreams occasionally about such things."

"Yeah, you're right," the Mayor chuckled. "Guess it's just male instinct to want one. Guess I'll never have one now." He patted his large stomach with his short, stubby hands that had become so fat that they looked like one piece of flesh. "Too fat! But, say, tell me about the ones you've been in." His voice had quickly become eager.

"I'll tell you about a little incident, leaving out names and places since you probably would know the person. While in Japan, I attended a dinner party given by a distinguished potentate. He was a brilliantly educated man who came from some place in the Far East. I became interested in his tales of the Yogi, their powers of concentration, and their ability to isolate themselves yet drawing all things toward them as a sensitized magnet. He saw that I was interested and he asked me to dine with him."

"You went, didn't you?"

"Most assuredly," I answered. "But I spent most of my time before going dreaming of having my own harem. I dreamed of an isolated tropical garden with about twenty young girls, training them in all of the new dances—and other things."

"Only natural," the Mayor chuckled and squirmed about in his chair, seeking a more comfortable position for his huge bulk. "What about the dinner? Was it in his harem?"

"Yes, I suppose it was. I went filled with curiosity and discovered that I was to be the only guest that evening. It was a splendid dinner, sprinkled with brilliant conversation. My host told me a great deal about the customs of his people that I didn't know, like the superiority of the male over the female. I can remember his words. He said, 'Females are instruments of pleasure—and mothers. They are fragile. Keep them behind walls and seek mental and spiritual companionship from men on the outside.'"

I paused to light a cigarette and noticed that the Mayor was eyeing me with great interest. He did not speak, but waited for me to continue. "It all seemed quite strange to me, as in America we feel quite the opposite about the woman."

"Yes, I know, but tell me. Did you meet any of his women?" The Mayor was definitely interested in my getting on with the story.

"I'm coming to that. Don't worry. At the end of the dinner, he took a small vial from his sash and put one drop from it in each of the small cups of black coffee which had been served to us. Since he sipped his, I began to do so, too, feeling assured that it could not be too powerful a drug. The aroma of an exquisite fragrance diffused my senses. I felt perfume going all through and down me.

"The potentate smiled and said, 'This must all be new to you. After dining and before enjoying other pleasures, it is well to cleanse the breath. And, now that I have so thoroughly enjoyed your companionship, I shall put you in the hands of my loveliest young girls so that you may experience the pleasures of the thousand and one delights.'"

"Ah! Interesting!" The Mayor had leaned forward so as not to miss a word of what was to come. To encourage me, he said, "Go on. What next?"

I continued, showing a little of my embarrassment. "He clapped his hands and an attendant appeared. He arose, bade me good night and wished me 'the pleasures of paradise' and left the room."

"I followed the attendant into an adjoining, dimly lit room, the walls of which were hung with silken draperies of a pale, iridescent green. An Oriental rug was on the floor, the colors shading from pale rose pink to soft green upon a gray background. A single couch occupied the center of the room."

The Mayor chuckled deeply and leaned closer, almost falling out of this chair in the process. "Don't leave out any details," he encouraged, showing his deep satisfaction in hearing such a story.

"This couch was covered with the petals of roses and gardenias, the perfume mingling with incense that was burning in an urn nearby. I stood there, completely bewildered. I thought I had either drunk too much champagne or the contents of the strange vial had transported me to some distant place. Six dancing girls entered silently, moving swiftly and with laughter like the tinkle of a bell. They began to encircle me, taking off my coat, then other garments, then others. I came too immediately and began to take an interest of a different sort in these entertainments."

The Mayor was listening intently, so lost in the scene described that he possibly felt that he was there.

"Soon they had me undressed. I laid upon this rose-petalled couch with two maidens at my feet, two at my head, and one on either side. They began to bathe me with delicate perfumes. Well, I can only stand just so much rubbing and—then I go to sleep."

"Honest, you didn't go to sleep, did you?" the Mayor demanded to know, infusing a bit of annoyance in his question. "How could you?"

I laughed, reassuring him, "I did stay until daybreak, and I did manage to learn something from the young ladies about the mysteries of life with its thousand and one delights."

"Gosh, but I would've liked to have been in your shoes." The Mayor sat for some time, looking into space as though transporting himself to such a scene. I watched him closely for some time, realizing that his huge size had made his whole life into a mental one. I could not help but wonder if the mental kick was as completely satisfying as the physical could have been. I knew from his whole-hearted responses to my story that, at the least, there was a certain amount of pleasure in the imagining, even a relief.

Chapter Twenty-One

Manila rapidly became as dance mad as the rest of the world. Perhaps the madness was even more so, as though everyone was frantically running away from something that could not be escaped. Men and women tried desperately to lose their tensions upon the dance floor. During these few weeks, the military personnel changed rapidly. Officers hurriedly left the Philippines upon the receipt of instructions; others appeared in their places unexpectedly. It was a rapidly changing, constantly moving group of people, anxiously awaiting developments, becoming more and more uneasy with each passing day and awkwardly trying to be casual. From everyone you heard the same thing, "It can't last long," but you felt that they did not really believe this in their hearts. It was a sort of military propaganda, repeated over and over to keep their spirits up. Each and all threw themselves into a mad whirl of life in an effort to forget the horrors descending upon the world. It failed.

The German merchant ships continued their silent vigil in the bay below my window. The officers and crew were interned and their lives must have been miserable. Watching them daily, as I did, I slowly developed a kind of sympathy for them and their situation. I often wondered, after America entered the war, just what became of them all.

I shared the anxiety of those around me. War, to me, was a horrible thing. My early childhood had been filled with the associations of those who had suffered greatly during the Civil War. The recovery of the South had been a slow and heartrending process. From my ancestors, I probably inherited a tendency to fight whenever it was necessary, yet war at close range seemed so futile. In all of history it had never accomplished the ideals for which it was fought. War is incited by greed, selfishness, and the ambitions of men who remain in safety and is fought by others, who, in giving all, gain nothing.

During our stay in Manila, we acquired the habit in the late afternoon of taking a drive around the prado in a coleta—a two-wheeled vehicle which was used in the Philippine Islands at that time. At six o'clock in the afternoon, the military band would strike up and play music from the Italian operas, interspersed with the Spanish music that was very popular there. At about seven o'clock, we headed for the Manila Club or the Army and Navy Club for what the local residents delightfully called "Sundowners," returning to the hotel around nine for a leisurely dinner. On the evenings that we did not have to dance, we attended parties. Everyone entertained lavishly, and revelry seemed to be the keynote of the day. History was once again repeating itself.

One balmy evening, I was taken by some men friends to a famous dance hall on the outskirts of Manila where sailors and soldiers met the native Mestiza girls and paid a dime to dance with them. These girls were all young and very pretty, gaily dressed in their native costumes, a relic of the stiff court costumes of early Spain. Their skirts were long, with flowing trails of some flimsy cotton material. Their bodices were cut low with puffed sleeves of tarlton, and around their shoulders they folded the pañuela in an intriguing manner. Their long black hair was slick and glossy and fell loosely down their backs. Upon their feet, instead of shoes, they wore a sandal called the "shinela," much like the ordinary mule without any fastening over the heel. This made it impossible for the girls to lift their feet from the dance floor when dancing, thus creating a gliding movement. For the first time in my life I saw a perfect smoothness upon the dance floor, a smoothness I had been trying to instill into every pupil I had taught. Even the Turkey Trot, which the enlisted men from the States had taught them, assumed a gliding smoothness.

I eagerly paid my dime and secured a partner who was one of the loveliest dancers I have ever had the privilege to dance with. I paid many more dimes that night. Here was a movement I could copy. I studied them closely. La Carinosa (The Flirtatious One), which I later created, was based upon the dancing of these Mestiza girls.

It was in Manila that I saw my first and only bullfight—a bloodless one. The fight itself, I took little interest in. The pageantry in connection with the entrance of the picadors, toreadors, and caparisoned horses against the background of boxes filled with Spanish families in full regalia was a sight to behold. The excitement and enthusiasm of the spectators was something I will always remember.

It was at this bullfight that I met the distinguished Spanish family of Rubio. The Rubios were a rare collection of sisters—six of the most beautiful women I have ever beheld. They were Mrs. Fox, the wife of an Englishman, Mrs. Davis, the wife of an American and a miniature Maxine Elliot, Lolita, Pepita, and identical twins Blanche Rose and Rose Blanche. There were several brothers, too, but naturally my interest stayed centered upon the girls.

Mrs. Davis was particularly fascinating. In a most entertaining manner, she explained to me the coquetry of the fan as practiced by the Spanish women. The opening, shutting, the sudden click, and every movement had meaning. To them it was a language of its own.

It was shortly after this time that I was presented to Mrs. Lorillard Spencer, of New York and Newport, and one of most beloved personages on the island. Mrs. Spencer was devoting her life and fortune to the education and advancement of the Moros, building numerous schools and hospitals. Untiringly she worked, earning in every sense her title as one of the world's greatest noblewomen.

It was close to the end of our stay in Manila that I was pleased and excited to receive an invitation from Captain Edward Fields to visit Fort Batangas in the interior. He was a fraternity brother of mine and had married my cousin, Mary Sivley. Natalie and I rode for several hours upon a small Philippine train, which was much like those in the States, through a very picturesque countryside. We arrived at the fort just in time for the dinner party that Ed had planned for us. All the officers and their wives were from the South, and they all made us feel very much at home.

Fort Batangas was much larger than I had expected it to be. It was quite old and, at that time, was being used for the training of colored enlisted men exclusively. The United States government had shown wisdom in selecting officers of the South to train these men. The Southerner has a love for the Negro and, they in turn, a respect that has never been understood by the Northern people. Probably one of the reasons that there was so much harmony and discipline at this fort was the complete lack of fear. These men understood each other, their places, and their duties.

After an excellent dinner, I retired with the officers for their customary smoke and liquor. It was only natural that the conversation should turn to war-clouded Europe—the big battle of Roye, the invasion of Belgium, the shifting of the capital from Antwerp to Oostand, the proclamation of President Woodrow Wilson for the whole nation to pray for peace. These men were sensibly facing facts and not seeking an escape in wild revelry, as the masses in Manila were doing. Their views were sound and their judgments sane. It was here that I came to the realization that the whole world was facing a monumental crisis which involved us indirectly at that time and most probably directly in the future.

We returned to Manila the next day. During the return trip, I spent much of the time lost in thought. From every angle of approach, I was forced to come to the same conclusion. The four of us must return to the United States before it was too late.

Upon our arrival back at the hotel that afternoon, we discovered that everyone was very agitated and concerned over the falling of Antwerp into the hands of the Germans. The intense bombarding from land and sky had caused untold damage and loss of lives, and the entire city was on fire.

I phoned Dorothy and my manager and asked them to have dinner with Natalie and me. As we all sat down, I immediately began to explain my recent decision.

"This may or may not surprise you," I began. "I know that we've only discussed this war in a casual manner, but I've been forced to face it squarely for the last twenty-four hours. The situation has become very serious and I feel that we should return to the United States at once. What do all of you think?"

My manager was the first to respond and so readily that I knew that he, too, had arrived at the same conclusion. "Yes, Tom, I agree. It's become more serious than anyone had expected. The death of the Rumanian king is a threat to the Balkan states. The sinking of the Russian cruiser, Pallada, by the submarines."

"Oh, those submarines," Dorothy interrupted. "They're terrible. Do you suppose that it will be safe for us to return?"

"I'm sure that the Pacific is still safe, Dorothy," I replied. "Even though Japan is in this war, the Germans are still pretty busy on the other side of the world. We should be safe sailing for home if we leave quickly."

Natalie interrupted. "Let's go right away then. Let's take the next boat. Can't we?" Her voice was mixed with both excitement and terror.

"What do you think?" I asked, turning to my manager. "Can you arrange it?"

"I'll do everything in my power. I'm just as anxious to get back on U.S. soil as anyone. I'll start first thing in the morning. Maybe tonight if I can find any offices open."

"Oh, I'll be so glad to get home," Natalie answered. "We've been away from home such a long time and so much has happened. It all frightens me."

"Then it's agreed," I cried jubilantly. "Let's skip the party tonight and start packing."

"The Robinsons are going home at the end of the week," Dorothy was saying eagerly. "Can't we go with them? They're such good friends of mine. I'd like to go back on the same boat with them if I could."

"All right. Find out the name of the boat and the sailing time and we'll try to arrange it for you," I replied. "We can't be too choosey just now, though, Dorothy. The main object of all this is just to get home safely as soon as possible."

It was almost dinner time the next evening before my manager returned. He looked worn and exhausted as he came to Natalie's room, where the three of us had gathered to wait for him.

"What news?" I asked immediately.

"Well, I managed to book passage for the four of us, but unfortunately not on the same boat. Most everyone else seems to have the same idea we do. I have two reservations for a boat leaving tomorrow afternoon and two for four days later." Then, turning to Dorothy, "Your friends are leaving on the second boat."

"But we mustn't be separated," I exclaimed.

"Listen, this is war, Tom. We have to accept what we can get," he grimly reminded me. "How shall we split up?"

"I'll not be separated from Tom," Natalie quickly and emphatically stated. "I don't care which boat we take, but the two of us must stick together."

"That's all right by me," my manager replied. "What about you,

Dorothy? Do you still want to go with the Robinsons? I can fix it up for you."

"Oh, yes I do, but I did want us all to be together." There was a slight choking in her voice. "But if we can't, let Tom and Natalie go tomorrow and I'll take the second boat."

There seemed to be nothing more to discuss and, as there was more packing to do, we all returned to our rooms and got busy. That evening the papers carried the grim story of the sinking of the British cruiser, Hawke, by a submarine. Three hundred and twenty-seven lives were lost.

The next afternoon, as the flaming sun sank into the sea, we sailed from the lovely city of Manila to the distant strains of the Constabulary band playing "La Paloma." Natalie and I stood on deck, waving good-bye to Dorothy, my manager, and all of our friends. Especially for Dorothy, I had a strange feeling about her leaving her at the time. It was a mixed feeling of love, appreciation, and sadness. Possibly it was a premonition that I would never see her again.

Chapter Twenty-Two

It was at this same time that money became quite a problem to most people. Gold was at a high premium. While I had bank accounts, both in Los Angeles and New York City, the cashing of a check had become quite a difficult situation. Fortunately, the steamship company had accepted my check for our tickets and, more fortunately, my good friend, Mrs. George Holmes, had secured for me five hundred dollars in twenty dollar gold pieces. This money I kept in a curious money belt I had purchased from a Hindu in a local public market. As soon as we were on board ship, I entrusted this belt to the care of the purser. This gold had been given to me with the greatest secrecy and, as far as I knew, no one else but my sister knew that I had it.

We were headed first for Hong Kong and then on to Shanghai, where we were to catch a final boat for America. As the first stage of our journey took only a few days, Natalie and I chose to remain entirely to ourselves. We were in no mood to trust casual acquaintances made on ship, especially the conglomerate crowd that surrounded us. Their harassed faces depicted the uncertainty of the times.

As we sailed into the harbor of Hong Kong, we were elated over the sight of the British men of war guarding the entrance. The city itself was most impressive, built upon terraces rising into the sky like a small mountain and crowned on the very top by a large hotel.

We had no trouble in securing rooms in a recommended hotel, very comfortable ones looking out into the harbor. Upon checking with the steamship offices, we were told that we would have to wait five days before our next boat would depart for Shanghai. When I gave Natalie this news she was quite dismayed at first, but then her face brightened up a bit.

"But, Tom, possibly Dorothy will catch up with us and be able to go back with us after all. I do hate the idea of leaving her on this side of the globe."

"I had thought of that same thing, Natalie," I replied, "and I hope that you're right. In the meantime, we might just as well enjoy ourselves and take in some of this fascinating city."

And that we did. I deposited my money belt with the hotel, first taking two, twenty-dollar gold pieces out and changing them into Mexican silver, which was the currency of the city. The rate of exchange was in my favor, so I told Natalie that we might buy a few things to take home with us.

The first evening after dinner, we decided to attend a cinema on a street called "Cat," just a short distance from the hotel. On our way there we passed many flower stalls, and I decided I would buy a few gardenias for Natalie to wear. Approaching the stall of a rather gnarled-looking old woman, I took out a silver Mexican dollar from my pocket, which is fifty cents in American money, and started to select a few blossoms. Almost instantly we were surrounded by a howling, shrieking mob. Almost all the flower vendors had pounced upon us to try to get this extravagant sale for themselves. Fortunately for us, two of the Sikh policemen appeared within moments and quelled the almost riot. These two men, magnificent specimens, were attached to the British government. They immediately escorted us back to our hotel and strongly suggested that we remain indoors for the balance of the evening.

It was a horrifying experience for us both, and it rather unnerved Natalie. We had been living through some rather tense days before our departure from Manila and on the boat, and this incident was of no help whatsoever. Natalie decided to retire to her room early and I remained behind in the lobby, purchasing an English newspaper and sitting down to read. I was absolutely stunned at the banner headlines across the front page. A Japanese cruiser, Takachiko, had struck a mine while patrolling the harbor at Tsing-Tau and sank. This was most alarming. I resolved not to tell Natalie anything and would use every precaution to see that she did not learn of the disaster from anyone else. I retired shortly but did not sleep, tossing in my bed considerably that night, worrying about what our journey home might bring.

The next day, feeling a little better in the morning sunshine, we started out upon a shopping expedition. The shops were interesting, usually small, and crowded from floor to ceiling with their wares. The vendors were desperate to make sales and would take almost anything one would offer. We bought tapestries, china, and several other interesting pieces to take home with us.

The table linens were of excellent materials and design. They were made by young Chinese girls whom a group of Belgian nuns had bought from their parents for fifty cents each when they were going to drown them. I understood that, in the course of about twenty years, these nuns had saved about thirty-eight thousand of these poor creatures and made them useful, happy beings. It was a horrible thought, especially since at this time the nuns' homeland was being treated so mercilessly by the Germans.

Prowling about in one little shop, I saw an antique altar cloth I was interested in. The price was fifty dollars and, while it was worth it, I hesitated because of the scarcity of cash at that time. Daily, this vendor called on me at my hotel, each time reducing his price and almost begging me to take the cloth. I continued my refusal. It was when we were aboard ship and about ready to set sail that he appeared again and offered the cloth to me for the reduced sum of fifteen dollars. I finally agreed to take the cloth and paid him. I have never seen such joy in anyone's face. I was told that this currency would probably provide him and his family with food for the next six months.

Poverty was everywhere, accompanied by its first cousins, dirt and filth. Through one of the side streets in Hong Kong, there was a deep gutter filled with almost stagnant water. At any time of the day, you could see a group of women washing clothes, another group preparing vegetables, and still more taking water home in jugs for drinking. The presence of a dead cat or dog made not the slightest difference to them.

During my days in Hong Kong, it was interesting for me to compare the Chinese with the Japanese, with whom I had spent so many weeks. These two yellow races, both Asiatics, are completely different in all respects. Most Japanese are short and squatty and walk awkwardly while the Chinese are often six feet tall and are graceful walkers. The Japanese love color in their clothes, while the Chinese clothes are very drab. The art of smiling is well known to the Chinese. They smile because they are friendly and enjoy laughter. The Japanese are taught not to smile. They share some aspects of the same religion, but their languages are entirely different. They have despised each other since the beginning of time. The Japanese teach their children to avoid and look down upon the Chinese, telling them elaborate stories of their uncleanliness and inferiority. The Chinese are taught that the Japanese are descendants of monkeys. This idea comes from an old legend that the greatest Chinese emperor of all times, Shih Huang-ti, centuries ago sent a cargo of young boys and girls to this island in the Pacific to find the fountain of youth. The cargo never returned but intermarried with the native monkeys and thus founded the Japanese Empire. Two neighboring races of the same color with utter contempt for each other.

When the day finally arrived for our departure for Shanghai, we were faced with the reality that we were going to have to leave without Dorothy, as her boat had not yet arrived in Hong Kong. The trip to Shanghai was rather short, the last part of which was up a very muddy river.

We had but a day to spend in this legendary city. We spent the morning sightseeing, lunching at the Astor. In the afternoon, we were taken on a shopping tour by a friend who was a business customer of the owner of one of the large silk manufacturing plants in Shanghai. It turned into a most interesting afternoon. I have never seen such an array of coloring, such texture in silk, as though all the colors of the rainbow had been imprisoned and enhanced. Their brocades were so soft and so beautifully blended that it seemed the accomplishment of almost the impossible. To me, the Chinese produce the rarest colors in the universe. Their greys resemble the breast of a dove, with a suggestion of mauve, blue, and pink perfectly blended. The brilliant jade green was so softened that the eye was not offended. The brick-dust red, a color I have never seen any place else, was soft, yet glowing with flames at the same time.

We had tea with the owner who proved to be revelatory in the dyeing and weaving process. He told us, too, of the SingSong girls who were similar to the Geisha girls of Japan. They appeared mostly at restaurants built upon barges anchored along the river and decorated with festoons of flowers.

He told me of the law of China which decreed that any foreigner who lived with a Chinese girl for three years or more had either to marry her or to make a settlement that would provide for her when her youthful charms had waned. What a humane way to look at it. Yet, these same lawmakers allowed the parents to drown their baby girls. To me this seemed typical of the race, thoroughly incongruous. Great lovers of beauty, perfect philosophers, absolutely honest, splendid sense of humor, yet with all of this they were utterly cruel.

With my gold again stored safely in the safe of the purser, we set sail for America. It was necessary for the ship to stop over in Japan at Nagasaki to refuel, obtain provisions, and take on more passengers. We arrived just before twilight, the small harbor and city presenting a rather dismal scene after the excitement and color of Hong Kong and Shanghai.

As soon as we docked, new passengers came aboard and also a number of Japanese civilians. I was preparing to go ashore to send a cable to my New York representative when a very pleasant looking Japanese man approached me.

"Is this Rector-san?" He spoke clearly and with rather a good accent. Upon replying that I was, he bowed and, in a most gracious manner, continued, "A great amount have I heard about you. Japan has been honored by your presence. To meet you I have been anxious."

"This is very nice of you," I answered, wondering just what he wanted with me, and, at the same time, amused at the way he put his English words together.

Noticing that I had my hat and coat on, he inquired, "Ashore are you going?"

"Why, yes. I wanted to send a message to the States." I started to move toward the door, then hesitated. "Possibly you could tell me where an office is?"

"I will be your guide," he answered, stepping to one side and bowing again. "The operator, maybe he no speak English. I can be of service to you."

This thought had occurred to me so I accepted his kindness and we went ashore.

Nagasaki was a large fishing village and well lighted. I was pleased to be able to see at least a part of the port as I had been more or less familiar with it from the story, "Madame Butterfly." The cable office was but a short distance from the docks, and my new found friend was most helpful in dispatching my message. As we left the office, I thanked him for his help, hailed a rickshaw, and rode off as he stood bowing upon the walk.

The rickshaw boy was young and a very husky Japanese. He started off at a rapid pace, and it was quickly apparent to me that we were headed in a direction away from the docks. I began to expostulate, and in pigeon English he replied something to the effect that he was taking me back another way, all the time running faster and harder.

I immediately grew alarmed. I had learned of their treachery all too well from my earlier visit to Japan. I stood up, attempting to jump, but realized it was too dangerous. The more I yelled, the faster he ran, and soon we had left the village behind and were in the countryside.

A great fear engulfed me. Fear, not only for myself, but for Natalie whom I had left innocently on board ship, saying I would be back shortly. Horrible thoughts flew through my mind in quickened tempo.

Suddenly my captor rounded a bend in the road and stopped before three other rickshaws. In the front one sat my recent friend. I was delighted to see him.

"This man had misunderstood me," I yelled and then started climbing out of the rickshaw. "Won't you please explain to him that I want to go to the docks?" My fear must have made this sound as a plea.

He did not answer me, but motioned to the two other men who had accompanied him. They advanced quickly toward me, grabbed me, pinned my arms behind my back, and pushed me into some bushes along the roadway.

"What do you want of me?" I cried, realizing that this all was a frame up.

"Gold," was the curt demand. "Give me. Quick." His voice had lost its earlier polish and was very now harsh and cold sounding.

I suddenly realized that my supposed secret had somehow leaked out. "But, I don't have any."

"He lies," the one I had supposed was my friend cried. Rushing forward, he began to search my pockets. I had but little money with me. Pushing me roughly, he hissed, "Where is it?"

The men holding me increased their grip and twisted my arm until the pain was excruciating. I lifted my right foot in agony and suddenly, without thinking, let go with a terrific wallop, striking the leader of this gang just below the belt. He fell backward in agony, writhing on the ground. I then let out a yell that I am sure would have normally been quite impossible of me except under such dire circumstances and must have been loud enough to have been heard on our ship.

Just at that moment, the brakes of a passing motor squealed with a sudden jamming. My assailants heard this and fled into the bushes before my unknown saviors came into view. I yelled again and quickly saw two men coming to the rescue. My lucky star was certainly shining that night. These two men were Spanish gentlemen whom I had met while in Manila.

"What's the matter?" they asked in unison.

"It's Rector," one exclaimed, recognizing me instantly. "What in the world happened to you?"

I quickly explained the attempted robbery and my desire to return to the ship at once. They assisted me into their car and it was but a few minutes before I was safely back aboard ship, rather upset from the shock, but grateful for the bungling Japanese and my lucky star.

I rushed to my stateroom and quickly bathed my face and hands and arranged my clothing. Steadying myself, I stopped for Natalie and we went to the bow of the boat, saying nothing of my recent harrowing experience as I did not want to frighten her.

We stood in the bow, along with numerous other passengers, and watched our boat being refueled. Barges filled with sacks of coal were brought up to the side of the boat and hundreds of women then carried these sacks onto the boat. It was a dreadful sight to see. Old women and young girls rapidly growing old struggled with the heavy sacks. All for a few pennies for their night's work. It was so noisy and so very hot that sleep was almost impossible. I, instead, stood on deck most of that night, watching these miserable creatures toil away. I was indeed happy to be an American where civilization was at least on a higher level. Yes, very happy that I was returning to that glorious country.

The next morning we began our sail through the inland sea, reaching Kobe, our first stop after dark. In this quaint harbor we were greeted by hundreds of fishermen in their sanpans lighted with colorful Japanese lanterns, giving the effect of thousands of butterflies. Fishing was the chief industry of this little city.

We dined with our American friends, Mr. and Mrs. St. John Chilton and took the midnight train to Tokyo. The sleeper, like everything else in Japan, was toy-like in proportion to our American accommodations. I remember particularly an almost sleepless night due to the lights. If you turned on your light in your berth, every light in the car was lighted. Considering the nervous strain most of the passengers were in, you can readily imagine how little sleep anyone had that night.

Shortly after arriving in Tokyo, we left for Yokohama where we were to board our final boat for the trip to the United States. To us, at this time, it seemed a very roundabout way to get home, but under the circumstances it was all we could do. Arriving early in the morning, Natalie and I went immediately to the Grand Hotel where I was assigned the same bedroom which I had occupied weeks before. Promptly at 8:30 in the morning, Ko, who had previously served me, appeared with a pot of black coffee, a papaya, and a small piece of lemon—the same breakfast I had always taken upon my former visit. The Japanese have excellent memories.

What a sad change we found in this colony, probably saddened more that morning by the official announcement from the Russian Embassy in Tokyo that Turkey had declared war upon Russia. Apparently the war was becoming even more complex. A heavy pall seemed to lay over the entire city. All of the young men—French, German, English, and Russian—had left for military duty. Apprehension and restlessness were left behind.

We were more than happy to board ship the next day. Yet, on board, we learned only too well the hatred and bitterness that had sprung up to divide families and separate friends. The ship was crowded to capacity with people of almost every nationality and walk of life. It represented a conglomerate cross-section of the world. Everyone was definitely unfriendly, even suspicious. Tension was high and the nervous strain was great. Each night, in the bar and other places, numerous rows would spring up, even fights that had to be quelled by physical force. Each time, everyone expected something disastrous to happen.

I was most fortunate in finding as a stateroom-mate a bright, young Scottish fellow who was returning from Siam to join the colors. He was just twenty-one and had recently learned of an inheritance from his father of about twenty thousand pounds. This had been great news for him, as his father had died when he was quite young, stipulating in his will that neither he nor his sister should be informed of their inheritance until they were of age. True to Scottish ingenuity, this matter had been kept a secret. And now, after many years in Siam, he was returning to receive his inheritance and join his fellow countrymen at the front.

Alec, for that was his name, and I succeeded in making the acquaintance of a young Western cowboy. What he was doing in the Orient, we never learned, but he did play a nice game of bridge and, with Natalie as a fourth, we spent almost our entire time together around the bridge table.

One afternoon Natalie was quite perturbed. "Before we play a single rubber, I want to tell you about a woman I just saw and talked to. She is a German woman and just as sweet and lovely as she can be. She has three daughters with her. They have been visiting her in China and now they are all returning home. One daughter is married to a German army officer, another to an English aviator, and the third to an Italian soldier. They all have a deep family affection and now this horrible war is coming between them. The mother is nearly frantic, but very brave. You have but to look at her face and see the tragedy there. Her sons-in-law are fighting each other and her daughters are torn between loyalties. My heart went out to her, yet by her calm dignity, I knew she would in some way keep them all together."

We played but a little bridge that afternoon. Our discussions turned to the Western world and the similar situations tearing apart many families.

Excitement reached a fever pitch two days before we reached Honolulu.

It was reported that there were German spies on board and that warships lay in wait for us. All the passengers were instantly thrown into pandemic confusion, and I am sure it was only the tactfulness of the Captain and his able crew that prevented disaster. The four of us remained in our rooms. We decided to meet our fate playing bridge, but nothing happened and we glided into the familiar Honolulu bay on a gloriously sunny morning. We felt quite at home and decided to enjoy the day while the vessel was being refueled and reprovisioned.

Having not forgotten the native dances and my desire to introduce them to America, I spent most of the day with the dancers and musicians. I was fortunate in finding a highly intelligent Hawaiian who helped me considerably with the steps and their interpretations. He gave me the name and address of the leader of a group of native musicians who were in California and who might be of further assistance to me. I was most grateful for this.

The trip from Honolulu to San Francisco was not quite so eventful. Unfriendliness and suspicion lurked in everyone's face, but the tension had been relieved. We four remained much to ourselves and continued our bridge games undisturbed.

At last the famous Golden Gate appeared upon the horizon and we were home again.

Thank God for America.

Chapter Twenty-Three

Home. The most joyous part of any trip is the returning home and this homecoming was certainly no exception. All across the Pacific I had been dreaming of a big juicy beefsteak and fresh crisp lettuce. I had had nothing but canned goods for so long that the thought of steak and lettuce threw me into a state of extreme anticipation—or possibly it was the return of the childhood desire of "I want meat." Ed Davey met us at the dock, and I must give him full credit for fulfilling our every desire that evening in so far as food was concerned.

It was necessary that I leave immediately for New York. As I was to return to the West Coast within a short time, Natalie preferred to remain in California with some friends at the Hotel Green in Pasadena. We hurriedly made these arrangements, and two days later I found myself in a train, speeding across the country.

What a wonderful feeling it was to be among my own people. What a feeling of contentment that we were not in danger of war. What beauty and friendliness I encountered everywhere. All the way across the States, I gave silent thanks that I was an American. Few people realize or appreciate the great privilege that is theirs to be an American citizen. Foreign travel and study will bring out the great opportunities that await every person in our own country, the limitless wealth within our own borders, the most priceless possession in all the universe—Freedom. I have no patience with people who do not recognize these glorious qualities. Nothing agitates me more than the soapbox orators denouncing this country, the government, or the people. This freedom of speech and activity can be carried too far. When men or women do not agree with our idea of peace and prosperity for all, they should be forcibly assisted in returning or going to that place which is more expressive of their ideals.

New York City looked more beautiful to me than ever before. Immediately upon my arrival, I got in touch with Beulah Livingston, my press agent. Beulah let forth her best efforts, and her best efforts were something to think about. She arranged interviews with the leading magazines and newspapers and featured articles were published and syndicated all over the country. I even endorsed a cigarette and toilet water. The latter was very funny as I never used perfume of any kind. The company sent a woman to my rooms to smell my personality and then concoct a special mixture to express my body odor or something. Anyway, when it was all mixed, I was presented with a large bottle. One whiff of it nearly knocked me over. It made me think of our stable at home! Of course, I never used it, and I do not think anyone else did for that matter.

I took temporary rooms at 2 East 33rd Street, over an English tearoom and settled down to real living once more. However, all of Beulah's publicity had made me a celebrity, and everywhere I went I was stared at and the gossiping tongues wagged a bit. I had a good sense of humor about it all, and some of the rumors that reached me were ridiculously funny. At least twenty rich women were keeping me. What a constitution the public must have thought I had! As a matter of fact, during this time I was working so hard that every night, well almost every night, I literally fell into bed. I was so tired I would have made a damn poor lover and could not have earned my keep very well. Do not misunderstand me. I am not trying to create the impression that I was a male virgin. I still had my moments.

I had difficulty in locating a suitable partner, finally accepting one temporarily. I missed Dorothy very much and was extremely grieved that I had not heard a word from her since our separation in Manila. All the efforts I had made to locate her had failed.

I was filled with the new ideas I had brought back from the Orient and Hawaii. I wanted to infuse new life into ballroom dancing. I arranged what I called the "El Parguaya," a combination of Manila, Spanish, and Oriental styles and danced to a very quick rhythm in picturesque costume. I also prepared the "La Carinosa," which was patterned after the ballerinas I had seen in Manila and was danced to a slow rhythm provided by a guitar and involved much use of the handkerchief. The Japanese dance I arranged was purely a story of a Geisha girl who mourned for her lover, his spirit coming back to her in the form of a bird. I danced this dressed as a white bird, and my partner wore a white kimono embroidered in silver. This dance was never very popular. I am sure it was because my partner looked so ravishing in her costume that no one could conceive of her being broken hearted or neglected. My Hawaiian ideas, I was forced to give up on for the time being due to the inability to obtain proper musicians. Probably the most popular dance I created was the "Globe Trot." This dance was accepted upon the dance floors and became very popular. Teachers added it to their repertoire, phonograph records were made, and the general public accepted it, much to my delight. The steps and movements were variations of those I had seen in Japan, China, and Manila.

My first public appearance was to be at the old Colony Club. What an opportunity. Since this was the most exclusive club in America, I could not help but feel that it was a rare privilege to perform there. This was to be the last affair held in the old home at 30th and Madison. The Club's new home at 62nd and Park Ave. was to be opened immediately. The old home was an unpretentious colonial type, filled with charm, romance, and social history.

This last affair was a benefit arranged by Mrs. Justus Ruperti, formerly Sally Nicoll, one of the most beautiful and popular belles of the gay nineties.

I had met both Mr. and Mrs. Ruperti the afternoon I had danced with Joan Sawyer at the Plaza. We had become friends, and it had been my pleasure to give dancing lessons to all of their seven children. As I knew her, she was a remarkable woman and a born social leader. Other patronesses that evening were Mrs. Hamilton Fisk, Mrs. DeLancey Nicoll, and others I do not recall at this time.

Mrs. Taft, the secretary of the club, had, in her efficient manner, arranged everything in the most perfect manner. The decorations were all influenced by the Oriental with a profusion of Oriental lilies throughout the room. I was to have my own orchestra and specially arranged music to present, for the first time, my new dances. It was a rare opportunity and a setting almost too good to be true, and I was elated.

Mrs. Ruperti was entertaining many of the season's debutantes and had asked me to dine with them. It was a delicious meal in a superb setting with the most charming companions. I ate heartily. Yes, heartily.

Did I say everything was perfect? Yes, everything was except my dancing. I gave the worst performance of my whole career that evening. I had sat at the dinner table for about two hours, forgetting myself in such entertaining company and eating the entire time. By the time I came out onto the floor to dance, I felt like a stuffed pig attempting to be graceful. I am sure that I must have conveyed that impression to everyone there. There was my golden opportunity and I had suddenly become a gormandizer. In my whole career I have never felt as disheartened as I did that evening.

The next day, my lovely sister, Leonora, whom I had not seen for several years, arrived from the South to spend a week with me. What a beautiful woman she had developed into, with regular chiseled features, definitely patrician, and a glorious suit of wavy golden brown hair. I was delighted to have her with me.

This was Christmas week and everything was in quite a whirl. I was making special appearances at the Ritz-Carlton, the Biltmore, and even the Hippodrome during a large benefit arranged by Frederick Townsend Martin. However, the most pleasing engagement was one to appear at the old Hotel Waldorf-Astoria under the auspices of most of the Metropolitan stars such as Caruso, Farrar, Destin, and others. Despite so many years away from it, my heart was still with the Metropolitan and I suppose that it always will be.

There were numerous dinner parties and other entertainments that I delighted in taking Leonora to, such as a performance of *Madame Butterfly* as the guests of Howard Potter and dinners by Mrs. James B. Grosvenor and Mr. George Boldt, the manager of the Waldorf. Mr. John Cort gave a lavish party at the opening of his Cort Theatre, turning the stage into a dance floor and installing a huge bar in the foyer.

Naturally, the crowning event of the year was New Year's eve. Several

Leonora Rector Crook with her daughter, Leonora
circa 1911

days previous I had received a telephone call from Mrs. Elizabeth Barbour, secretary to Mrs. Stuyvesant Fish, asking my partner and me to dance at a large ball Mrs. Fish was giving. The invitation also graciously included Leonora as a guest. Mrs. Fish was the social leader preeminent of the Four Hundred, and her affairs were always both original and brilliant. For an artist to be asked to appear at one of her parties was the social significance of his arrival at the top of the ladder.

Mrs. Fish was probably the most benevolent of the social leaders that New York has known. She always paid all the performers she asked to appear at her affairs. Other social leaders often took advantage of the prestige that went with appearing at their homes and engaged artists even, at times, forgetting to thank them. To further illustrate her benevolence, I must tell you the following story.

Mrs. Barbour had been with Mrs. Fish but about a year when Mrs. Fish learned that she had a son. She immediately went to her.

"Mrs. Barbour, I have just learned you have a son. How old is he and where is he now?"

"He is five years of age, Mrs. Fish, and he is in Louisville, Kentucky with my people."

"A child's place is with his mother, Mrs. Barbour. You sit down and send a telegram and have your child come here to live with you until he is old enough to go to school. I'm only sorry that I did not know about him before."

It is needless to say that she did this. Mrs. Barbour remained with Mrs. Fish for twenty years, taking charge of her New York and Newport homes and other estates.

It had been requested of my partner and I to be at the Fish mansion by eleven o'clock on New Year's Eve. As I had already made reservations at the Waldorf-Astoria for that evening, I decided that, rather than cancel them, Leonora and I would join my party immediately after the dance. To expedite matters, I put on my dancing costume at my apartment and carried my evening clothes in a bag so as to change at the Fish home as soon as we were finished and not be delayed.

My partner's costume for the evening had been designed for me by one of New York's leading artists and was a combination of silver, greenish metal draped over her body and trimmed with long fringe. My costume was a combination of the Oriental and Spanish, the background being of heavy crepe, profusely covered with embroidered bands of red and gold and studded with imitation jewels. From my shoulder hung a dark-purple brocade, embroidered in flowers of every color of the rainbow. The effect of the two costumes together was a dazzling sight to behold.

At about 11:30, as we were standing by the huge stairway waiting for our cue, Mrs. Fish appeared for her entrance into the ballroom. She was beautifully gowned and wore a small tiara of diamonds in her hair. Just before reaching the last step, she tripped slightly and knocked the tiara out of place. Unlike most women, she did not return to her dressing room but simply grabbed the ornament and pushed it back into place with a simple but expressive, "Oh, hell!"

Seeing us standing there, she stopped and looked us over from head to toe. Feeling that some words were necessary, I stepped forward and said, "I hope that you like our costumes. This is the first time we've worn them. And our dances. They, too, are new."

She made no reply but nodded her head in apparent approval and entered the ballroom. I had learned that Mrs. Fish was a woman of but few words—expressive words.

Standing where we were, we were able to get a prospectus of the party. There were more than one hundred guests, and they were entertained on three floors. The room before us was strictly modern American; however, another floor was decorated in strict Italian and another Russian. The costumes and jewels of the women guests were dazzling. Champagne was flowing like water and while the gaiety was at high pitch, no one was the least bit drunk. It was said of Mrs. Fish that one of the secrets of her success as a great hostess was that she always gave her guests something to drink the minute they arrived and managed to get them out before they had too much.

At about 11:40 we made our appearance and, inspired by such a setting, we danced well. We gave several encores as the elite were most generous in their applause that evening, which was a little unusual for their usually blasé attitudes. I remember that Mrs. George Gould, blazing in emeralds that set off her dark beauty to great advantage, said to us as we left the room, "My dears, you were simply marvelous."

At twelve o'clock, a sumptuous buffet supper was served and, believe it or not, by one o'clock the last guest had departed. Mrs. Fish's parties always stopped at their zenith, an accomplishment any hostess would love to attain.

As soon as the last guest left, I hurriedly changed into my evening clothes. Leonora was waiting for me, and we were anxious to join our friends at the Waldorf. Imagine my chagrin in discovering that I had neglected to pack my dress studs. Mr. Fish's valet was assisting me and very kindly offered the loan of a pair belonging to his master. I promptly returned them the next day, often wondering if Mr. Fish knew of the great service he had been to me.

When we arrived at the hotel, the festivities were at their height. The entire hotel was packed and jammed. Mr. Boldt, in his usual casual manner, greeted us. Turning to Leonora he said, "This is your first New Years with us. I hope that you have a most enjoyable time."

"I hope so, too, but I am a little frightened, " Leonora replied. "You see, I don't know anyone and I'm afraid that I'll be a wall flower."

About an hour later, Mr. Boldt came to our table, leaned over Leonora's shoulder and smilingly said, "So this is the young lady who knew no one to dance with, yet she has not missed a single dance. I think that our wallflower has budded into an American Beauty."

Leonora laughed. "I still don't know them. They just ask me to dance, and it seems in the spirit of the New Year to dance."

"Well, it takes a Southern beauty to get away with that," he replied and walked away.

We didn't return home until about daybreak. At noon, my valet awakened me by handing me an open page of "The Sun" exhibiting a large picture of my partner and me in costume with this caption, "Blazing in jewels in superb costumes, this couple danced at the ball given by Mr. and Mrs. Stuyvesant Fish last night." This photograph was syndicated in many important papers throughout the United States, publicity that was really worthwhile, publicity that could not be bought.

The next day Leonora returned South and I left in a blinding snowstorm for Pasadena to fulfill numerous winter engagements.

Chapter Twenty-Four

I arrived in California in the late afternoon, just as the sun was dropping into the mountains, leaving wave after wave of changing color behind. The crimson sky was staging a flamboyant show for me. I stepped gingerly from my train, completely intoxicated with the champagne-like atmosphere. To me, California was a veritable fairyland where everything was continuously new—always spring with seemingly no death or decay.

I joined Natalie at the Hotel Green in Pasadena, which was to be my headquarters for the winter season. I had stayed in New York longer than I had planned and as a sort of peace offering, I had brought Natalie several new gowns that a close friend of mine had selected.

"Tom, these gowns are the loveliest I've ever seen," she said, glowing with delight.

"I'm glad that you like them. By the way, isn't there any mail for me? I haven't heard a word from Dorothy, and I'm a little worried." I tried to make my inquiry sound casual, not wanting her to know just how upset I had actually become.

Her face instantly betrayed the news she had to give me. "Yes, a cable came for you yesterday, and I opened it right away. I hope that you don't mind, but I thought I should. It was from Dorothy. She's not coming back, at least not right away. I don't like her staying in the Orient during these times, Tom. I'm uneasy about her."

"That doesn't seem at all like her. What excuse did she give?"

"Oh, something about an offer to dance in Shanghai. Wait, I'll get the cable for you."

This was quite a shock to me. I was completely at a loss to understand this sudden change in Dorothy's plans. What had caused her to remain in the Orient at a time like this? Try as hard as I could, I could not find a plausible answer to that perplexing question. Years later, when I learned of the taking of her own life, I realized there was more to her remaining in the Orient than I had even suspected. This act of hers had a great affect upon me. The Gypsies of my early years had predicted correctly. I had loved Dorothy, and I had not brought her happiness.

I was now faced with a new problem, or rather an old one, just under different circumstances. What should I do now? Whom would I get for a partner? I had but little time as the dances were scheduled at the Hotel Green in about two weeks time. It was Natalie who suggested the solution.

"Why don't you get one of the girls that assisted you at the Booster's Festival?" was her question that turned my thoughts in the right direction.

I remembered one girl in particular, Hazel Allen, a solo dancer. I knew she had studied dancing since she was a child, specializing in acrobatic and ballet work. I recalled, in dancing with her, that she was just the right height, extremely graceful, with a simplicity that radiated charm. I immediately got in touch with her and, to my delight, she readily accepted my offer.

We began rehearsals at once. Hazel quickly learned the new dances I had arranged, adding much to their interpretation by her agile, acrobatic ability. We opened on schedule and she was an instant success. I had, again, found a wonderfully gifted partner.

We remained at the Hotel Green during February and March, also appearing at numerous country clubs and private engagements. In addition to all of these commitments, we were also engaged to appear every other week at the Hotel Coronado, where, at the end of March, I had the misfortune to sprain my ankle, which interrupted our performances for four weeks.

During this period, Natalie and I had been living in a furnished apartment which overlooked the Pacific ocean. There we had many delightful neighbors and friends who made our lives very happy and contented. Madame Pavlova was making her first moving picture at that time, with Sascha Voline as her leading man and the two of them often joined us in picnic lunch parties on the beach. The three Talmadge girls—Norma[43], Constance[44], and Natalie[45]— were also living in Hollywood with their mother. Norma was already an established name in the movie colony. Constance was about sixteen and of the greatest tomboys I have ever met. She was very anxious to become a dancer and often begged me to take her on as my partner. It was the following year, after which I am sure that she forgave me for not honoring her request, that she made her first major success in the picture "Intolerance."

Two other girls stand out very vividly in my memory from this time. They were Doris Pawn[46] and Mildred Adams. Doris was from Nebraska with corn-silk hair, blue eyes, and marble-like skin. Mildred was from Colorado, a great outdoor girl with a fascinating figure, gray eyes, and brown hair. I liked these two girls, probably more than they ever realized.

At the beginning of May, Hazel and I were engaged by the Board of Trade of Santa Monica to appear for two months at a huge pavilion built over the Pacific Ocean. It was there that I fulfilled the promise I made to myself to introduce to the American public my interpretation of the rhythmical beauty of the Hawaiian Hula dance. I went to my trunk for the guitar arrangements of two Hawaiian waltzes that I had obtained in Honolulu and created what we called the "Mohina Mo Ko Aloha" (Moonlight and Love) dance. Our costumes deviated somewhat from the stiff straw skirts worn by the natives. Hazel's skirt was composed of strips of chiffon, arranged in color from the palest to midnight blue, sewn on a band around her waist. I wore short, ragged trunks made of deep, rich red crepe, which I had brought from China, with a flowing scarf of royal purple. As leis, we used dried seaweed, gilded with silver and gold. We wore no shoes or stockings. This was a bit daring for those times and I must admit that both Hazel and I were a bit dubious as to its reception. Endowed with a full moon and a still night, we entered arm in arm as two young lovers, spellbound by the mystery of the moonlight and our love, to the plaintive playing and singing of our Hawaiian orchestra. Our interpretation of the hula was an instantaneous sensation and nearly every program after that included this dance. Over the course of time, we performed it nearly a thousand times. Although it was inevitable that the Hawaiian music would sweep this country, I feel that I had no small share in its introduction. If I had done nothing else, I would have felt some degree of success.

All artists encounter, from time to time, outbreaks of professional jealousy. It was shortly after our presentation of the hula that such an outbreak nearly terminated my dancing career. Previous to our engagement, a local team had been dancing at the pavilion with only a mild degree of success. Displeased with the termination of their engagement, and probably infuriated with our success, they decided to take strenuous measures against us.

In order to execute our dances, which often required high leaps, we not only insisted that the floors not be waxed, but usually dampened the soles of our pumps as a precaution against slipping. Just before our second appearance, my valet rushed into my rooms, highly agitated.

"Mr. Rector, the ballroom floor has been waxed." Stopping for a moment to catch his breath, he continued. "One of the workmen saw the couple who danced here last week thoroughly waxing the floor this afternoon. They worked on it for over two hours."

I immediately sent for the manager. He called his crew of cleaners and had the entire ballroom floor scraped and mopped, removing about two pounds of wax. From this time on, a guard was positioned at the door during the hours when there were no performances. A calamity had been avoided; the jealous efforts of our retributors had been thwarted.

Two days later all the newspapers carried the horrible story of the sinking of the Lusitania by torpedo with the loss of 1,198 lives, 124 of which were Americans. This was a huge shock to the civilized world, but I believe California was more stunned than the rest of the United States. Up until this time, the Californians that I had encountered had been so utterly absorbed in their own lives and problems that they had considered the war a European struggle, which would only affect them indirectly, if at all. This great tragedy brought the war home to California in a very real way. The fighting in central Europe took on new meaning; everyone became greatly incensed and aroused.

Hollywood, then only a small village, was but five miles distant by motor.

We made many trips there and met most of the moving picture celebrities, such as Mr. and Mrs. Wallace Reid[47], Ruth Roland[48], Henry King[49], and others. I was impressed by their sincerity and ceaseless efforts dedicated to their particular art form. They all earned their crowns by hard work.

I had the pleasure of knowing Felice Lyne, the young American girl who had captivated London singing the roles of Juliet and Marguerite under the direction of Oscar Hammerstein. She was a miniature Melba with a voice as clear as crystal.

I also met Marcella Craft[50], the prima donna who had created the role of Salome in Richard Strauss' opera of that name in Munich. This meeting was at a dinner party given at the Mission Inn at Riverside. This inn was one of the most interesting spots I found in California. Originally it had been a Spanish mission. Some farsighted men had restored and modernized it into this inn, ingenuously retaining its atmosphere of calm and peace. Just inside the entrance there was an enormous bowl of large oranges. Proceeding further you entered a Spanish patio filled with exotic flowers and splashing fountains. The music of soft chimes filled the air. After the dinner, we would adjourn to the roof of the hotel, overhung with pepper trees, for coffee. It was only natural that the conversation should include the opera *Salome*, and to our delight, Miss Craft, without any accompaniment, sang and danced the climaxing scene from this opera. In fancy, I was transported to the Kingdom of Judea where the real Salome danced, probably in just such a setting, for the head of John the Baptist. We lacked, however, a Herod and Herodious.

The next day I received a telephone call from Martin Hansen, one of the outstanding impresarios of New York City.

"Rector, I have an interesting proposition to talk over with you. How about your driving up to Los Angeles after your performance this evening and having a talk with me?"

"I could do that, " I replied, wondering just what he could want with me. "Tell me, what's this all about?"

"Can't tell you over the phone," was his rather decisive answer, "but it's about a dance tour. I have someone to introduce you to. One of the biggest names in the world. Can you make it around eleven thirty, here at my hotel?"

"I'll be there. Probably before then." I spent the rest of the afternoon and evening trying to figure out just what he wanted from me.

I arrived at his hotel at exactly eleven thirty. Before we had hardly exchanged civil greetings, I had propounded the question, "What's all the excitement about?"

"Don't be so anxious. I have a car waiting for us. I'm going to take you to see a truly great artist. Come on, we haven't any time to lose."

I followed him into the waiting car, and we drove to the outskirts of

Los Angeles, up a very steep hill, and into a large garden that overlooked the city with its pageantry of lights. I sat upon a bench beneath a pepper tree, deciding to ask no further questions but to just wait and see what happened next.

Suddenly, like a moth, an enchanting woman appeared, swathed in white, filmy chiffon.

"Well, Mr. Hansen, I see that you are on time." Her voice was soft and musical. Her outstretched hand was very white, with long, tapering fingers. Her manner was that of a princess.

"I'm always on time," he laughingly replied. "I've brought Tom Rector along, just as I promised." Turning to me, he continued, "Mr. Rector, this is Maud Allan[51], of whom I am sure you have heard."

"Indeed I have. It's a pleasure to meet you, Miss Allan. I'm very familiar with your success in London as Salome and your famous dance of the seven veils."

"Thank you very much, but I'm afraid that I shocked quite a few people. I don't think they quite understood me." This was indeed true. The entire continent had been scandalized over the seven veils dance, declaring it rather naughty, but at the same time proclaiming her artistry.

We had a most pleasant hour and a half with Miss Allan, discussing the dance, theatre, and other arts. I found myself watching her hands and later in the evening I summoned the courage to remark upon the graceful manner in which she handled them. She then told me that her first love had been the piano. She had initially studied to become a concert pianist, but later, through a twist of fate, had turned her attention to dancing. Our visit was purely a social one and no plans were discussed.

The ride back to the hotel was made in silence. Mr. Hansen seemed gloomy and quiet—probably thinking and planning was my interpretation. I turned my thoughts to the two famous Salomes that I had met in rapid succession, the first primarily an operatic singer and the second a modern dancer. Each one was outstanding, yet totally different from the other. They were an excellent example, I thought, of self expression.

As we reached the hotel I finally broke the silence by asking, "Just what are your plans, Mr. Hansen? Miss Allan is a charming woman, and I am interested."

"It won't work. It won't do," he answered quietly.

"What do you mean?" My voice must have expressed my disappointment.

"I had hoped to interest you and Miss Allan in a concert tour with a symphony orchestra, but I see now that it can't be done."

Failing to follow him in his thoughts, I asked, "But why?"

"First, there is a noticeable difference in your ages. Second, you are too slight in build. You are fully an inch shorter than she. It wouldn't look right."

I realized that he was right. It was just another disappointment.

However, a few days later, a telephone call from Mr. Oliver Morosco changed my plans materially. At his request, I called his office.

"Mr. Rector, I have a proposition to offer you and Miss Allen. One, which I hope you will accept."

It was only natural that my curiosity should be aroused. "We're at liberty now to accept anything that's attractive." I did not want to appear too anxious.

"Good!" He paused for a moment as though trying to make up his mind as to what to say. "As you know, William Rock and Frances White are handling the dance routines and specialties in *Nobody Home*. They are both leaving the cast to go on a vaudeville tour, and I would like for you and Miss Allen to take over their roles."

This proposal came as quite a surprise. *Nobody Home* had been running for several weeks starring Blanche King and Charles Winniger, ably supported by these two young artists.

After talking the matter over with Hazel, we accepted Mr. Morosco's offer, fully realizing our problem in supplanting two such popular people. We were to do three specialty dances—a waltz, a Hungarian czardas, and a cakewalk. We had but two weeks to prepare our dances and, strange as it may seem, the cakewalk presented the greatest problem. The waltz we had done in many variations. The czardas already had special music, so to create our interpretation was fairly simple, but the cakewalk presented a difficulty. In memory, I flashed back to my early childhood days on the banks of the Mississippi River, and I copied some of the steps I had seen the roustabouts do. One, "You buck up to me and I buck up to you," was often used, but another, "De passa ma la," I do not think had ever been used professionally before. I cannot tell you the origin of this step, the meaning, or even if I have spelled it correctly, as all of that was lost long ago. We made our exit doing an original cakewalk step of the levee where the girl puts her foot on the man's knee and he dusts off her shoe with a very gaudy handkerchief.

We were, to a degree, successful in filling the parts of Mr. Rock and Miss White. Our engagement with *Nobody Home* lasted for ten weeks. During this time, Miss White was taking the country by storm with her youth, dancing, and singing of "Mississippi."

I had, at last, arrived on the stage in a musical comedy. After several attempts, Fate had shown me that she, and she alone, was the master and in control. What else did she hold in store for me? Would I go on? Would I fail? I had long since decided not to guess, but just to wait and see.

Chapter Twenty-Five

Natalie and I arrived back in New York in time to be greeted by the first snowfall of the season. There was great unrest everywhere. The major topic of all conversations was the war. Could we possibly stay out of it, was the much debated question. Edith Cavell had been recently executed in Brussels; Bulgaria had declared war on Serbia and in rapid succession Great Britain, France, and Italy had declared was on Bulgaria. All Europe was involved and the rest of the world was being threatened. The World War was on its way.

Relief drives for the children of Belgium were in almost constant progress and other charitable enterprises for the war stricken Europeans were the chief thoughts of New Yorkers.

It was only natural that I should be drawn into these charity pageants. The first one I assisted with was held at the Biltmore Hotel and proved to be little more than a conflict of its own. The main object, to raise funds for the sufferers of the war, was apparently forgotten to the petty jealousies, committee rows, and private fights of the organizers. One of the chief promoters of the event was a man who had recently made a great deal of money. As a result of his success, he had been bitten by the social bug for his only daughter, who was could be very pleasant when she forgot to be a snob. He and his daughter, losing sight of everything but to meet the right people, caused most of the unpleasantries. I tried my best to remain strictly neutral.

There were two bright spots in the entire affair, luminous through personalities. The first was Madame Paderewski, wife of the famous pianist, who worked with earnesty and devotion for the cause. It was through her graciousness and tactfulness that many difficulties, such petty difficulties, were smoothed away and the pageant finally staged. The other bright spot was the kindness of Mrs. Robert Hilliard. It was through her that I obtained an imposing array of the best-known actors and actresses appearing upon Broadway at that time to lend their assistance. Through the efforts of these two outstanding women, the fussing, squabbling, and backbiting were quelled and the pageant was a success financially, which, of course, was the original purpose. Personally, I felt as though I had been through hell.

I needed diversion after this and it came quite unexpectedly in the form of the Beaux-Arte Ball, the first naked ball given by fashionable New York society. It was held at the Hotel Astor on Lincoln's birthday and called "The Ball of the Gods." It was a magnificent, extravagant affair and acclaimed the finest thing of its kind ever given in New York up to that time.

The large ballroom, on the main floor of the hotel, lent itself perfectly to the occasion. Long draperies, the edges stenciled with mythological designs, covered the walls. The huge chandeliers were decorated in a complimentary manner. The boxes surrounding the ballroom were profusely decorated in brilliant hues, blatantly displaying the legendary symbols of the evening. The stage had been enlarged and adorned with a backdrop of blue and gold. A single tree occupied the center of the stage. (Just why I never learned.) India, Egypt, and Greece were symbolized on one side of the stage, while the other side revealed steps leading to a temple bathed in artificial moonlight. It was a fabulous setting and very artistically arranged.

The pageant began at eleven o'clock with Miss Edith Synne Matthewsen appearing as Sybil, the spirit of prophecy, and speaking a prologue with music by Kirt Schindler.

Immediately following this, a scene was depicted of the Gods of India upon a mission to Mankind. Mr. Theodore Steinway represented the magician. Mrs. Hinman Bird was the goddess of Dawn and Miss Albertina Rasch portrayed the Goddess of Night. The scene closed with Miss Rasch giving a dance to the moon, assisted by her ballet girls dressed as stars.

The second part of the pageant represented the Gods of Egypt and honored Osiris, who signified divine goodness, and his sister-wife, Isis, the symbol of pantheistic divinity. Mrs. Alexander Dallas Bache Pratt (now Mrs. Charles Aubrey Cartwright of London), a beautiful woman with a superb figure, magnificently portrayed Isis, looking every inch a goddess. Mrs. Ogden Mills and Messers. Oliver Harriman and Donn Barber were also in this scene, winning praise for their portrayals.

Greece was next to be honored, with a scene revealing the gods and goddesses worshipping at the shrine of Aphrodite on the enchanted island of Cyprus, where all was love and beauty. Mr. Malcom Whitman was Apollo and Mrs. John Jacob Astor as Herecere were assisted by Mrs. Leonard Thomas and Mrs. Lydia G. Noyt, all displaying a combination of dignity and talent.

After the pageant, we lesser lights, which numbered about fifteen hundred, joined the Gods and Goddesses on the dance floor. It had been decreed that everyone must be in appropriate costume. Just what the word appropriate meant in such a case, I doubt if anyone took the trouble to discern. Most of the costumes were very extreme and exotic and probably would have shocked those whom they were representing, but this detail had not been considered. Revelry and gaiety were the keynote of the evening. Inhibitions were flung to the winds and the masquerading desires were completely satisfied. What sights you began to see. Fat women draped in scanty, flowing robes skipped in dance; skinny bald-headed men, with their bodies stained and decorated with a fur rug or a goat skin, awkwardly grabbed first one partner and then another, somewhat self-conscious of their nudity. Within half an hour, the dance floor was crowed to capacity with a seething mass of would-be immortals. Nymphs, slaves, and swarthy Egyptians with blue beards were all dancing together.

The bar became an oasis, and numerous trips were made by the great majority of participants to quench their insatiable thirsts. The Gods and Goddesses became less dignified; nymphs flitted all over the place. The blue beards became more bold and those in leopard or goat skins, overheated by alcohol and strenuous dancing, began to emit strange odors which, together with an itching sensation, created a problem heretofore not thought of. It was a strange picture. The madness of the dance that had preceded all the great wars was at its height. I wondered if the Duchess of Richmond, from some distant shore, was watching and smiling, yes, smiling sadly.

Like many other people, I made a mistake in choosing my costume, taking this opportunity to wear an exotic creation that had been given to me while I was in the Orient. Superb though it was, that is what there was of it, I look back and realize that only a very daring youth would have appeared in it. A few tabs of gold beads, embroidered with imitation jewels and set off by and elaborate headdress, were intended by the creator to represent the Hindu god, Krishna, the incarnation of Vishnu. Maybe it did. I don't know. My fatal mistake was in not staining my body brown as most of the men had done. My white skin, plenty of which was showing, attracted an undue amount of attention. To say that I became embarrassed is putting it mildly.

My first embarrassment was just as I entered the ballroom. I encountered an enormously fat woman, weighing at least two hundred and fifty pounds, with bulging breasts, dressed as Diana. She gave me one good look and, throwing her nose in to the air, haughtily remarked, "Disgusting. You should be in bed."

"But not with you, darling," I replied, hurrying on into the ballroom, not daring to look back.

My progress through the room was humiliating, as I felt hundreds of eyes following my every step. I was rescued by an artist who asked if he might sketch me. Whatever his motive was, I did not care. I was more than glad to retire to a corner and just watch the proceedings.

While sitting there, a young Southern fellow approached me with a look of complete bewilderment upon his face. "May I sit with you?" he more stammered than asked.

"Of course," I answered, moving over a bit. "Aren't you enjoying the party?"

"Well, no, to be quite frank, I'm not. I've never been in New York before, or to a party like this, for that matter. I just don't know how to treat the ladies."

I laughed. "I think I can give you the key to success with women. Treat the ladies like tarts and the tarts like ladies."

He smiled quizzically. Whether he took my advice or not, I do not know, but he did become one of the most popular young men in New York that season.

I left the ball early and awakened the next morning with a very bad cold. I wondered just how many other participants of New York's first naked ball were recipients of the same reward.

Chapter Twenty-Six

I spent ten days in my rooms, nursing my cold. During this time, I was delighted to receive an invitation to attend a musical at the Fifth Avenue home of Mr. and Mrs. William K. Vanderbilt[52]. Their affairs were always ultra-conservative, and when the invitation was sent to a person not of the Four Hundred, such as myself, it was a real compliment and recognition. It would have taken more than the blizzard that was raging over the city that night to keep me away. Dressing carefully and bundling myself warmly in a heavy fur coat, I braved the fury of the elements. Entering the mansion, I checked my coat and, with my tails flying in the breeze, I boldly entered the huge drawing room. There, I was greatly surprised to find everyone wearing coats—that is, nearly everyone. This seemed a rather strange custom for society, and I became a little embarrassed, but I soon discovered the reasoning behind it. This marble home, attractive and modern as money could make it, presented quite a problem to its owner, and that problem was heating. Those who had been to the Vanderbilt home before knew about this and, probably at Mrs. Vanderbilt's own suggestion, always wore their coats. It was easy to pick out the newcomers and for the others to recognize my own debut. I soon began to chill, then practically shiver and shake. Feeling that a cumbersome fur coat would be much out of place, I left early. I caught a second cold and was confined to my rooms for ten days more.

During this second imprisonment, I read considerably, especially the newspapers. They were filled with descriptions of the intensive fighting that was taking place at Verdun, the great loss of lives, and the ruthless destruction. The horrors of modern warfare stunned me. It seemed inhuman, uncivilized, and barbarian. My blood began to boil at the lasciviousness. I wanted to give what aid I could.

It was just at this time that I was asked to help stage another benefit for the war sufferers. I accepted gladly, only to find myself in another squabble of petty jealousies and desires for personal social greed. It was even worse than my previous experience. I began to wonder if they were all like that.

However, like the previous pageant, there was a redeeming feature. This time it was Miss Anna Fitzhue and her niece, Miss Edna Kellogg. Miss Kellogg had just arrived in New York to create the leading role in the opera *Gousscas*, by Granades, who had just met such an untimely end on a torpedoed ship as he was returning to his home. She had had great successes, both in Spain and Italy and had every qualification for an outstanding prima donna; a lovely voice, youth, beauty, and most gracious mannerisms. When she spoke with you, she had that rare gift of making you feel as though there was no one else in the world at that moment. The opera itself did not create much of a furor at that time, although the beautiful intermezzo and other numbers have been used many times since. It is regrettable that this was the only appearance of Miss Kellogg with the Metropolitan Opera Company when other women, less gifted, were thrust into parts for which they were inadequate.

My partner, Hazel Allen, who was to have followed me to New York, had written that she was ill and was forced to postpone her arrival until a future date. This was a bad jolt. I decided, rather than try to locate and train a temporary partner, to wait until she was able to join me. Therefore, I had plenty of free time on my hands.

During this idle time, I was asked to a Sunday morning breakfast, which is really of no particular importance except that I did get into a scrape. I was introduced to a very attractive woman whose photographs I had seen in magazines and newspapers. She was stately and very dark, but with a certain look in her eyes. How or why, I don't remember, but I found myself maneuvering this siren into the pantry where I mixed a special type of drink just for the two of us. After the first one, we clinched. Suddenly, pain shocked my whole system. I had been bitten, and bitten well, upon my lip! Whether this was in anger or in great passion, I have never figured out. One look in the mirror showed me that my lip was swollen all out of proportions. I made a hasty exit down the back stairs to the nearest butcher shop for raw meat, then straight home where I remained for several days. I never saw the woman but once after that. I detected quite a sadistic gleam in her eyes on that occasion and gave her a wide berth.

Recovering from this, I still found myself with plenty of time upon my hands. I was invited, among other people, to be a guest at a women's club luncheon at the Hotel Astor. I was seated next to a most engaging young woman, and we became immediately engrossed in an interesting conversation regarding various the arts. She was, she told me, a very well-known prima donna in Europe, having sung at a number of the leading opera houses. The fact that I had never heard of her did not disqualify her statement. She was now in America, beginning a concert tour, chiefly in fashionable houses for a "very large fee." In spite of her self-interest, which most artists have anyway, I liked her. After the luncheon, she suggested that I drive with her, as the afternoon was one of those radiant, sunny afternoons that proclaim spring is near at hand. During the drive, which was quite prolonged, I suggested that she dine with me. It was during dinner that the conversation again returned to her numerous successes.

"I should enjoy hearing you sing. Are you giving a recital in New York?" I asked.

"No, I'm not, at least I don't have one booked at the present," she modestly answered. "Probably in the very near future I will accept an offer."

"That is really very indefinite." I hesitated, thinking. "I have a good piano at my apartment. Would you care to stop by now and sing for me?"

"I would like to, if that is quite the thing to do here in America. On the Continent, we think nothing of it, but I am not too familiar with American customs."

"I assure you that it's perfectly all right," I laughingly replied.

She did have a nice voice and sang several charming songs. At the conclusion, she surprised me by requesting, "Now that I have sung for you, you must dance for me."

"How did you know I was a dancer," I responded, showing surprise as we had not mentioned the fact.

"Oh, I've heard about you," she giggled in a flirtatious way.

"I would like to very much, but you see, I'm not a soloist. I can't dance alone."

"I'll dance with you," she quickly replied.

Fortified with another good whiskey and soda, we began to dance to the phonograph, deciding upon a spring dance. Now, to execute a spring dance properly you must be comfortably attired. That is, the clothes should be loose and not too many of them. So dressing properly, we executed a most exotic ode to the coming season. It was probably a bit different than usually seen, inventing steps and holds, but still, I insist, a spring dance. We sank upon the couch, breathless but exhilarated.

The next morning, when I phoned her apartment to pay my respects, her maid informed me that she was quite ill with laryngitis and a very bad cold. For ten days, the prima donna could not speak above a whisper and had to cancel, so I was told, $8,000 worth of engagements. It had been a delightful but expensive spring dance!

I made several appearances at a new dance club called Club de Vingt, formed by my old friend, Mrs. Hawkesworth. I met many interesting people there and took on a few as pupils. One of the most interesting pupils I had at that time, although not through the Club de Vingt, was Mrs. Frederick Vanderbilt. I would arrive at her home around 5 o'clock in the afternoon and have tea with her and her secretary, after which we would begin our lessons in the waltz, as that was the only dance she was interested in. She was a graceful dancer and one of the most interesting women I have ever met. At that time, she was very much interested in horticulture and had a small garden in the back of her home where she grew a canary-yellow carnation with a spicy fragrance, the only one I had ever seen.

I also had as a pupil, Miss Rita Jolivet[53], who had just come to New York to play the feminine lead in Otis Skinner's new play, *Kismet*. She had been a passenger on the ill-fated Lusitania and was talking with Charles Frohman when the vessel was torpedoed and sunk by a German submarine.

I also met the great pianist, Leopold Godowsky[54], his wife, and his two daughters, Fonita and Dagmar. I renewed my acquaintance with Charles L. Wagner, who was managing McCormick, Mary Garden, and other great operatic stars. At a benefit at the Ritz-Carlton, I was presented to Mrs. Wheeler Wilcox.

But of all the people that I met that winter, or at any other time, there is one that stands out vividly, one whom I have been privileged to call my friend ever since. It came about rather unexpectedly.

One day I received a telephone call from Miss Julia Carroll, asking me to an informal dinner. "I have someone that I want you to meet," she told me, without divulging the person's identity. Now, Miss Carroll came from a very aristocratic family of Louisville, Kentucky, and anyone whom she thought was worthwhile was indeed someone.

Arriving at her apartment that evening, I was ushered into her living room.

"Tom, it's so nice to see you. I'm delighted that you could come." Julia had a cordiality about her that was most flattering. Turning to a young woman who was sitting on a divan and adding dignity and beauty to the small room, she continued, "Miss Ferguson, may I present Tom Rector? Tom, this is the Elsie Ferguson[55] who has created such a sensation in 'Outcast' and has everyone talking about her."

"I'm delighted to meet you, Mr. Rector. Julia had told me a lot of nice things about you." Her voice was deep, like a cello; her smile was most genuine.

"Miss Ferguson, this is indeed an honor." I was delighted and wanted to show it. Miss Ferguson was then the reigning beauty of the American stage and was being acclaimed by the critics as the American Muse. To meet her was a privilege.

We had a most enjoyable evening—in fact, one of the nicest I can remember. It is seldom in life one meets a woman that has charm, beauty, and intelligence. She had all three. Her hair was like spun red-gold, worn with a peculiar swirl. Her features were like chiseled marble, with a tip-tilted nose that suggested sauciness. I was attracted by her from the first moment. Something within me seemed to say, "Here is a great woman."

I did not meet Miss Ferguson again for almost two years, when I was very happy over the news that my sister, Natalie, had become her secretary. Through this, a friendship for all three of us was begun. One which still lasts, one which I still treasure.

I continued for the balance of the winter to do many things, none of which were very important, and I longed to get back to real work. When I received a telegram from Hazel that she and her sister were on their way to join me, I was ecstatic.

"Now we will show New Yorkers some real dancing," I said, feeling very confident.

Elsie Ferguson

Chapter Twenty-Seven

Hazel and I signed a contract to appear under the management of Marinelli, who was attaining considerable success at that time handling principally foreign artists of high caliber.

Vaudeville was at its height. Specialties acts of all kinds were on all the bills at every theatre. Material was in great demand and the salaries were very alluring. To meet this increasing demand, green, inexperienced, and untalented people were signing to sing a song badly and wave a flag. Discretion was flung to the winds and vaudeville was preparing its own taps.

Influenced by Mr. Marinelli and Mr. Avid Samuels, who was our personal manager, we, too, went vaudeville. We secured an orchestra of seven of the original Russian Baililika, who had come to this country at the outbreak of the war. We mapped out a program that was to last for twenty minutes, opening with a Russian Polka to the music of Strauss's "Violete." It was gay and very light, with much pantomime. My partner wore a white chiffon gown, light in texture as thistledown. Wetzel designed a suit of white broadcloth for me. The result was like snow-white butterflies flying through the air and was most effective. We followed this by our Hawaiian waltz, which we first presented in California, and then a Spanish number. We closed with the "Globe Trot," which I had created. With almost breath-taking speed, we did this two and three times a day.

Our little orchestra of splendid musicians could only speak two English phrases when we first met—"good morning" and "apple pie." The latter they relished with all of their sensitive souls. This typical American dessert, they ate at every meal and often between meals. As a matter of fact, the influence of apple pie almost closed our vaudeville career on the first day. As the time approached for our early evening performance, Dave began to worry about their absence. Scouts were sent out and they were finally corralled and hurried into their costumes, actually making their entrance with a slip second to the good. The next day I decided not to take any more chances with our musicians. Between the afternoon and evening performances, I locked them in their dressing room with a deck of cards and several apple pies. They were quite satisfied, and I don't believe they ever knew they were literally prisoners!

Two weeks were spent playing the smaller theatres around New York, breaking in the act. We were well received and all our notices were favorable. Then we were booked for the Palace, the seventh heaven of all vaudevillians. The two weeks we had been on the road, I had heard a great deal about this theatre. As a matter of fact, about ninety per cent of the conversations of my fellow artists were about the playhouse. I was somewhat dazed by it all and

Hazel Allen & Thomas Rector

certainly anxious to experience this most thrilling of all thrills possible on this earthly planet, as pure friends on the circuit would have had us believe, but that evolved into a deferred pleasure. As the time neared for our appearance, we were approached by management with the announcement that they could only pay us one third of the original salary agreed upon, giving us their reason as it was near the end of May, which was late in the season, and that was all their budget would allow. This was utterly preposterous, as I was under very heavy expenses with such a large company and two managers. I think that my refusal to continue came as quite a surprise to them. Many vaudeville artists would have accepted any type of contract for the glory of appearing at the Palace, but I was not that eager, so our little group disbanded and thus ended my vaudevillian days.

Hazel and I had several offers, but we decided to accept the one to appear at the Hotel McAlpin. Although the hotel was under the management of Mr. Lucius Boomer, it was really through Ted Baur that we accepted this engagement. A few months before, I had met Mr. and Mrs. Theodore Baur. Ted was a Hungarian by birth, a splendid gentleman, and quite a connoisseur of the arts. Mrs. Baur was a Southern woman whose family I had known in the South.

It was a very happy reunion, made especially so by Kabon Franko conducting the orchestra. We were to appear once in the afternoon at the tea Dansant and once in the evening during the supper dance, dividing time with another couple, Leonora Hughes and a young man. The young man has since, I understand, become quite successful in business.

We opened our engagement with our interpretation of the Hawaiian waltz with a Hawaiian stringed orchestra, as we had done in Santa Monica. This was all new to New York and somewhat on the daring side. The exhibition we had previously given had been very successful and so we hoped that New York, too, would appreciate our efforts. I decided to try and influence the dancing-minded youths with its captivating beat, hoping they would respond to the simplicity of movement, the beauty, and the sensuous rhythm. They did. The audience seemed to radiate a soft tenseness, as if they felt that all that was lovely had not been lost on the glare of the million lights outside and in the heartaches of the city.

Two great gentlemen of an almost vanished race were present at our opening. I refer to Colonel B. B. McAlpin, whose name the hotel bore, and General Coleman T. DuPont,[56] whom I had previously met in Pasadena. After our first number, they rushed over to us, like a couple of young boys bursting with enthusiasm, and insisted that we accompany them to another room in the hotel which was also crowded with dancers, and show them, as they expressed it, "something beautiful." So, orchestra and all, we accompanied these two fine men and repeated our dance before a strictly social gathering. They, too, received it with great enthusiasm.

And so my dream had come true. I had introduced the Hawaiian dance to New York, and they had accepted it with open arms. Soon the music was heard in every café in the city. It soon swept the entire country like a huge fire.

Our engagement at this fine hotel was a most pleasant one. We made new friends and met many interesting people. One afternoon, Mr. John Aspregen, a well-known business and social leader at that time, brought a young man to our table. He was dark, with oily skin, black hair, short in stature, and very interesting looking.

"Miss Allen and Mr. Rector, I would like you to meet Mr. Rudolf Valentino[57], who dances quite well himself."

They sat at our table for some time. Mr. Valentino was struggling with his English at that time and was quite good-natured about it all. Hazel and I were both impressed with his charm, especially his low bow as he took his leave from us. Little did we realize that this young, almost unassuming man, would typify the great lover to romantic America.

Mrs. Thomas Cary Welch, whom I had known in Manila, was often a guest at the tea Dansant. She was a brilliant writer and was then associated with *Town and Country.* One afternoon, she had as her guest, Mrs. Pankhurs[58], who was fighting so valiantly for women's rights. She was a fragile, feminine type of a woman and most interested in the dance, especially the Russian Polka. I was quite surprised when she remarked," You know, Mrs. Welch, I should like to dance the polka with his young man."

I am absolutely sure that she would have done very well.

One evening, Mr. Boomer, the manager, approached me by saying, "Tom, ex-president Taft is here tonight. He's interested in your dancing and he has asked me that you come over to his table."

Again, I experienced pangs of stage fright. To have such a request from a man of so great importance was such a surprise, complimentary as it was, that I felt inhibited. I stammered my acceptance, but my nervousness showed itself plainly as I walked toward his table. However, he soon put me at ease. His radiant smile and genial manner quickly made me feel that he was my friend. He was especially interested in my experience in Manila and the Mestizo dancing girls. Although brief, my personal contact with Mr. Taft made me a staunch admirer of him, his high ideals, and his excellent judgment.

They say that everyone had a counterpart, and it was during this time that I began to discover that mine was not only in New York, but that we had mutual acquaintances. Often, on the streets and other public places, I was greeted with a "Hello, Frank!" I never realized just what this salutation meant until acquaintances of mine explained that Frank Ridge resembled me physically very much. This naturally piqued my curiosity, and I insisted upon an introduction.

The introduction came rather unexpectedly. One evening, while at the McAlpin, I looked up from my table and actually saw myself walking toward me. If I had a few more drinks, I am sure that I would have thought the DTs had me. Just behind this apparition, I saw a friend of mine beaming smugly.

Reaching my table, he introduced us. "Mr. Rector, meet your double, Mr. Ridge."

"So, you're the man I've been mistaken for so often."

"Well, I've been called Tom and Rector so often that I felt as though I had lost my identity."

We both laughed and proceeded to have several drinks to our meeting.

Frank was from Atlanta and was then appearing in the light opera, *The Soldier Boy*, starring John Charles Thomas[59], later taking over the lead when Thomas withdrew from the cast. Frank enlisted promptly upon declaration of the war, giving valiant service to his country. At the close of the war, he was put at the head of a musical organization of doughboys and toured the Continent. After his discharge, he returned to his career under Chubert management, appearing with Ed Wynn[60] and other stars. Through all of this and up to the present day, we have remained staunch friends, even though we have ceased to look alike. In this respect, Frank had the distinct advantage over me. We often get together for a powwow and have much fun remembering persons and incidents. Together, we could furnish very interesting data about people, both social and artistic, but there is always the question of getting such a thing published.

Of the young ladies I met at this time, there is one that was very outstanding. When my sister announced that she was to have a visitor from Virginia, I had but a passing interest, but when I met her, the interest quickly advanced to admiration and desire. Her name was Margaret Scott, although I always called her Margarita. She was truly beautiful, with honest-to-goodness blond hair and the figure of a goddess. Besides this, she was very young, bubbling with charm, wit, and humor, yet she possessed a brilliant mind and understanding that created a balance which is so often lacking. Need I say that I was captivated by her? But, she had little time for me. All the other men about town, and other towns, saw these same qualities, and she was the recipient of countless invitations, bounteous flowers, and the most ardent attentions, all of which she accepted most graciously.

Yes, she married—someone else. She is now Mrs. John Carl Hobbert of Stockholm, Sweden, and I can well understand the reports of her charming the social circles of Europe.

Several years after she married, she brought her younger brother to dine with us. He was only a lad then, but his distinct personality made quite an impression upon all of us. We were not surprised when the movie world discovered Randolph[61] and made him the star he is today.

One by one, I met all of the Scotts—five girls and two boys—each one more attractive than the other. I instinctively think of them as the "Scintillating Scotts."

One of the greatest experiences of my whole career occurred this winter when I met and came to know the famous Nijinski[62]. Madeleine and Laurence Steinhardt, the niece and nephew of Samuel Untermeyer, had become friends of mine, possibly being as their mother was a Virginian. Madeleine was a beautifully educated and cultivated girl, interested in all forms of art. She had spent several years at school in Europe and had had as one of her schoolmates, Romola Nijinski, wife of the famous dancer. He had just recently come to America and was creating quite a sensation. Laurence Steinhardt was handling his business affairs and doing exceedingly well.

I was greatly excited one evening when Laurence phoned to say that he was bringing the great artist and his wife to the hotel to see our Hawaiian dance. I should say that I was almost petrified as I felt that our dancing was so simple and childlike compared to his. The hotel was in great excitement and everyone was on the qui vive. They arrived and, of course, were given a choice front table. As we danced, I noticed that he kept his eyes glued upon our feet. In fact, he never took them away. We were nervous to begin with, and his scrutiny made us even more so. But the surprise of the whole event was his reappearance the following night with his wife and Lydia Lopokova[63], whom I had previously met. This time, Madame Lopokova, watched our feet while the great Nijinski glued his eyes to our hands. Many times, this trio returned and each time they watched us as before. Of course, we talked with them each time they were there and soon became well acquainted. I finally found the courage one evening to ask him why he watched our hands and feet so closely. I remember the seriousness with which he replied.

"I have never seen, anywhere in the world, movements like you make with your hands and feet in your Hawaiian waltz. It is most fascinating." As he answered, he was not looking at me, but rather looking into a remote distance, seeing more, thinking more, but remaining quiet.

Of course, I was pleased, but I never really knew what he meant. There was an intensity about every movement—yes, every thought—and I wondered if he ever relaxed, even in his sleep.

Hazel was showered with attentions. She was such a charming little person, retaining that delightful girlishness that first attracted me so much. In almost childish simplicity, although inwardly she had become quite sophisticated, she stole her way right into people's hearts. Of course, she received a certain measure of, shall I say, attentions. I remember particularly an engagement when we had to dance at a small dinner party that Mr. Albert Gould Jennings was giving. It was small in size, having only fourteen guests, but a great portion of the wealth of the universe was represented. After our performance, as we were preparing to leave, Hazel said to me, "Several of these men have asked me to give them dancing lessons, insisting that they be private. What would you do?"

"Give them, by all means. Charge them $100 per lesson," I replied, and winking slyly. "Your mother will be an excellent chaperone."

She only smiled in return.

The next day, one of the gentlemen promptly appeared for his promised lesson. He took only one. None of the other gentlemen ever appeared.

Another interesting person I met while dancing at this hotel was Leslie Stuart[64], the English composer who had written that masterpiece of musical comedy, *Floradora*. At that time, he and Cosmo Hamilton[65] were collaborating on a new musical comedy that was to be produced the following season. Stuart came to the hotel often and our friendship became somewhat intimate. I thoroughly enjoyed his keen wit and subtle humor.

One day, he surprised me by saying, "Cosmo and I have been talking about you. We have both decided that you are quite the type for our lead in our new show. We were wondering if you would be at all interested?"

"Of course, I feel quite flattered with your offer." I smiled. "I had quite a similar offer several years ago, which had left me a bit skeptical. My hopes rose to the sky, only to be dropped with a terrific thud." Then I continued by telling him of my experience with Mr. Charles Dillingham.

"Well, I don't blame you. However, it does seem to me that they passed up a good box office attraction in you. Suppose you do this. Take the script home and read it. We'll not say anything more about it until the time for casting comes, but then, if you are free, you shall have the first opportunity."

"That I will be happy to do," I replied and that was that. As a matter of fact, I was so pleased with the comedy and the libretto of Cosmo Hamilton's that I very quickly learned the part.

I planned a supper party for Stuart. As a sort of novelty, I asked Leonora Hughes and her partner to join in the fun. We teamed together, exchanging partners and arranged a specialty dance done to his famous sextet. What fun we had. I have always rejoiced in Leonora's great success. She later became the partner to the renown Maurice, and, after his death she married a wealthy Argentine gentleman and is now residing in Buenos Aires.

Of course I knew the members of the press quite well. Anyone is public life contacts them constantly. I want to say this about these gentlemen. Upon every occasion within my knowledge, they have given the artist or the performer, especially if they were new, the breaks. There is something in their makeup that likes success, and I am sure that the writing of a success story is one of their greatest joys. To my knowledge, they often went out of their way to create an opportunity for some deserving unknown. I often think of the day that Dr. Sigmund Spaeth[66], who was then connected with one of the leading newspapers as a musical critic, approached me about, the since very famous, Mainbocher, quite unknown then as Main Bocher[67].

"He's an exceedingly clever artist," Dr. Spaeth said. "He needs publicity and needs it badly. I'm going to try and do something about it. I wonder if you would help?"

The outcome of this helping was the painting of Hazel and me in our Hawaiian costumes by Bocher, which was hung conspicuously in the lobby of the hotel. Sigmund ran a lengthy article in his paper about the Hawaiian dancing and Hazel and me, featuring a reproduction of this portrait and climaxing the article with quite a boost to the artist himself. I believe that this was the first bit of publicity that Main Bocher ever received. However, he was too clever with colors and designing ideas to be hidden for long. Had it not been Sigmund, it would have been someone else who would have launched his career. The world knows him today as the famous Mainbocher, an outstanding designer of Paris, who received so much publicity so recently through his serving H.R.H. the Duchess of Windsor.

And, I knew Marie Dressler[68]. It was a very great privilege to know a person as genuinely sincere as she—a privilege that no one could possibly share without gaining a worthwhile note in their lives. It all happened through my old friend, Alice Neilson, who asked me to dine with her one evening. Marie was planning to produce a small musical play for Mrs. Oliver Belmont, in which women's rights was to be the keynote. I was honored with the staging and the planning of the dances. Naturally, our association became somewhat intimate.

Marie was extremely popular with the Newport-New York society sets. In social history it is written of an intense fight she had at this time with Mrs. Belmont, wherein, she is reputed to have thrown an umbrella at this great social leader. I never believed it, but I am sure that if it did occur, both women would have had many great laughs together over the incident. The public knows Marie's superb sense of humor and what little I saw of Mrs. Belmont, I took notice of the fact that her humor had not gone uncultivated.

Marie was probably the most unselfish person I have ever known. She would literally move mountains to obtain recognition for some unknown. I am sure that one of the reasons for her own great success was that she was willing to share her success with everyone worthy. At this time she was living at the Ritz-Carlton and had issued invitations to a gala affair in the grand ballroom, all in the interest of introducing to America some unknown artist. The room was filled with great social lights, including Mrs. Belmont, Mrs. Reginald DeKoven, Mrs. James Louell Putnam, the Duchess of Richlieu, Mrs. Jerome Napoleon Bonaparte, Mrs. Frederick Kohl, Mrs. Malcom Whitman, and many others that I do not recall at this instance.

The concert was going beautifully and, of course, Marie was doing her share of comedy and singing. The highlight of the evening, however, was as much a surprise to Marie as it was to the others present. She was in the middle of a grand imitation of a then famous person when some unplanned movement of her body loosened her drawers, heavily weighted with ruffles of lace, and they fell, unabashed, to the floor. Unhesitatingly, and with the most complete composure, she reached down and picked them up and tucked them in place without losing a single beat of the music or a line of the words, even though the rest of her imitation was lost to her audience in their convulsions. She appreciated the fun as much as her friends did!

It was through Marie that I met Nella Webb, the very fine astrologist who had just then cast Marie's horoscope and predicted her great success. With an uncanny foresight, she saw through the veil into the future and detailed her life. It was shortly after this meeting that Nella refused to let Marie sign a most attractive contract, saying, "Wait. Wait until the first of the year. A far greater opportunity is on the way. It is in a different field. It will be a great surprise. Wait."

Marie waited, even though she was very hard up at that time. At the turn of the year an opportunity opened up that resulted in Marie's going to Hollywood.

For the first time since I had left my home in the South, I was enjoying a home life. My sister, Leonora had become a widow and was left with a five-year-old daughter. They had come up from the South, bringing along Mandy Myers, a typical Southern Darky and endowed with the finest culinary skills. Mandy was quite a character, a rather large one at that, being of enormous height and size. Mandy brought three of her many children along. One was a daughter named "Idalena Istabula Ione," who became a waitress. Another was a son she called "Flaubert Filanamo Fondelas," who readily took to odd jobs, and the third was a small child who, in a poetic mood, she had christened "Valerian Vulcano."

What a cook Mandy was! It makes my mouth water to this day to think of her waffles, fried chicken, hot breads, yams, and her pièce de résistance—chicken dumplings. My friends soon discovered Mandy, and their visits became more and more numerous, always ending up in the kitchen with some fresh delicacy Mandy had just prepared.

Nijinski and Mandy became bosom buddies. He often came by for dinner, after which he usually disappeared, only to be found in the kitchen, perched in some corner with another plate of food and engaged in some sort of conversation that evoked laughter and guffaws. I never discovered the real basis of their friendship as Mandy spoke only English and Nijinski, at that time, knew almost nothing of our language. Some how or other, they found much favor in each other's company.

Mandy's pet was the lovely Anna Fitzhugh[69], who often came to our house and charmed us all with her captivating personality. Living with Anna at that time, was her niece, Edna Kellogg. They made a delightful pair as they were very close in age. Edna was very solicitous of her famous aunt—always watching her diet and protecting her from colds, the two arch enemies of artists.

Anna and Edna lived in the country, and I remember with much joy a certain weekend when we were all invited to their house—an invitation that included Mandy as mistress of the kitchen. The other guests included Antonia Scotti, Andreas de Signola, Main Bocher, Sigmund Spaeth, and several others.

The specialty for dinner was Anna's favorite—Mandy's irresistible chicken dumplings. We all ate heartily, with the exception of Anna who was forcing herself to remember that she was a prima donna. Or maybe it was Edna's watchful eyes that radioed, "Watch your starches."

After dinner, we were all in the living room having music and playing bridge when someone spoke up, "Where's Anna?"

Edna, who had been playing bridge, looked up with a start. In an almost rage, she cried out, "I'll bet I know where she is," and rushed out toward the kitchen. We all followed. There sat Anna at the kitchen table, putting away chicken dumplings as fast as she could!

"Anna, aren't you ashamed of yourself? What will happen to your figure," Edna almost yelled.

"I don't care, Edna. I lost complete control of myself with the first taste of these dumplings. I'm going to finish this plate of them if I have to go without food for the coming week."

One evening, toward the end of our engagement at the McAlpin, I was especially attracted by a certain young woman who was a member of a party at a ringside table. She was strikingly lovely, with pearl-white skin, midnight hair, and dark eyes like twin stars. She sat at the table with a calm, almost serene-like manner. Her personality actually caused people to gape at her. Yet, so great was her poise, she apparently was unaware of anyone else's presence in the room. I watched her from my side of the table and felt a great desire to know her. I instinctively knew his young woman, hardly more than a girl, had come into my life to play some role. I hoped it would be filled with romance and experience. I began to ask people who she was, but no one seemed to have the answer. Surely someone knew her. There must be someone who could introduce us, but all I questioned gave the same negative response.

Later in the evening, my diligence was finally rewarded. As I was in my dressing room changing to my street clothes, a boisterous rap upon my door was followed by an old friend bursting into my room.

"Rector, I hear there is a certain party outside you would like to meet."

"Do you know her?" I quickly interrupted.

"You know me. I know everybody." His eyes were dancing mischievously. "Maybe I could fix it up for you. What's in it for me?"

"Name your reward. That is, anything within reason."

"Well, you do want to meet her, don't you?"

"I most certainly do." My reply was definitely positive. "Tell me, who is she?"

"Hold on, just cool your excitement. That young lady has asked to meet you." He was thoroughly enjoying his role of intermediary.

"What?" I could hardly believe what I heard. "Stop quibbling. Who is she?"

"Well, Tom, that young lady is Roshanara[70]. She has just arrived from England. She had been watching you dance and is most interested in your interpretations. She has asked to talk to you. However, I'm quite sure that it's strictly from an artist's viewpoint, so don't get too excited over it."

"Well, whatever the reason, take me to her."

So this little goddess was Roshanara. I knew her history well. She was born of English parentage, but had spent most of her life in India and Burma where she had completely absorbed the Oriental atmosphere. Her name, too, was one of the East, meaning "Light Adorned," which was certainly most fitting. She was a gifted dancer and had taken her interpretations to the Continent, winning praise with every performance.

Upon being presented to her, I found that her charm was even greater at close range. She spoke with an exquisitely modulated English accent, emanating a certain aloofness that one inherently associates with royalty. There was no artificial posing that you so often find in the less-cultured artist, but a thoroughly sincere expression. We talked at great length, discussing the dancing of all countries and ages. She was greatly interested in our Hawaiian waltz, which pleased me greatly. When she left, I felt as though I had known, at least for a short time on this earthly sphere, a true goddess.

But the next morning brought me an even greater surprise. Answering the ringing of the phone, which had annoyed me with its early ringing, I heard the quick, sharp voice of a man.

"Mr. Rector, I am Roshanara's manager. We are planning a special matinee performance at the Hudson Theatre. Would you consider being her partner?"

Would I? What a question! It seemed all too good to be true, but I accepted instantly. My joy was boundless. My happiness was complete.

Chapter Twenty-Eight

Roshanara's dancing was entirely new to me, being of a different school and arranged by a true artisan, but she was endowed with limitless patience and we worked very hard rehearsing. I am sure that it was my great desire to please her that incited any success that I may have made in this new type of dancing.

In her first performance in America, which was at the Hudson Theatre, I appeared with her in two numbers. The first one was called "On the Way to the Temple" and was done entirely in silhouette, the effect being created by our shadows thrown upon a large screen at the back of the stage. At no time did the figure of Roshanara or myself or the company of twelve girls ever appear upon the stage—a feat harder to perform than the dance itself. She used the music of Remsky-Karsekoff's "Song of India," which, if I am not mistaken, was the first time it had ever been used as a dance number. Our second number was her famous "Snake Dance." I took the part of a snake charmer. The music of my flute, which was actually played behind the scene, enticed what appeared to be the head of a white cobra from behind the curtain. As the music continued, another head appeared, creating a rather uncanny effect for it was nothing other than the hands of the great dancer about to burst forth in an exotic dance. The story was that the music of the flute player charmed the vicious snakes and lured them away. I do believe that it was the most effective routine I ever had the pleasure of assisting in. Roshanara completely won the hearts of her audience. The critics used all of the superlatives in their praise of her. I was happy in my assisting role, and I must tell you again that I continued to think of Roshie, as I came to know her, as a goddess!

As the winter season advanced, it became evident that the novelty of the ballroom dancing was on the wane. Ideas were giving out and there was very little new in the way of arrangements of exhibition numbers. The public was becoming bored. Then, too, a vast number of young men and women had sprung up everywhere, like mushrooms, as full-fledged exhibition dancers. The market was flooded; the novelty of the idea had worn out and the public wanted to dance themselves, rather than watch other dancers. And they wanted to dance with the professionals. The result was inevitable. A great many undesirable young men and women were given an opportunity of dancing and meeting men and women of social importance and wealth. The gigolo had become a recognized pest. I know of many cases where older women paid men to dance with them regularly, just as you would hire a secretary or a chauffeur. One case, especially, was that of a young man who was paid a weekly salary, all entertaining expenses, and even his laundry bill, just to dance with a certain woman whenever and wherever she desired. She even took him to resort hotels in the summer. Older men were employing young ladies in a similar capacity, and it became a booming business. But the seriousness of the war, especially since the United States had severed diplomatic relations with Germany, was occupying people's thoughts and, in turn, affecting the dance. Vernon Castle had joined the English air forces. America was worried. What had happened to the world? Were we being drawn into a war in which no one wanted a part? Would we have to fight to save the present civilizations? Questions like these were heard everywhere, but no one had the answers.

With Hazel and myself, the situation was becoming exceedingly difficult. While, in our capacity as exhibition dancers, we were not required to dance with the guests, we were meeting so many people and making so many friends that we were dancing almost continuously. The result was that, in addition to our exhibition numbers, we were dancing every dance during the afternoon and evening, besides our several hours of rehearsals each day and coaching lessons to a few other professionals. We found ourselves averaging about ten to twelve hours of dancing a day, which was beginning to take its toll upon us both physically. We had to make a change.

Leonora Hughes was anxious to have Hazel join her in a few specialty numbers. We talked the matter over, and it seemed the most plausible thing for her to accept. While this meant separation, we both felt it would be for only a short time. At least I hoped that this would be so. What a splendid artist she was. What an understanding person she had been. How greatly I admired her. I have never told anyone, but I am telling you the secret now. I loved her for all the fine things of young American womanhood she stood for.

As for myself, my success with Roshanara had caused us to consider more extensive work. We signed a contract to tour the principle cities of the East, under the personal management of Mr. R. R. Herndon. He was a keen businessman with the ability to see both the artistic side as well as the commercial angle of the theatre. He had previously arranged, very successfully, the American tours of Pavlova and Nijinski.

Mr. Herndon organized a company to compromise besides Roshanara and me, Michio Ito[71], the celebrated Japanese dancer, Tulle Lindohl, a protege of the Royal Opera in Copenhagen, a ballet of twenty girls, and a good sized orchestra. It was to be a very intimate dance review to include, besides the two previous ballets I had done with Roshanara, a very elaborate number called "The Festival of Lights." The story was taken from an old Hindu legend in which Roshie was to play a slave girl and I to portray Krishna, a god. Strangely enough, this same god I had most likely embarrassed at the Beaux Arts ball the winter before. In addition to this, Roshie arranged for me a pantomime to be danced to the tune of "Madame, Will You Dance with Me?" I played the role of a young French lieutenant, assisted by five of the young ladies of our ballet, out for an afternoon stroll and adventure. It was a very catchy routine and a role I enjoyed thoroughly.

Naturally, Roshie did solo numbers, as did Ito and Lindohl. Ito created a ballet to include, besides himself, Tulle and me, which he called *The Little Red Shoe*. It was extremely modernistic with special music. Ito played the part of the broken-hearted lover whose sweetheart I had, in a most villainous manner, seduced. I enjoyed the seduction scene and found it much simpler to stage than I had ever encountered in real life.

We rehearsed for about four weeks, night and day; every rehearsal I thoroughly enjoyed. Roshie and I became fast friends. We were friends that never at any time had cross words, which is a good deal to say about any dance artist. She was aloof, without being prudish, and most considerate of all who worked with her. I understood, at that time, that I was the only male partner she had had, with the exception of Adolph Bolm[72]. During rehearsals, I was very circumspect in my love scenes—much more so than I really wanted to be.

We travelled to Boston where we were to open, in a private car which the company was to use on tour. We opened at the Tremont Street theatre on a very cold, wintry night. Our program ran along smoothly, the first half closing with the ballet, *The Festival of Lights*. It was a lovely story in a perfect setting. The curtain rose, showing the interior of a Hindu temple, with Krishna (me) sitting upon a throne at the back of the stage. My costume, or what there was of it, was the same mass of glittering jewels embroidered on bands of gold that I has worn at the ball. My headdress was elaborated upon, including ropes of pearls hanging around my neck and, falling from my shoulders a huge scarf of golden tissue, which had been added to make more color and to serve in the dance. Special lighting was used, centering upon Krishna, and the effect was most dazzling. To the accompaniment of slow music, the girls came in in a procession, carrying candles which they lighted, received the blessing of Krishna, and then placed them in a frail boat to float down the river Ganges to attract a lover before the year has passed. Roshanara appeared as a beggar girl dressed in rags, too poor to even buy a candle to wish for a lover. She sees the golden tissue falling from Krishna's shoulders and believes that if she had a golden robe and some jewels, she, too, would find a lover. Slowly she approaches Krishna and begins to drape herself in the golden tissue. Krishna smiles and she climbs into his arms and relaxes, having found her lover. He then comes to life and, carrying her in his arms, slowly descends the throne. Then the dance of seduction begins, slowly at first and then working into a tremendous climax, literally chasing her around the stage. I could not withhold myself any longer. I began to play the part, not as I had rehearsed it, but as I wanted to play it. I caressed her cheeks, her eyes, and her breasts in the most lecherous manner. With my passion unleashed, Roshanara became frightened. She cried, "What are you doing?" and darted away from me. I followed right after her. Roshie was panic stricken, thinking

I had suddenly gone mad. Finally, I caught her in my arms with a mad kiss of death, flinging her to the floor and ascending the throne.

As we took our curtain calls, Roshie, still somewhat frightened, asked me, "What on earth were you trying to do? You acted as though you were either mad or drunk!"

"I was only acting the part as it should be," was my reply.

The papers vindicated me the next day as each one, in their praise, said that they had never seen Roshanara act with so much fire or passion or give such a dramatic performance.

We played one week in Boston and began our tour. Our first stop was Newport, Rhode Island. Roshie and I went to the theatre in the early part of the afternoon as we wanted to rehearse a certain scene that we felt could be improved. It was NOT the love god scene, however. As I entered the theatre, I heard a distinctly Southern voice saying to the man in the box office, "Be sure and see that Mr. Rector gets this note the minute he comes in. It's very important."

Turning around I saw an extremely handsome woman, of middle age, very smartly gowned. I instantly knew that it was not the usual mash note. Stepping up to her, I said, " I am Mr. Rector."

Quite surprised, she hesitated and, smiling, answered, "Tom, I would never have known you, for the last time I saw you, all you had on were the pink ribbons on your wrists."

"My dear lady," I replied, "I won't have on much more at the performance tonight."

What a charming laugh she had. "I must explain myself," she continued. "I was one of your mother's bridesmaids and a life-long friend of hers. When I saw you were to dance here tonight, I arranged a theatre party followed by a small supper, hoping that you could attend."

"I would be most happy to," was my response and the details were arranged.

That evening, it was easy to spot my hostess and her party of about twenty of Newport's smart set. I was most anxious to dance my best so that my mother's friend would be proud of me, having known me when. The performance went along smoothly until I came to the pantomime, where I dressed as a young French lieutenant, wearing black patent leather leggings. I had danced but a few steps when I heard a snap and felt something dangling around my ankle. I looked down and there was my right legging, hanging from the sole of my shoe. My very big number had been spoiled on the very night I so desired it to be perfect. My leg was bare to the knee, certainly detracting from any romantic spell I wished to convey as the dashing young French lieutenant. Every step I took, I would kick out to try and loosen the legging and, thereby, be relieved of my trailer, but it stuck tight and flopped and flopped without any sense of rhythm. How I managed to finish the number, I never knew as my embarrassment almost unnerved me, but the audience was most polite and there was not one sound of recognition of my dilemma.

The next number I danced was in the ballet with Ito and Tulle. It was extremely modernistic for the time. In the scene where I seduced the lady, I had to bring her on the stage, riding a frightful looking wooden horse hat was painted with brilliant red spots and wore a sickly expression as if he thought it was he I was going to seduce. This fiendish looking, make-believe animal was on rollers of some kind, and Tulle was riding it sideways. About halfway across the stage, our horse balked and refused to even budge one inch. No horse in the flesh could have balked more effectively. You almost expected to hear a snort after struggling to encourage him to move on. In an awkward attempt at tenderness, I lifted Tulle from the wild animal and carried her to a nearby table and began to ply her with wine, which was acknowledged as the proper approach to seduction. I believe that this method is a very ancient one that is still in use. By the time we reached the table, we had lost all count of the music as each step was paced. We hurried through our stage business and finally caught up with the music just as I reached for wine to encourage her to take a drink—which is no different from the present form. The stage pitcher was rather large and ornate, and with a grand gesture I raised it in the air with the proper beats of the music and began the action of drinking heartily. But, instead of wine coming forth, I was covered with the accumulated dirt of the 20-year-old Newport Opera House. It spattered all over Tulle and filled my eyes and throat. I spat and sputtered. Tulle began to laugh and the audience shrieked. Continuance of the seduction was impossible, so folding her in my arms, I signaled for the curtain to be lowered. The audience enjoyed the fun, and they called us before the curtain so we all could have a good laugh together. My attempt at perfection for my mother's old friend had been met with opposition at every step.

But I went to the party just the same. My hostess of the evening was most charming as were all of her guests. They had enjoyed the comedy of errors, and I soon lost the sting of my recent embarrassment. I remember meeting that evening one of the famous twins, Frances Burke Roche. Also Mr. and Mrs. Reginald Norman, Miss Roberta Willard, now Mrs. Robert Goelet, and many other charming people.

From Newport we went west to Pennsylvania to appear for a week of one-night stands before opening in New York. Our first engagement was in Reading. During the night, one of those sudden blizzards developed, and when we reached this little city it was bitter cold and not one of us felt particularly well. Roshie developed a slight temperature and looked very tired and listless. She immediately went to bed for rest, but like the good trooper she was, when curtain time came, she was there for her performance. The theatre was a very old one and quite cold. In our first dance number, the minute I touched Roshie's hand I realized that she had a burning fever. As I took her in my arms, I knew she was a very sick woman. I grew panicky, but she somehow finished the performance. How she managed, I do not know.

During the night, it grew colder and the temperature dropped below zero. Very early I rose to inquire about Roshie, only to find that she was quite ill and had been rushed to the hospital during the night. She had left us all a message that we must "carry on" without her. Calling at the hospital, I was not allowed to see her as she was supposedly resting. I was again given the message to continue the tour. But how, was the question. She was the star. She was the person the audiences all wanted to see.

Lancaster was our next stop. One of the girls of the ballet had been specially trained by Roshanara, and she danced her solo numbers. However, she was not an actress in the least and was not competent to do the dramatic parts in the two ballets. We were at our wits end. Ito made the suggestion that he and I work out some routine where he could do a dance in worship of the god, Krishna, on his throne. While it robbed the ballet of its dramatic value, it was the best we could do under the circumstances.

In the meantime, it grew colder and colder. When we reached the theatre, it seemed as if we were in an old barn. There was actually frozen ice in my dressing room. I absolutely refused to strip and stain my body with cold brown liquid. I would have been encased in ice, I am sure. So whether the audience liked it or not, they were going to have a white Hindu that evening, a Nordic Hindu—possibly the sort whose father had been a blonde Britisher.

There were at least ten people in the audience that evening. Probably there, we thought, incited by the conservative Dutch instinct to get what they had paid for, regardless of the weather. We were foolish to even attempt a performance, as all sensible people were home between blankets, trying to keep warm. Or maybe the audience was not the Dutch residents at all, as we had first thought, but consisted of those poor unfortunates who had no fires to run home to and the management had invited in to save us the embarrassment of playing to an absolutely empty house.

The performance started very smoothly, in spite of the shiverings from the cold and the fright of Roshie's absence. Her understudy was a nice little dancer, and she executed her solos in a most pleasing manner. After each number, there was thunderous applause accompanied by the stamping of feet. The little understudy almost cried with joy. We were all amazed. Yes, amazed, until it suddenly occurred to us that the tramps were probably trying to keep warm by clapping and stamping, rather than expressing any real appreciation for our performances.

Our stage manger, Eddie Fennell, was the hero of the hour. I had known him when I was associated with the Metropolitan Opera House. He had thoughtfully brought along a nice supply of whiskey, which he was passing out to some of us to help keep our blood flowing. I know that I had several good drinks.

Finally, the big moment arrived, the time for *The Festival of Lights*. Just before I was seated upon my throne, Eddie gave me another swallow of whiskey. Possibly it was one too many. I had begun to feel a little dizzy and had more than a little trouble ascending my throne. I finally made it up and the curtain rose. There I was, sitting in a terrific draft and half naked. It reminded me of the gory illustrations of a frozen hell that I remembered seeing in our copy of *Dante's Inferno*, illustrated by Dore.

I shivered and I swayed. It must have looked like I was doing the hoochie-koochie dance on the throne. I was freezing cold and probably more than a little tight. I thought the girls would never finish their number. When they did and I looked up for Ito's appearance, I was completely aghast. There, before me, was the weirdest looking sight I had ever beheld. Arrayed in a long Japanese garment with yards of trail was the petite Ito. In his hands he was carrying an object which he was moving up and down as if it were a ladle out of soup. Eddie Fennell was standing in the wings. I caught his eye, looked again at Ito, and burst into laughter. I reeled and shook and became almost became hysterical. Ito solemnly continued with his dance and I continued my hysterics. The audience must have enjoyed it all as they clapped and stamped as I have never heard before or since. Ito was infuriated. As an artist without a sense of humor, he felt that I had spoiled the act that he had always secretly dreamed of. Maybe I had, but I failed to see it. Anyway, he barely spoke to me for a week.

After the afternoon performance, Mr. Herndon told us that we would return to New York the next day. Roshie was too ill to appear with us for a month, at the very least. He was taking no chances in the meantime, and I do not blame him. I was not a good one-night trouper. We returned to the city and disbanded. Again, I was without a partner or engagement.

Roshie returned in a little more than a month. She called me immediately, and I went over to see her. She looked pale and thin. The biggest shock came when she said, "Yes, Tom, I was quite sick. You know, I had a bad case of smallpox. But, isn't it wonderful? It did not leave a single scar."

The war news at this time was becoming more tragic. All Europe was engaged in the bitterest of conflicts. And, what's more, it was coming closer and closer to our shores as the days and weeks passed.

It is but history that upon April 6th, the United States declared war, that all red-blooded Americans rushed to the colors. On April 26th conscription began and on June 25th the first U.S.A. contingent arrived in France. It is but history—tragic and barbaric.

My dancing days were over. That was certain. Filled with patriotism, the desire to serve humanity, the hope of continuing our present civilization, and inspired by the slogan of the time to physically aid in this "war to end all wars," I looked about to see in just what niche I might fit most effectively. A friend of mine, who was in the service of the government, gave me the proper inspiration and direction. I said goodbye to my friends, to New York that I had learned to love, and to the dancing that had become such a part of me and entered the service of my country. Whatever I did, how little or how big, I did it willingly and sincerely. I was completely filled with the desire to end all wars.

Chapter Twenty-Nine

It is Indian summer. The trees flaunt their brilliant hues, red and yellow leaves drift listlessly here and there like faded women whose lovers have grown weary of them. The air is soft; the song of the bird is hushed. Nature is fulfilling another year in its endless cycle. It is the Indian summer of my life.

As I sit in my living room on the south side of Central Park, in the hazy blue of the late afternoon, I find myself in a meditative mood. Countless motor cars are continuously passing by, carrying their human loads, some in the joyous anticipation of the cocktail hour, others being tired business men going home to the suburbs. An occasional car passes, presumably on an errand of mercy, and still others drive by in the gay quest of adventure. My eyes wonder through the park. I see the young lovers strolling, vowing the pledges that have been sworn throughout all eternity. Or perhaps they are working out their budgets, which has become one of the necessary evils of these times. They pass by without noticing the derelicts sitting hopelessly on the benches, beaten by life, too wounded to take up the struggle, too downcast to ever care if tomorrow ever comes. Some of them have known success; others have felt only the sting of failure. But each of them has lived and loved. They seem now to be returning as ghosts of warning.

Sitting here in the twilight of the day and of my life and in a reflective mood, I recall the lines of the immortal Victor Hugo:

"Life is but a slumber and love is but its dream, for
Life is worth its pain if love has filled your heart."

Perhaps those on the benches are remembering only the pain.

My attentions are directed to the little children—our future, our hope—entering an era where youth is so supreme, filled with its glorious vision, superb courage, and resiliency. I notice several groups of well-dressed, correctly trained children being watched over by governesses. A little boy falls. Two others rush to his aid. A larger boy puts him on his feet. He wants to cry, but he does not. A little girl brushes him off. How kind children are to each other. Why do so many of them lose this golden quality as they grow older? Why must only a very few remember? Why must others mature into self-centered individuals? Will some of them resort to trickery or become thieves, probably in a most gentlemanly fashion? Perhaps some will live idle lives and become social mongers. Fate may even lead a few to the benches of the derelicts, now so unnoticed. I am happy to feel that many will retain a semblance of the ideals of youth and go forth, carrying a banner. They are the golden few who make life beautiful.

As these children are eastward bound to their Fifth or Park Avenue homes, they meet and pass other groups leisurely returning to their Ninth and Tenth Avenue tenements. For them there is no great hurry as their lives are not built upon schedules. They stare at each other. Some caustic remarks are passed. Curiosity is in their eyes. Envy is probably in their hearts. My eyes focus upon a little sister-mother, no more than ten years of age. She has a young baby in her arms and is holding a little brother by the hand. She stops to watch a Rolls Royce pass. I wonder what her heart feels as she contrasts the sole occupant of that car, folded in satin and furs, with her own mother at home, tired, worn, and sick from a seemingly helpless struggle. Little does she realize that some day she, too, might be wrapped in furs or that small hand she clutches might be that of a genius. The gifts of this great universe are within the reach of all, awaiting some understanding heart with a clear, steadfast vision. The earthly background is of no importance. Some call it opportunity. Others refer to it as the hand of fate. A few will believe in the rare distribution of genius. But, I like to think that it is a soul-vision.

And so, day after day, this panorama of life unfolds before me. I subconsciously drift into the years that have fled. The oft repeated lines of Swinburne come to me again and again:

"Forget that I remember and dream that I forget."

It is more than two decades since I stopped dancing. The great war came, and I did my insignificant bit. In its wake followed that great demoralizing era called prohibition, pushing us further back and attempting to wreck the standards of our youth. What horrible sights one saw. After the fine dancing, dignified tea Dansants, and cultured dinner and supper parties, we were flung into a wild orgy of night clubs and speakeasies. Drunk, sodden men and women packed basements, entering into the wild abandon spirit of breaking the law. Bands began to scream blatantly like souls in torment. Dancers turned to violent contortions, wiggling like a can of worms. Life became an orgy of animals. Civilization had about-faced and was due for a tumble. Whether you want to believe it or not, dancing has in the past, and always will, reflect the trends of the times. The great depression was inevitable.

Time has marched on and brought its countless changes and adjustments. Most of my contemporaries have passed the great divide—Pavlova, Vernon Castle, Maurice, Wallace McCutcheon, and many others. My three outstanding partners have left me. Dorothy Smoeller and Roshanara both died in great physical agony after having expressed so much beauty throughout their lives and showered kindness on so many. Hazel Allen, time has separated us and I have long since lost track of her.

Many new artists have taken their places. I have tried to see most of them and to keep up with the modern trends. As for the dances, such as the Big Apple, the Shag, Trucking, the Lambeth Walk, La Conga—they all have turned dancing into either acrobatics or interpretations of the old folk dances, losing the gracefulness and stateliness of the tango or the waltz. Some of the dancers have remained artists though. Ramon and Rosita have done some fine exhibition work. Escudero, I believe is a great artist. Also L'Argentina. Medrano and Maria Montero are a great couple. The team that has given me the greatest pleasure is that of Moss and Fontana. To me they are the greatest of their style since the Castles and Maurice and Joan Sawyer. They seem the personification of grace, especially in their waltz when Fontana lifts Moss in the air like a ball of thistledown. It is extremely lovely, but, again, it is not the ballroom dancing of my day. It is more like ballet.

My Indian summer is rich with friendships. Many of my earlier associates are still my friends. The telephone rings often; the postman rings much more than twice with messages, greetings, and invitations from all corners of the globe.

Strangely enough, many of the sons and daughters of the intimate companions of my youth are my closest friends now. They often drop in for a cocktail or to play bridge. The boys will ask me to go with them to a prizefight or to play bridge. The girls will ask me to their parties. They all call me "Tom." At bridge, they do not lose their tempers; their conversations are not malicious; their sports are based upon fairness; sex is discussed in a frank, clean, decent manner and accepted as a natural function of life. We never discuss the past. They are not interested. The present is too occupying for them. They are interested in the present political situations, the present war, the new books, the current plays. They are all charming, polite, and most considerate. They seem to have regained that something that those of my generation lost during the prohibition era. Their companionship has brought me a richness that is very rare, indeed. I ask myself why. Perhaps the answer came the other day from a little boy, aged four, my grand-nephew. Rushing into my study and putting his hand upon my knee, he looked up into my face in a most solemn manner and said,

"Uncle Tom, my mamma says that you are not really an old man."

I could not imagine what had prompted this remark until his mother, who had followed him into the room, smilingly explained.

"Gerard just said that he thought you were an awful nice old man. I was just trying to explain to him."

I smiled. Perhaps I am not really an old man. I probably never will be because my heart still sings. It is true that the songs are sometimes a bit slower, the cadence not quite so lilting, but then again, the old cosmic urge will swell up within me and there will be a few moments of wild, unlicensed song. It is then that I feel my old pal looking at me in a quizzical manner. Returning that look squarely in the eye, I again remember Swinburne, who so truthfully said:

"We twain cannot remember the paths that once we trod."
Life seems to laugh. I smile, but the heart keeps on singing.

The past few months have been delightful. My life-long friend, Norval Richardson, has been spending the summer with me during the absence of my sister, Natalie. He has long since retired from the diplomatic service and has become one of our well know writers. He has been working on his new novel, soon to be published and it was through his encouragement that I have written these lines. Only this morning, he came to me with great news.

"Tom, an old friend of yours is moving into this building."

"Life is full of surprises, Norval. What is this one?"

"As I was going out for a walk, whom should I meet but Dick Barry directing moving men in bringing in furniture. He was greatly pleased to hear that you were living here. He's stopping in this afternoon for a cocktail."

"That is a surprise. There's no one I would love having more for a neighbor."

"We had just a few moments chat about you, Tom. A couple questions he asked, I couldn't answer, even though we've been close friends all these years. It seemed funny to me. Tom, how did it happen that you quit dancing so young? Right at the zenith of your career you suddenly stopped and you have never done anything about it since. It didn't seem strange to me at the time, but when Dick asked the question, I couldn't help but wonder."

"That's a very easy question to answer," I replied. "When in my student days with the Metropolitan Opera Company, I witnessed an attempted return of a famous Queen of Song. She had been in retirement for several years, but the old urge seemed to have gotten the better of her judgment. Against the advice of her friends, she was trying to portray one of her greatest roles. After the first act, which did not go well, I watched her backstage pacing the floor with tears in her eyes and wringing her hands. Then and there I made a solemn vow to myself that, if I ever accomplished anything in my artistic life, I would stop at the right time. I ...

Afterword

And so the story that Tom Rector started comes to an end. The final pages of his manuscript have been lost over the course of the years. His final thoughts, as he looked back upon his performing career will never be known.

After World War I, Tom went on to become a successful businessman. He traveled the world over, living in Paris and the Orient, as well as New York, conducting business, but never failing to appreciate the performing arts that each of his adopted homes had to offer.

Upon his return to New York and before the start of World War II, Tom took up residence with his sister, Leonora Crook. She was doing very well for herself at that time, serving as the manager of the Waldorf-Astoria tea room and was receiving her own fair share of publicity in the society pages, receiving praise for the efficient, creative, and gracious manner in which she arranged and managed the many events there. Tom and Leonora kept up an active social life together, often gathering together their friends from the entertainment and arts worlds, both old and new.

Tom's sister, Natalie, continued to play a large part in Tom's life. As he mentioned in an earlier chapter, Natalie became the personal secretary of the actress, Elsie Ferguson. Not only was she her secretary, but her closet friend. With Tom in tow, the three of them were often off on worldwide jaunts, promoting Elsie's career or just enjoying each other's company. The friendship among the three of them survived and flourished throughout their lifetimes, with Natalie serving as Elsie's secretary and companion until her death, and Elsie becoming Godmother to Gerard, Tom's grand-nephew.

Tom Rector's final years were spent in New York, often visiting with his niece, Leonora Crook Wayland-Smith, daughter of his beloved sister, Leonora, in the small town of Oneida, in upstate New York. His grandnephew, Gerard (my father), had vague memories of a rather eccentric old man periodically visiting them. Just what this old man had done to deserve such admiration from his mother, he was never quite clear on. Obviously his mother's admonition that Uncle Tom was not an old man did not convince him that he was otherwise.

Thomas Allen Rector died in 1954, at the age of 73 and was buried in a small cemetery in Oneida, New York, next to his sister, Leonora, who died in 1947 at the young age of 60. Natalie, died at the age of 97 in 1987 and rests next to Tom and Leonora.

Tom's tombstone reads, "Fear no more the heat of the sun, nor the furious winter's rages."

I often wonder if Tom would approve of his final resting place. His niece, my grandmother, always talked of the love her mother, uncle, and aunt had for Vicksburg, their old home, and the gentle Southern ways. I believe that

Tom would have wanted to return there at the end, to lie close to the banks of his beloved Mississippi, the same river that had brought such joy and tragedy to his childhood. I know that he is there again in spirit. His heart continues to sing.

References

Chapter 1

1. **Isabella "Belle" Boyd (1843-1900)** was a famous Confederate spy who operated in the Shenandoah Valley from her father's hotel in Front Royal. She provided valuable information to Generals Turner Ashby and Stonewall Jackson during the 1862 spring campaign in the Valley, was betrayed by her lover, and was arrested on July 29, 1862, and held in the Old Capitol Prison in Washington. Exchanged a month later, she resumed her work and was arrested again in June 1863. Belle was released in December 1863, suffering from typhoid, and six months later was sent to Europe by the Confederacy as a letter courier for Jefferson Davis. She attempted to return to the South on a blockade runner that was captured by the Union Army, and during this adventure fell in love with the prize master, Samuel Hardinge, who later married her in England in 1864. Hardinge died in 1865. Belle stayed in England for another year and started a career as an actress and lecturer.
2. **George Barr McCutcheon** (1866 - 1928) was a popular American novelist and playwright. His best-known works include a series of novels set in Graustark, a fictional East European country, *Brewster's Millions*, a play, and several films.
3. **Maxine Elliott** (1868 - 1940) was an American stage actress. It is said that reviewers disagreed over whether it was her beauty or her acting ability that attracted attention. Elliott made her first appearance in 1890 in *The Middleman*. In 1895, she got her first big break when Agustin Daly hired her as a supporting actress. Elliott married her second husband, comedian Nat C. Goodwin, in 1898, and the two starred together at home and abroad in such hits as *Nathan Hale* and *The Cowboy and the Lady*. She was billed alone when Charles B. Dillingham's production of *Her Own Way* opened on Broadway in 1903. From then on, Elliott was a star. When the production moved to London in 1905, King Edward VII asked that she be presented to him. Goodwin divorced Elliott in 1908, and around this time she became friendly with financier J. P. Morgan. Morgan gave her financial advice that enabled her to become a rich woman. Shortly after divorcing Goodwin, she returned to New York, and with Morgan's help opened her own theater *The Maxine Elliott*, opening with *The Chaperon*. Elliott experimented with acting in silent films in 1913, but soon returned to London.

Chapter 2

4. **Stuart Armstrong Walker** (1888 - 1941) was an American film producer and director.

5. **David Belasco** (1853 –1931) was an American playwright, impresario, director, and theatrical producer. He arrived in New York City in 1882 and worked as stage manager for the Madison Square Theater while writing plays. By 1895, he was so successful that he set himself up as an independent producer. Between 1884 and 1930, Belasco wrote, directed, or produced more than 100 Broadway plays, making him the most powerful personality on the New York City theater scene. Although he is perhaps most famous for having penned *Madame Butterfly* and *The Girl of the Golden West* for the stage, both of which were adapted as operas by Giacomo Puccini, more than forty motion pictures have been made from the many plays he authored, including Buster Keaton's *Seven Chances*.
6. **Griffin Barry**, American journalist. Griffin Barry was a talented and charming man. As a free-lance reporter, he roved the world in the 1920s and '30s, and later worked for the U.S. government in New Deal and wartime agencies. But while many friends of his went on to notable literary achievements, Barry's life became focused on a fruitless quest for love and stability with the mother of his two children, Dora Black Russell, author, feminist, and wife of philosopher Bertrand Russell.
7. **Alexander Humphreys Woollcott** (1887 - 1943) was an American critic and commentator for *The New Yorker* magazine and a member of the Algonquin Round Table. He was the inspiration for Sheridan Whiteside, the main character in the play *The Man Who Came to Dinner* (1939), and for the far less likable character Waldo Lydecker in the classic film *Laura* (1944). Woollcott's review of the Marx Brothers' Broadway debut helped move the group to superstardom and started a life-long friendship with Harpo Marx.
8. **William "Billy" Armstrong** (1858 - 1942) was an American music critic, lecturer, and writer. He received piano lessons as a child in Germany and later began playing professionally and teaching lessons. Armstrong published musical reviews in major newspapers such as the *Chicago Tribune*, where he was the music editor (1893 - 1898), and *The New York Times*. He also published reviews and essays in periodicals such as the *Saturday Evening Post* and the *Saturday Review*. Armstrong wrote several books, including the novels *Thekla* and *An American Nobleman*, and the essay series *The Romantic World of Music*.
9. *Florodora*, an Edwardian musical comedy that became one of the first successful Broadway musicals of the 20th century. The original London production opened in 1899 where it ran for a very successful 455 performances. The New York production, opening in 1900 was even more popular, running for 552 performances. After this, the piece was produced throughout the English-speaking world and beyond. The show was famous

for its double sextet and its chorus line of "Florodora Girls."

Chapter 3

10. **Alice Nielsen** (1872 - 1943) was a Broadway performer and operatic soprano had her own opera company and starred in several Victor Herbert operettas.
11. **Enrico Caruso** (1873 –1921) was a famous Italian tenor who sang to great acclaim at the major opera houses of Europe and North and South America and a key pioneer in the field of recorded music. His tremendous record sales and extraordinary voice—celebrated for its power, beauty, richness of tone and remarkable technique—made him arguably the greatest male operatic singer in history.
12. **Lina Cavalieri** 1874 –1944) was an Italian operatic soprano known for her great beauty.
13. **Emma Calvé** (1858 –1942) was probably the most famous French female opera singer of the Belle Époque. She had an international career and sang regularly and to considerable acclaim at the Metropolitan Opera House in New York, and the Royal Opera House, Covent Garden, London. She possessed a potent stage presence and was noted for her acting ability, stormy personality, and dramatic intensity. Contemporary accounts of her soprano voice describe it as extraordinary, with a first-rate technique.
14. **Emma Eames** (1865 - 1952) was an American soprano. She sang major lyric and lyric-dramatic roles in opera and had an important career in New York, London, and Paris during the last decade of the 19th century and the first decade of the 20th century.
15. **Louise Homer** (1871 –1947) was an American operatic contralto. She created the witch in Engelbert Humperdinck's opera, *Königskinder* and the title role in Horatio Parker's *Mona*. Nellie Melba hailed her as "the world's most beautiful voice." She made her operatic debut as Léonore in Donizett"s La Favorite at Vichy in 1898. Her American debut was at the Met in 1900 singing Amneris in *Aida*. Her last Met appearance was in 1929.
16. **Geraldine Farrar** (1882 – 1967) was an American soprano opera singer and film actress who created a sensation in the German capital with her debut as Marguerite in *Faust* 1901. Her admirers in Berlin included Crown Prince Wilhelm of Germany, with whom she is believed to have had a relationship beginning in 1903. Farrar made her debut at the New York Metropolitan Opera in *Romeo et Juliette* in 1906 and remained a member of the company until her retirement in 1922, singing 29 roles in nearly 500 performances. She developed a popular following, especially among New York's young female opera goers, who were known as "Gerry-flappers."

Farrar starred in more than a dozen films from 1915 to 1920, including Cecil B. De Mille's 1915 adaptation of Georges Bizet's opera *Carmen*. One of her most notable screen roles was as Joan of Arc in the 1917 film *Joan the Woman*.

17. **Arturo Toscanini** (1867 –1957) was an Italian conductor and one of the most acclaimed musicians of the late 19th and 20th centuries. He was renowned for his brilliant intensity, his restless perfectionism, his phenomenal ear for orchestral detail and sonority, and his photographic memory. He is widely considered to have been one of the greatest conductors of the 20th century.

18. **Emmy Destinn (Emílie Pavlína Věnceslava Kittlová)**, (1878 - 1930) was a renowned Czech operatic soprano who became internationally famous in 1901 when she sang the part of Senta in *Der Fliegende Holländer* at Bayreuth. She made her Metropolitan Opera debut in 1908 with a performance of *Aida*. Destinn returned to her homeland after the start of World War I, but her links with the Czech resistance caused her passport to be revoked, and she was interned at her chateau for the remainder of the war. She returned to the Metropolitan Opera in 1919, but had been replaced by a new generation of singers, although she did still sing with the company until 1921.

19. **Feodor Ivanovich Chaliapin** (1873 - 1938) was a Russian opera singer. With his large and expressive bass voice, he is often credited with establishing the tradition of naturalistic acting in his chosen art form. Early in his career, Chaliapin endured direct competition from three other great basses: the powerful Lev Sibiriakov, the more lyrical Vladimir Kastorsky, and Dmitri Buchtoyarov, whose voice lay between the extremes exemplified by Sibiriakov and Kastorsky. The fact that Chaliapin is the best remembered of this magnificent quartet testifies to the magnetic power of his personality, the acuteness of his musical interpretations, and the vividness of his performances.

20. **Marcella Sembrich** (1858 - 1935) was the stage name of the Polish coloratura soprano, **Prakseda Marcelina Kochańska**. She had an important international singing career, chiefly at the New York Metropolitan Opera and the Royal Opera House in London.

Chapter 4

21. **Richard Bennett** (1870 - 1944) was a star of the stage and early silent movie era and probably best-known for his role as Major Amberson in Welles' motion picture adaptation of *The Magnificent Ambersons* (1942). Bennett is also known for adapting socially conscious works of Eugène Brieux, such as *Damaged Goods* and *Maternity*. He married actress Adrienne Morrison

in 1903 and they had three daughters—Constance, Barbara, and Joan. Constance and Joan became successful movie stars. Barbara was also briefly an actress, but with less success. She married the popular singer, Morton Downey, and their son was the controversial television talk show host, Morton Downey, Jr.

22. **Laurette Taylor** (1883/4 - 1946) was an American stage and silent film actress. In 1912, she married British playwright J. Hartley Manner, who wrote *Peg o' My Heart*, a major triumph for Taylor, who toured in it extensively throughout the country. Based upon the popular novel by Mary O'Hara, the play's success inspired a 1922 film version starring Taylor and directed by King Vidor. Laurette Taylor's great-granddaughter, Chloe Taylor, is an actress in Los Angeles.

23. **Charles Bancroft Dillingham** (1868 - 1934) was a Broadway producer who started his career as a theater reviewer for the *New York Evening Post*, then became a manager for such actors as Julia Marlowe. He began his producing career in 1902, with a production of *The Cavalier*, starring Julia Marlowe, William Lewers, and Frank Worthing. He also produced several musicals and musical reviews during his career, including *Watch Your Step*, the first musical by Irving Berlin, which featured Vernon and Irene Castle in their Broadway debut. In 1915, Dillingham hired the famous Russian prima ballerina Anna Pavlova to perform in New York City for six months.

Chapter 5

24. **The McAlpin Hotel** was constructed in 1912 at the corner of Broadway and 34th Street in New York City by General Edwin A. McAlpin. When opened, it was the largest hotel in the world. The hotel was designed by the noted architect Frank Mills Andrews.

25. **Dansant,** a **tea dance**, or *thé dansant* (French: literally *dancing tea*) is an afternoon or early-evening dance. The function evolved from the concept of the afternoon tea, and books on Victorian Era etiquette even included instructions for hosting such gatherings. A frequent feature of tea dances was the presence of a live orchestra playing light classical music. The types of dances performed during tea dances included waltzes, tangos, and, by the late 1920s, The Charleston. Tea dances were a common cultural reference in early 20th century fiction as a staple of genteel society, where people normally attend these receptions while visiting resort towns—like Brighton, Saratoga, the Hamptons, and Provincetown.

26. **Vernon and Irene Castle** were a husband-and-wife team of ballroom dancers of the early 20th century. They are credited with invigorating the popularity of modern dancing. British born **Vernon Castle** moved to New

York in 1906. **Irene Foote Castle** was born in New Rochelle, New York, and studied dancing and performed in several amateur theatricals before meeting Vernon Castle at the New Rochelle Rowing Club in 1910, and with his help, she was hired for her first professional job. In 1911, the two were married, traveled together to Paris, and were hired as a dance act by the Café de Paris. Performing the latest American dances, they soon became the rage of Parisian society. Returning to the U.S. in 1912, their success was repeated on a far wider scale. In 1914, the couple opened a dancing school in New York called "Castle House," where they taught New York society the latest dance steps by day, and a nightclub called "Castles By the Sea" and a restaurant, "Sans Souci," where they performed at night. They also were in demand for private lessons and appearances at fashionable parties.

Chapter 6

27. **Chancellor "Chauncey" Olcott** (1858 –1932) was an American stage actor, songwriter and singer. In the early years of his career, Olcott sang in minstrel shows and Lillian Russell played a major role in helping make him a Broadway star. Amongst his songwriting accomplishments, Olcott wrote and composed the song "My Wild Irish Rose" for his production of *A Romance of Athlone* in 1899. Olcott also wrote the lyrics to "When Irish Eyes Are Smiling" for his production of *The Isle O' Dreams* in 1912. His life story was told in the 1947 movie, *My Wild Irish Rose*.

Chapter 7

28. **Joan Sawyer** was one of the most successful female dancers in the nightclub circuit in the 1910s. Her shrewd business sense and self promotion garnered her top billing among her dance partnerships, some who were famous dancers themselves very such as Rudolph Valentino, with whom she partnered for months in the Vaudeville circuit until Valentino became involved in a complex sex scandal. She was popular with New York's "400." Around 1914, she managed, taught, and performed at the very popular "Persian Garden" and had her own band called "Joan Sawyer's Persian Garden Orchestra (PGO.)" Sawyer is said to have created the Aeroplane Waltz and Joanelle dance. In 1913, Lew Quinn and Joan Sawyer made the first real attempt to introduce a new dance to the United States called the "Rhumba."

29. **William Randolph Hearst** (1863 - 1951) was an American newspaper magnate and leading newspaper publisher. He entered the publishing business in 1887 after taking control of *The San Francisco Examiner* from his father. Moving to New York City, he acquired *The New York Journal* and engaged in a bitter circulation war with Joseph Pulitzer's *New York*

World, which led to the creation of "yellow journalism"—sensationalized stories of dubious veracity. Hearst created a chain of newspapers in major American cities that numbered nearly 30 at its peak. He later expanded to magazines, creating the largest newspaper and magazine business in the world. His life story was a source of inspiration for the lead character in Orson Welles' classic film *Citizen Kane*

30. **Nahan Franko** (1861 - 1930) was an American violinist, conductor, and concert promoter. As a violinist, he played with leading American and European orchestras. He later became the first American-born conductor to work at the Metropolitan Opera in New York City, conducting 68 performances at the Met and 33 performances with the company elsewhere. Beginning in 1908, he led open-air concerts in Central Park, and it was largely through his efforts to make good music popular by performing these al fresco concerts did NYC and the Metropolitan Opera begin the habit of performing free outdoor performances.

31. **Theodore Herman Albert Dreiser** (1871 - 1945) was an American novelist and journalist. He pioneered the naturalist school and is known for portraying characters whose value lies not in their moral code, but in their persistence against all obstacles, and literary situations that more closely resemble studies of nature than tales of choice and agency.

Chapter 8

32. **Anna Pavlovna (Matveïevna) Pavlova** (1881 - 1931) was a Russian ballerina of the late 19th and the early 20th century. She is widely regarded as one of the finest classical ballet dancers in history and was most noted as a principal artist of the Imperial Russian Ballet and the Ballets Russes of Serge Diaghilev. Pavlova is most recognized for the creation of the role *The Dying Swan* and, with her own company, became the first ballerina to tour ballet around the world.

Chapter 9

33. **James Truslow Adams** (1878 -1949) was an American writer and historian. He was not an academic, but a freelance author who helped to popularize the latest scholarship about American history, especially New England, and his three-volume history of New England is well regarded by scholars. Adams coined the term "American Dream" in his 1931 book *The Epic of America*. His American Dream is "that dream of a land in which life should be better and richer and fuller for everyone, with opportunity for each according to ability or achievement."

34. **Winsor McCay** (1867 - 1934) was an American cartoonist and animator. A prolific artist, McCay's pioneering early animated films far outshone the

work of his contemporaries, and set a standard followed by Walt Disney and others in later decades. His two best-known creations are the newspaper comic strip *Little Nemo in Slumberland*, and the animated cartoon *Gertie the Dinosaur*, which he created in 1914.

35. **Dorothy Smoller** was a dancer and motion picture actress. On December 9, 1926 in New York City, the 25-year-old motion picture actress committed suicide by drinking poison in her hotel room. She left several notes, one addressed to Benjamin Strong, governor of the Federal Reserve Bank of New York. In the notes she gave ill health as the cause. Another note was addressed to her mother, Mrs. Rose Smoller, informed her mother that suicide had been decided upon because she has learned she was tubercular.

Chapter 10

36. **Oliver Morosco** (1876 - 1945) was an American theatrical producer, director, writer and theater owner. He worked as a child in an acrobatics act led by Walter Morosco, from whom he took his stage name and went on to work in and manage theaters in San Jose, San Francisco, and Los Angeles, California. He began producing plays in 1909 and mounted over 40 productions on Broadway including *Peg o' My Heart* and *The Bird of Paradise*. In 1926, Morosco filed for bankruptcy, his fortune lost in part due to a large speculative purchase of land in California where he planned to create a development called "Morosco Town."

Chapter 11

37. **Mary Pickford** (1892 –1979) was a Canadian-born American motion picture actress, co-founder of the film studio United Artists, and one of the original 36 founders of the Academy of Motion Picture Arts and Sciences. Known as "America's Sweetheart," "Little Mary" and "The girl with the curls," she was one of the Canadian pioneers in early Hollywood and a significant figure in the development of film acting. Because her international fame was triggered by moving images, she is a watershed figure in the history of modern celebrity. And as one of silent films' most important performers and producers, her contract demands were central to shaping the Hollywood industry.

Chapter 12

38. **Samuel Parker**, known as **Kamuela Parker,** (1853-1920) was a major landowner and businessman on the island of Hawaii. He became involved in politics at a critical time of the Kingdom of Hawaii. Despite his American-sounding name and upbringing, he had three-quarters native

Hawaiian ancestry. Parker made social connections among the Hawaiian nobility there that would be valuable throughout his life.

Chapter 14

39. **Grand Hotel** in Yokohama, Japan, burned to the ground during the Great Kanto Earthquake in 1923.
40. **Miyanoshita** is an *onsen* (inn) in the town of Hakone, Kanagawa Prefecture, Japan. The hot springs have been an attraction for tourists and pleasure-seekers for hundreds of years going back to the beginning of the Edo period.

Chapter 17

41. Tokyo's **Imperial Hotel** was the best known of Frank Lloyd Wright's buildings in Japan. The original Imperial Hotel in Tokyo was built in 1890. To replace the original wooden structure, the owners commissioned a design by Wright, which was completed in 1923. In 1968, the facade and pool were moved to The Museum *Meiji Mura*, while the rest of the structure was demolished to make way for a new hotel on the site.

Chapter 20

42. **Thomas Henry Barry** (1855 –1919) was a Lieutenant Colonel and Adjutant General of the 8th Army Corp during the Spanish–American War. He was appointed Brigadier General of volunteers and served in the China Relief Expedition and in the Philippine-American War during 1900–1901. In 1907, he was chosen a commander for the army of Cuban occupation and pacification by President Theodore Roosevelt. In 1914, he was sent to the Philippines and China as commander of all the American troops.

Chapter 24

43. **Norma Talmadge** (1893–1957) was an American actress and film producer of the silent era. A specialist in melodrama, she was one of the most elegant and glamorous film stars of the roaring twenties, and in the early 1920s she ranked among the most popular idols of the American screen. After her two talkies proved disappointing at the box office, she retired a very wealthy woman. Talmadge married millionaire and film producer Joseph Schenck and they successfully created their own production company.
44. **Constance Talmadge** (1897 - 1973) was a silent movie star and the sister of fellow actresses Norma and Natalie Talmadge. She began making films in 1914, in a Vitagraph comedy short, *In Bridal Attire* (1914). Her first major role was as The Mountain Girl and Marguerite de Valois

in D.W. Griffith's *Intolerance* (1916). With the advent of talkies in 1929, Talmadge left Hollywood and invested in real estate and other business ventures.

45. **Natalie Talmadge** (1898 - 1969) was an occasional silent-film actress who was more well-known as the sister of her movie star siblings Norma and Constance Talmadge until her marriage to silent film actor and comedian Buster Keaton.

46. **Doris Pawn** (1894 - 1988) was an American actress who appeared in films of the silent era. She was offered work as a *fill in* in the film *Trey of Hearts* (1914) while the company was on location in San Diego. The filmmakers were so impressed that she was offered additional work if she came along to Los Angeles. Pawn worked for a period of three months as an extra. She was also very well known for her extremely high singing voices.

47. **Wallace Reid** (1891 - 1923) was an actor in silent film referred to by *Motion Picture Magazine* as "the screen's most perfect lover." He appeared in several films with his father and, as his career in film flourished, he was soon acting and directing with and for early film mogul Allan Dwan. He was featured in both *Birth of a Nation* (1915) and *Intolerance* (1916) both directed by D.W. Griffith, and starred opposite many leading ladies such as Gloria Swanson, Lillian Gish, Elsie Ferguson, and Geraldine Farrar en route to becoming one of Hollywood's major heartthrobs.

48. **Ruth Roland** (1892 - 1937) was an American stage and film actress and film producer. Her father managed a theatre in San Francisco, and she became a child actress who went on to work in vaudeville. She appeared in her first film for Kalem Studios in 1909 and was soon billed as a "Kalem Girl." Roland was eventually sent to Kalem's West Coast studio where she was the lead actress and overseer of "Kalem House" where all the actors lived. Roland left Kalem and went on to even more fame at Balboa Films, and in 1915 she appeared in a 14-episode adventure film serial, *The Red Circle*. A shrewd businessperson, she established her own production company and signed a distribution deal with Pathé to make six new multi-episode serials that proved very successful. Between 1909 and 1927, Roland appeared in more than 200 films. She left the film business until 1930 when she made her first talkie. Although her voice worked well enough on screen, she returned to performing in live theatre, making only one more film appearance in 1935.

49. **Henry King** (1886 - 1982) was an American film director, directing over 100 films in his career. Before coming to film, King worked as an actor in various repertoire theatres, and first started to take small film roles in 1912. He directed for the first time in 1915, and grew to become one of the most commercially successful Hollywood directors of the 1920s and 1930s. He

was nominated for the best director Oscar twice, but did not win on either occasion. In 1944, he was awarded the first ever Golden Globe Award for best director for his film *The Song of Bernadette*, based on the novel of the same name by Franz Werfel. King was one of the 36 founders of the Academy of Motion Picture Arts and Sciences.

50. **Marcella Craft** (1874 - 1959) was an international soprano opera singer in the late 1800s and early 1900s. After voice training in Boston, Massachusetts, Craft traveled to Italy were she was given leading operatic roles. Later she moved to Germany and became a lead with the Munich Opera.

51. **Maud Allan** (possibly 27 August 1873–7 October 1956) was a pianist-turned-actor, dancer, and choreographer remembered for her "famously impressionistic mood settings." In 1900, in need of money, Allan published an illustrated sex manual for women titled *Illustriertes Konversations-Lexikon der Frau*. Shortly thereafter she began dancing professionally. Although athletic, and having great imagination, she had little formal dance training. She was once compared to professional dancer and legend Isadora Duncan, which greatly enraged her, as she disliked Duncan. She designed and often sewed her own costumes, which were creative. In 1906 her production *Vision of Salomé* debuted in Vienna. Based loosely on Oscar Wilde's play, *Salomé*, her version of the "Dance of the Seven Veils" became famous (and to some notorious) and she was billed as "The Salomé Dancer." Her book *My Life and Dancing* was published in 1908 and that year she took England by storm in a tour in which she performed 250 performances in less than one year.

Chapter 26

52. Anne Harriman Vanderbilt. In 1903, Vanderbilt married Anne Harriman, daughter of banker Oliver Harriman. She was a widow to sportsman Samuel Stevens Sands and to Lewis Morris Rutherfurd, Jr. Her second husband died in Switzerland in 1901. She had two sons by her first marriage and two daughters by her second marriage. She had no children by Vanderbilt.

53. **Rita Jolivet** (1890 - 1971) was an actress in theater and silent movies in the early twentieth century. Known in private life as the Countess Marguerita de Cippico, she was one of three children of Charles Eugene Jolivet from Carmansville, New York, an owner of extensive vineyards in France and his French wife, Pauline Hélène Vaillant, a talented musician. Jolivet's great-great grandmother was the only member of her family to avoid the guillotine during the French Revolution. Her grandmother Vaillant was among the *beauties* in the court of Napoleon III. She was also a singer. On November 14, 1908 Jolivet married Alfred Charles Stern, but the marriage

failed soon.

54. **Leopold Godowsky** (February 13, 1870 – November 21, 1938) was a famed Polish-American pianist, composer, and teacher. He has been described as "a pianist for pianists."

55. **Elsie Louise Ferguson** (August 19, 1883 – November 15, 1961) was an American stage and film actress. Born in New York City, Elsie Ferguson was the only child of Mr. and Mrs. Hiram Benson Ferguson, a successful attorney. Raised and educated in Manhattan, she became interested in the theater at a young age and made her stage debut at seventeen as a chorus girl in a musical comedy. She quickly became known as one of the most beautiful women to ever set foot on the American stage. For almost two years (1903-05), she was a cast member in *The Girl from Kays*. In 1908 she was leading lady to Edgar Selwyn in *Pierre of the Plains*. By 1909, after several years apprenticeship under several producers including Charles Frohman, Klaw & Erlanger, Charles Dillingham, and Henry B. Harris, she was a major Broadway star, starring in *Such A Little Queen*. In 1910, she spent time on the stage in London. During World War I, a number of Broadway stars organized a campaign to sell Liberty Bonds from the theatre stage prior to the performance as well as at highly publicized appearances at places such as the New York Public Library. Ferguson, noted for her great beauty and as one of the "Park Avenue aristocrats," on one occasion is reputed to have sold $85,000 worth of bonds in less than an hour. At the peak of her popularity, several film studios offered her a contract but she declined them all until widely respected New York-based French director, Maurice Tourneur, proposed she appear in the lead role as a sophisticated patrician in his 1917 silent film, *Barbary Sheep*. Producer and director Adolph Zukor then signed her to an eighteen film, 3 year, $5,000.00 per week contract. Following this first film, Ferguson was highly billed in promotional campaigns, and starred in two more films directed by Tourneur under a lucrative contract from Paramount Pictures that paid her $1,000 per day of filming in addition to her weekly contract income. Her only surviving silent film is *The Witness for the Defense* (1919) co-starring Warner Oland and performed as a play in 1911 by her friend Ethel Barrymore. Continuing to play roles of elegant society women, Ferguson was quickly dubbed "The Aristocrat of the Silent Screen," but the aristocratic label was also because she was known as a difficult and sometimes arrogant personality with whom to work. Elsie Ferguson eventually followed the move west and bought a home in the Hollywood hills. In 1920, she traveled to the Middle East and Europe. She fell in love with Paris and the French Riviera and within a few years bought a permanent home there. In 1921, she accepted another contract offer from Paramount Pictures to star

in four films to be spread over a two-year period. One of these was the 1921 film entitled *Forever* in which she starred opposite the leading heartthrob of the day, Wallace Reid. In 1925, she made only one film before returning to the Broadway stage. In 1930 she made her first talkie that would also be her final film, titled *Scarlett Pages*, which is now preserved in the Library of Congress. Although her voice came across well enough, at age 47, she was well past her prime for fans who wanted to see her as the great youthful beauty she had once been. Despite her wealth and fame and glamorous lifestyle, Elsie Ferguson's personal life had more than its share of turmoil. Well known behind the scenes as difficult to work with, temperamental, and argumentative, she married four times. Following her final marriage at age 51, she and her husband acquired a farm in Connecticut and divided their time between it and her Cap d'Antibes home on the Mediterranean Sea in the south of France. Ferguson's final appearance on Broadway in 1943, at the age of 60, met with critical acclaim. She played in *Outrageous Fortune*, a play written by her neighbor Rose Franken. The play closed eight weeks after it opened. Critics hailed Ferguson's performance as "glowing" and having "the charm and winning manner of old." She lived on an estate called "White Gate Farms." A very wealthy woman with no heirs and a lover of animals, on her passing in 1961, she left a large part of her considerable estate to a variety of charities including several for animal welfare. She also made sure that her faithful lifetime friend and personal secretary, Natalie Rector, was taken care of, allocating to her the interest from her estate to live on until her death, which was in 1987.

Chapter 27

56. **Thomas Coleman du Pont** (1863 - 1930) was an American engineer and politician. He was President of the of E. I. du Pont de Nemours and Company and a member of the Republican Party who served parts of two terms as United States Senator from Delaware. He was known by his middle name.
57. **Rudolph Valentino** (May 6, 1895 – August 23, 1926) was an Italian actor, sex symbol, and early pop icon. Known as the "Latin Lover," he was one of the most popular stars of the 1920s, and one of the most recognized stars from the silent film era. He is best known for his work in *The Sheik* and *The Four Horsemen of the Apocalypse*. His death at age 31 caused mass hysteria among his female fans, propelling him into icon status.
58. **Emmeline Pankhurst** (née **Goulden**; 1858 - 1928) was an English political activist and leader of the British suffragette movement, which helped women win the right to vote. In 1999, *Time* named Pankhurst as one of the 100 Most Important People of the 20th Century, stating: "she shaped

an idea of women for our time; she shook society into a new pattern from which there could be no going back.

59. **John Charles Thomas** (1891 - 1960) was a popular American opera, operetta, and concert baritone known for his exuberant singing style and virile, well-trained voice.

60. **Ed Wynn** (1886 - 1966) was a popular American comedian and actor noted for his *Perfect Fool* comedy character, his pioneering radio show of the 1930s, and his later career as a dramatic actor. Wynn became a headliner in vaudeville in the early 1910s and was a star of the Ziegfeld Follies starting in 1914. In The Ziegfeld follies, W. C. Fields allegedly caught him mugging for the audience under the table during his "Pool Room" routine and knocked him unconscious with his cue, but this may be apochryphal. Wynn also wrote, directed and produced many shows.

61. **Randolph Scott** (1898 - 1987) was an American film actor whose career spanned from 1928 to 1962. As a leading man for all but the first three years of his cinematic career, Scott appeared in a variety of genres, including social dramas, crime dramas, comedies, musicals (albeit in non-singing and non-dancing roles), adventure tales, war films, and even a few horror and fantasy films. However, his most enduring image is that of the tall-in-the-saddle Western hero. Out of his more than 100 film appearances more than 60 were in Westerns; thus, "of all the major stars whose name was associated with the Western, Scott most closely identified with it."

62. **Vaslav (or Vatslav) Nijinsky** (1890 - 1950) was a Russian ballet dancer and choreographer of Polish descent. He grew to be celebrated for his virtuosity and for the depth and intensity of his characterizations. He could perform *en pointe*, a rare skill among male dancers at the time, and his ability to perform seemingly gravity-defying leaps was also legendary. Choreographer Bronislava Nijinska was his sister.

63. **Lydia Lopokova, Baroness Keynes** (1892 - 1981) was a famous Russian ballerina during the early 20th century. She is known also as Lady Keynes, the wife of the economist, John Maynard Keynes. Lydia trained at the Imperial Ballet School, and her chance came when she was chosen to join the Ballets Russes on their European tour in 1910. She stayed with the ballet only briefly. Knowing that she had little future in Russia, she accepted an American offer of £16,000 per month and, after the summer tour, left for the United States, where she remained for six years, enjoying tremendous success. In America she was basically a novelty act, and she rejoined Diaghilev in 1916, dancing with the Ballets Russes, and her former partner Vaslav Nijinsky, in New York and later in London.

64. **Leslie Stuart** (1863 - 1928) was an English composer of early musical theatre, best known for the hit show *Florodora* (1899) and many popular

songs. Stuart began writing songs in the late 1870s, including songs for blackface performers, songs for musical theatre and ballads such as "Soldiers of the King."

65. **Cosmo Hamilton** (1870 – 1942) was an English playwright and novelist. Born Henry Charles Hamilton Gibbs, he took his mother's maiden name when he began to write. His London musicals include *The Catch of the Season* (1904), *The Belle of Mayfair* (1906), *The Beauty of Bath* (1906). He went on to write a number of Broadway shows, and many screenplays.

66. **Sigmund Gottfried Spaeth** (1885 – 1965) was a musicologist who traced the sources and origins of popular songs to their folk and classical roots. Presenting his findings through books, lectures, liner notes, newspapers, radio and television, he became known as "The Tune Detective." He taught school and worked for *Life*, *The New York Times*, the *Evening Mail* and the *Boston Evening Transcript*. He composed music scores for early sound films, and his books include *Read 'Em and Weep*, *Weep Some More, My Lady*, *A History of Popular Music in America*, *The Common Sense of Music*, *Fifty Years With Music*, *The Importance of Music* and *Stories Behind the World's Greatest Music*. On NBC, his program of piano instruction, *Keys to Happiness* (1931), brought an avalanche of 4,000 fan letters each week. In November 1931 he began his 15-minute NBC program, *The Tune Detective*, continuing until 1933. Beginning in 1932, NBC also carried his *Song Sleuth*. On Mutual, he did *Sigmund Spaeth's Musical Quiz*, and he also appeared on *Metropolitan Opera Quiz*.

67. **Mainbocher** is a fashion label founded by the American couturier Main Rousseau Bocher (1890 - 1976), also known as Mainbocher. Established in 1929, the house of Mainbocher successfully operated in Paris (1929-1939) and then in New York (1940-1971). Main Bocher was a native of Chicago where he studied art at the University of Chicago and the Chicago Academy of Fine Arts. He served in the Army in the first World War and stayed on in Paris after the war, working as a fashion illustrator for *Harper's Bazaar*, as Paris fashion editor for *Vogue* (1922-1929), and eventually became the editor-in-chief of the *French edition of Vogue* in early 1927. Mainbocher's decision to become a couturier grew out of his years as editor at *Vogue*; he realized that his critical eye and his feeling for fashion might also serve him as a designer. It is Mainbocher's painting of Tom Rector and his partner, Hazel Allen, that graces the cover of this book.

68. **Marie Dressler** (1868 - 1934) was a Canadian actress and Depression-era film star. She won the Academy Award for Best Actress in 1932 in *Min and Bill*. Dressler began her acting career when she was fourteen, and in 1892 she made her debut on Broadway. At first she hoped to make a career of singing light opera, but then gravitated to vaudeville and became a major

star. In vaudeville she was known for her full-figured body—fashionable at the time. She appeared in a play called *Robber of the Rhine*, written by Maurice Barrymore. Years later, she would appear with his sons, Lionel and John, in motion pictures. In addition to her stage work, Dressler recorded for Edison Records in 1909 and 1910.

69. **Anna Fitziu** (1887 - 1967) was an American soprano who had a prolific international opera career during the early 20th century. After her singing career ended, she embarked on a second career as a voice teacher. Fitziu began her career as a chorus girl and concert soloist in New York City in 1902. At this point in her career she worked under the name "Anna Fitzhugh," taking the last name from an old Virginia family that she was related to. She went to Chicago in early 1903 to portray a number of smaller roles in the musical comedy *The Wizard*. She remained in Chicago through 1904, appearing in leading roles in operettas and musical comedies. In 1905-1906 she performed on the American vaudeville circuit.

70. **Roshinara** (actually spelt, 'Roshanara') (1894-1926) was the stage name for Olive Craddock. She was born in Calcutta and was the daughter of a British Army officer. Roshanara's adopted stage name reflected her exotic dancing style, which stemmed from her familiarity with Southeast Asian culture. She appeared on stage in London, toured with legendary ballerina Anna Pavlova, performed throughout India, and gave movement lessons to the young Bette Davis.

Chapter 28

71. **Michio Ito** (1892-1961) was a Japanese dancer, choreographer, and an associate of William Butler Yeats, Ezra Pound, Angna Enters, Isamu Noguchi, Louis Horst, Ted Shawn, Martha Graham, Vladimir Rosing, Pauline Koner, Lester Horton, and others. He was interned and eventually deported from the United States after the outbreak of World War II.

72. **Adolph Rudolphovitch Bolm** (1884 - 1951) was a Russian-born American ballet dancer and choreographer. He graduated from the Russian Imperial Ballet School in Saint Petersburg in 1904 and that same year became a dancer with Mariinsky Ballet. In 1908-09, he ran a European tour with Anna Pavlova and then collaborated with Diaghilev's Ballet Russes in Paris. In 1916, Diaghilev's Ballet Russes toured the USA, and while on tour Bolm was injured and left the tour to stay in the US. He went on to organize Ballet Intime in New York and later collaborated with the New York Metropolitan Opera. He continued work, staging ballets until 1947.

www.ingramcontent.com/pod-product-compliance
Lightning Source LLC
Chambersburg PA
CBHW020800160426
43192CB00006B/388